T0305044

Infrastructure's Role in Lowering Asia's Trade Costs

Infrastructure's Role in Lowering Asia's Trade Costs

Building for Trade

Edited by

Douglas H. Brooks

Senior Research Fellow, Asian Development Bank Institute, Japan

David Hummels

Professor of Economics, Krannert School of Management, Purdue University and Research Associate, National Bureau of Economic Research, USA

A JOINT PUBLICATION OF THE ASIAN DEVELOPMENT BANK INSTITUTE AND EDWARD ELGAR PUBLISHING

Edward Elgar
Cheltenham, UK • Northampton, MA, USA

Published by
Edward Elgar Publishing Limited
The Lypiatts
15 Lansdown Road
Cheltenham
Glos GL50 2JA
UK

Edward Elgar Publishing, Inc.
William Pratt House
9 Dewey Court
Northampton
Massachusetts 01060
USA

A catalogue record for this book
is available from the British Library

Library of Congress Control Number: 2008937423

Mixed Sources
Product group from well-managed
forests and other controlled sources
www.fsc.org Cert no. SA-COC-1565
© 1996 Forest Stewardship Council

FSC

ISBN 978 1 84844 162 0

Printed and bound in Great Britain by MPG Books Ltd, Bodmin, Cornwall

Contents

Contributors

Adina Ardelean, Lecturer, Santa Clara University, CA, USA

Douglas H. Brooks, Senior Research Fellow, Asian Development Bank Institute, Tokyo, Japan

Prabir De, Fellow, Research and Information System for Developing Countries, New Delhi, India

Evelyn Devadason, Senior Lecturer, Faculty of Economics and Administration, University of Malaya, Kuala Lumpur, Malaysia

Jon Haveman, Principal, Beacon Economics, San Rafael, CA, USA

Loke Wai Heng, Senior Lecturer, Department of Economics, Faculty of Economics and Administration, University of Malaya, Kuala Lumpur, Malaysia

David Hummels, Professor of Economics, Krannert School of Management, Purdue University, Indiana; Research Associate, National Bureau of Economic Research, Cambridge, MA, USA

Liqiang Ma, Associate General Manager, Treasurer's Department, China Vanke Co., Ltd., Shenzhen, People's Republic of China

Nanda Nurridzki, Researcher, Institute for Economic and Social Research, Department of Economics, University of Indonesia (LPEM-FEUI), Jakarta, Indonesia

Arianto A. Patunru, Research Director, Institute for Economic and Social Research, Department of Economics, University of Indonesia (LPEM-FEUI), Jakarta, Indonesia

Rivayani, Researcher, Institute for Economic and Social Research, Department of Economics, University of Indonesia (LPEM-FEUI), Jakarta, Indonesia

Tham Siew Yean, Director and Principal Research Fellow, Institute of Malaysian and International Studies, Universiti Kebangsaan Malaysia, Bangi, Selangor, Malaysia

Christopher Thornberg, Principal, Beacon Economics, Los Angeles, CA, USA

Jinkang Zhang, Associate Professor of Economics, Yunnan University of Finance and Economics, People's Republic of China

Foreword

Trade-related infrastructure has given Asia's economies access to, and made them accessible for, trade with the rest of the world. Growth has both followed from and contributed to this process. The same has become true for regional cooperation and integration. The Asian Development Bank (ADB) and its subsidiary for research and capacity-building, the ADB Institute (ADBI), have contributed to expansion of the region's infrastructure and understanding of how that infrastructure contributes to trade and resulting growth in the region.

While trade is primarily a private sector activity, much of it relies on infrastructure which, in turn, is primarily financed by the public sector in acknowledgement of trade's contribution to growth, development and poverty reduction. Infrastructure, both physical and institutional, facilitates trade by lowering the costs of moving goods, information and payments from economic agents in one country to those in another. As tariff barriers have fallen in successive GATT/WTO (General Agreement on Tariffs and Trade/World Trade Organization) rounds of negotiations, infrastructure-related trade costs have become comparatively more important. At the same time, production and trade patterns have evolved as technology and infrastructure have lowered absolute and relative trade costs while timeliness of delivery has increased in importance as a factor in demand.

Most of the analysis of infrastructure's impact on trade costs has focused on conditions in more developed countries. This volume contributes to our understanding by examining the situation in developing Asia, the world's most populous and fastest-growing region. Chapters explore topics ranging from Asian trade patterns and trade costs to port competitiveness, congestion and foreign direct investment (FDI) in trade-related infrastructure. Empirical estimates complement the analysis of issues to inform the policy-making process.

Asia's trade is found to be expanding at both the extensive and intensive margins. The new trade flows at the extensive margins in particular are often in the form of small shipments from small firms, of goods with lower weight–value ratios, and facing greater demand for timeliness of delivery and air shipment. At the intensive margin, enhanced port efficiency and greater competition between ports and between different modes of transport are seen to have augmented trade flows. Improved physical infrastructure has lowered trade costs for intraregional trade, spurring development of production fragmentation. The importance of service links in this process highlights the importance of institutional infrastructure for further trade expansion.

The chapters in this volume were prepared, discussed and refined as part of an ADBI research project on infrastructure's role in reducing Asia's trade costs. Prema-Chandra Athukorala, Fukunari Kimura, Fausto Medina-Lopez and Toshiro Nishizawa provided valuable comments on drafts of the chapters, as did staff from ADBI. Ms Kayo Tsuchiya's excellent assistance in preparation of this manuscript is gratefully acknowledged.

Masahiro Kawai
Dean, Asian Development Bank Institute

Abbreviations

ADB	Asian Development Bank
ADBI	Asian Development Bank Institute
AFTA	ASEAN Free Trade Area
ASEAN	Association of Southeast Asian Nations
BAF	bunker adjustment factor
CES	constant elasticity of substitution
c.i.f.	cost, insurance, freight
DWT	dead weight tons
EDI	electronic data interchange
FAF	fuel adjustment factor
FDI	foreign direct investment
f.o.b.	free on board
FTZ	free trade zone
GATT	General Agreement on Tariffs and Trade
GSP	Generalized System of Preferences
ICT	information and communications technology
IPC	Indonesian Port Company
OLS	ordinary least squares
PRC	People's Republic of China
PRD	Pearl River Delta
PSO	public service obligation
RTG	rubber-tyred gantry
SAARC	South Asian Association for Regional Cooperation
SAFTA	South Asian Free Trade Agreement
SEZ	special economic zone
TEU	twenty-foot equivalent unit
THC	terminal handling charge
TRT	turn-round time
WTO	World Trade Organization
YAS	yen appreciation surcharge

1. Infrastructure's role in lowering Asia's trade costs

Douglas H. Brooks

Infrastructure services can reduce distribution margins, narrowing the gap between prices faced by producers and consumers, and thereby facilitating welfare improvements for both. On the supply side, the expansion or quality improvement of infrastructure services can lower marginal costs, raising the minimum efficient scale of production, transportation, or marketing. These lower costs and greater economies of scale raise the potential for increased sales overseas, as well as domestically. Indeed, a significant part of infrastructure's contribution to growth and poverty reduction in Asia comes through its facilitation of international trade expansion. It expands both the scope for domestic absorption and supply to export markets, while stimulating linkages with and between different sectors and industries, and encouraging innovation.

Asia benefits from market-driven integration, where large trade and FDI (foreign direct investment) flows respond to infrastructure development, outward-oriented policies and international production networks. Both Asian and non-Asian multinational corporations have developed international supply chains in the region. Financial integration has supported these developments by increasing access to credit and innovative financial instruments. Tariffs and quotas have been reduced under successive rounds of multilateral negotiations under the General Agreement on Tariffs and Trade (succeeded by the World Trade Organization) and the recent plethora of bilateral and regional trade agreements, and openness to FDI is promoted. In this economic environment infrastructure-related trade cost reductions have become relatively more important than direct policy barriers as sources of further cost savings (Brooks et al., 2005).

Efficient infrastructure services lower transaction costs, raise value-added and increase potential profitability for producers while increasing and expanding linkages to global supply chains and distribution networks. In a study incorporating threshold effects, Francois and Manchin (2006) found that infrastructure is a significant determinant not only of export

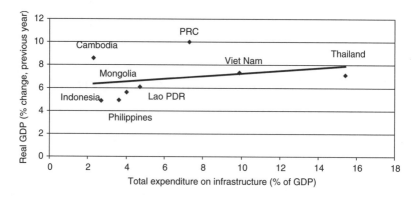

Sources: World Bank, *World Development Indicators 2007*; Asian Development Bank, *Asian Development Outlook* (2005, 2006, 2007).

Figure 1.1   GDP growth and total expenditure on infrastructure in 2003 (per cent of GDP)

levels, but also of the likelihood of exporting at all. Moreover, a country that is more deeply involved in global production networks will probably benefit more from trade-related infrastructure investment than one that is not. Investments in expanding and upgrading transport and telecommunications infrastructure are particularly important in this regard, but FDI, while closely linked to trade, is unlikely to finance and develop significant amounts of infrastructure by itself.

Public investment accounts for most physical infrastructure outlays, particularly where fixed network infrastructure has public good and natural monopoly characteristics. Francois and Manchin (2006) illustrate the complementarity between greater government involvement, domestic transport and communications infrastructure, and export performance. Figures 1.1 and 1.2 reflect the positive correlation between infrastructure expenditure and growth, and infrastructure expenditure and trade, respectively.

The ability of a nation to finance infrastructure projects is complicated by the dynamics of trade balances, debt and reserve accumulation, among other factors that constitute important feedback loops between trade and infrastructure. Consequently, the modality chosen for financing infrastructure investment can have macroeconomic implications which vary depending upon initial conditions (Brooks and Zhai, 2008). Demographics, government debt levels and intergenerational equity are all relevant concerns in the decision-making process for infrastructure expansion and financing.

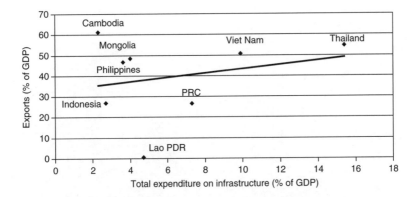

Sources: World Bank, *World Development Indicators 2007*; International Monetary Fund, *Direction of Trade Statistics 2007*.

Figure 1.2   *Exports and total expenditure on infrastructure in 2003 (per cent of GDP)*

Often, and particularly in developing countries, too little is spent on maintenance of existing facilities relative to new investment. Allocation of infrastructure expenditures across the various infrastructure subsectors also poses numerous challenges, not the least of which stem from the political economy of such decisions. Furthermore, allocation of spending between different infrastructure subsectors and different modes of transport (for example) requires careful analysis of potential risks, externalities and scale effects. Unfortunately, the necessary data for productive analysis are often sorely lacking. The studies in this volume contribute to filling that gap for trade-related infrastructure.

A common theme throughout these studies is that while infrastructure often evokes images of large-scale physical projects, soft (or institutional) infrastructure is equally important. A supporting environment of predictable legal and judicial rights and procedures, equitable and enforceable competition policy, a sound but not unduly restrictive regulatory framework etc. are crucial for physical infrastructure investment to be efficient. Financial services, including financial intermediation, risk management opportunities, and payment and clearing services, are especially important. Bond markets capable of supplying long-term finance in local currencies play a particularly central role in infrastructure finance, but are still in an early stage of development in most of Asia, although efforts are under way to broaden, deepen and strengthen these markets.

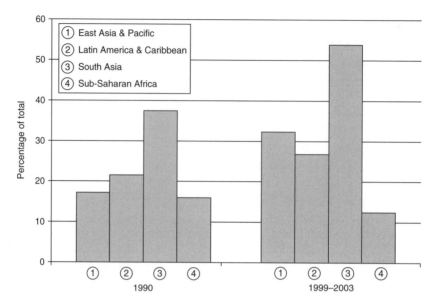

Source: World Bank, *World Development Indicators 2007.*

Figure 1.3   Paved roads

TRENDS IN ASIA'S INFRASTRUCTURE AND TRADE COSTS

Overall, Asian infrastructure has expanded relatively quickly to support the region's rapid trade growth and economic integration compared to other developing regions (Figure 1.3 and Table 1.1). The growth has not always been smooth and symmetrical. Just as the financial balance of trade flows is frequently uneven, so is the physical balance. Unbalanced international trade volume creates additional costs for managing shipping capacity, utilization of infrastructure adjacent to port areas, and cargo clearance, as well as possible macroeconomic imbalances. With berth space in ports now becoming a greater constraining factor in Asia's trade expansion, exploiting complementarities with other modes of transportation infrastructure becomes even more important. At the same time, shifts in production and trade are affecting modal usage. For example, greater shipments of goods with higher value per unit of weight and sharply higher rewards for timeliness of delivery are reducing the relative importance of sea transportation *vis-à-vis* air, although sea shipments still dominate overall.

Table 1.1 Intraregional comparisons

	Period	Africa	East Asia	South Asia	Latin America & Caribbean
Merchandise trade (% of GDP)	2005	57.8	74.6	31.2	44.2
Gross fixed capital formation (% of GDP)	2004	18.4	33.8	22.9	19.5
Gross domestic savings (% of GDP)	2004	17.9	37.9	20.1	23.8
Cumulative inward FDI flows (billion US$)	1990–2005	125.0	1340.0	65.0	725.0
Intraregional trade shares (%)	2003	12.2	55.0	6.0	15.0
Infrastructure					
Electricity consumption (kWh per capita)	2003	513.0	1184.3	393.9	1614.5
Fixed line and mobile subscribers (per 1000)	2004	90.6	431.7	75.3	496.0
Internet users (per 1000)	2005	29.0	88.6	49.0	156.1
Electric power transmission and distribution losses (% of output)	2003	12.0	7.3	26.4	16.1
Paved Roads (% of total)	1999–2003	12.5	32.3	53.9	26.8

Source: World Bank, *World Development Indicators 2007.*

Both the quantity of infrastructure investment and the quality of infrastructure services influence trade performance (see, e.g., Limao and Venables, 2001; Clark et al., 2004). This occurs through infrastructure's impacts on pecuniary transaction costs, loss, damage and spoilage to goods in transit, and timeliness of delivery, among other factors.

Nordås and Piermartini (2004) characterize four dimensions of the relationship between infrastructure and trade transaction costs:

1. *Direct monetary outlays* on communications, business travel, freight, insurance and legal advice are partly determined by the quality of infrastructure and the cost and quality of related services.
2. *Timeliness*, even more than freight rates, is probably influenced by geography and infrastructure.
3. *Risk* of damaged cargo and resulting increased losses and insurance costs is higher when infrastructure is of poor quality.

4. *Lack of access* to a good transport or telecommunication service can have a high opportunity cost, restricting market access and limiting the likelihood of participating fully in the benefits of trade.

In Chapter 2, David Hummels looks at four types of recent changes in the composition of trade and their effects on demand for transportation: (1) changes in the weight–value ratio of traded goods; (2) demand for timeliness and the shift towards increased air shipping; (3) new trade flows (of both products and geographical routes) and variation in the size of shipments; and (4) production fragmentation. The relationships are complex since the developments are interlinked. For example, declining weight–value ratios and vertical specialization in the fragmentation of new production supply chains generate new trade flows and patterns that spur the rapid growth in Asian air cargo shipments.

When infrastructure development lowers the marginal cost of trade, there can be increases in exports at both the intensive and extensive margins. The expansion at the extensive margin, typically through small shipments from small firms, influences the types of infrastructure demanded, and especially transportation infrastructure demand, differently than does the deepening of existing trade flows. The resulting growth in exports from shipping new goods to new markets (trade at the extensive margin) has been greater than that due to increasing current exports to existing markets (trade at the intensive margin). When the new markets are inland, air transport may be an alternative to a combination of sea and land freight to avoid and reduce potential port congestion. In addition, the shipping time savings are positively correlated with the shipping distances involved.

As infrastructure expanded in Asia, particularly in East Asia, trade costs fell and altered the comparative advantages of countries in the region, making greater fragmentation of production supply chains possible and spurring the region's intraregional trade in intermediate products. The subsequent economic integration in East Asia is sharply higher than in other developing regions (Figure 1.4). When inputs are being sourced from wherever costs are lowest (including trade costs), and the production process increasingly dispersed geographically, then timeliness and reliability of delivery become critical factors and the influence of both physical and institutional infrastructure services is even more apparent. In this context, East Asia's performance stands out relative to other developing regions (Table 1.2).

Among different indicators of infrastructure services' contributions to trade, port efficiency appears to have the largest influence, reflecting the fact that the vast bulk of developing countries' trade (by weight) goes through seaports. The dominance of sea freight over land transport and associated

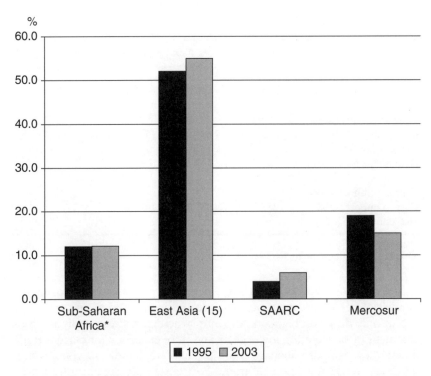

Notes: * 1998. SAARC: South Asian Association for Regional Cooperation; Mercosur: Southern Common Market.

Sources: World Bank African Database 2005; Asian Development Bank, *Regional Cooperation and Integration Strategy*, 2006.

Figure 1.4   Intraregional trade (per cent of total exports)

cost savings emphasize the need to address the challenges faced by land-locked countries attempting to compete in global markets, as well as the importance of improving port efficiency in countries with amenable coastal areas.

Jon Haveman, Adina Ardelean and Christopher Thornberg confirm through detailed estimation in Chapter 3 that specific types of infrastructure investments are highly correlated with reductions in port costs for a subsample of Asian ports. While Penang (Malaysia) currently has the lowest costs of those ports studied, Mumbai experienced the greatest improvement in relative costs between 1997 and 2005. Operating with a new harbour, wharf, or terminal, and procurement of a new crane are found to

Table 1.2   Border trade costs

	Sub-Saharan Africa	East Asia & Pacific	South Asia	Latin America & Caribbean
Documents for export (number)	8.2	6.9	8.1	7.3
Time for export (days)	40.0	23.9	34.4	22.2
Cost to export (US$ per container)	1561.0	885.0	1236.0	1068.0
Documents for import (number)	12.2	9.3	12.5	9.5
Time for import (days)	51.5	25.9	41.5	27.9
Cost to import (US$ per container)	1947.0	1037.0	1495.0	1226.0

Source: World Bank, *Doing Business 2007*.

reduce port costs by 2 per cent and 1 per cent, respectively. Increasing the number of berths and deepening channels at ports have less effect.

Not only do investments in port infrastructure, and especially the procurement of new cranes, lower costs and raise efficiency for current trade flows; they can also increase port capacity to handle new flows and influence the composition of trade. Port costs vary significantly across products even at a single port and new infrastructure can, for example, differentially influence the costs for loading/unloading containers versus bulk commodities. Given the inherent advantages in containerization for certain product categories, relevant port infrastructure developments can potentially reduce unit costs further as the container share of trade rises.

Interactions between changes in the composition of trade, mode of product packing (container or bulk, for example), and the capacity expansion effect of new port infrastructure all influence the potential profitability, and hence bankability, of port infrastructure investments. In planning port expansion or improvement projects, both the efficiency and capacity effects need to be taken into account when projecting potential benefits. This is true for all modes of transport, through sea-, dry and airports.

The relative weights of different aspects of trade costs are often surprising. As Prabir De notes in Chapter 4, in 2005 the ocean freight rate for importing a container to India was about two-thirds greater than for exporting. At the same time, the ocean freight rate for importing a container to China from six Asian countries was far lower than for exporting. Auxiliary shipping charges (documentation fees, container handling charges, government taxes and levies, etc.) are sometimes greater than the ocean freight charges, particularly where shipments experience congestion at ports or borders. This highlights great potential for infrastructure's contributions to lowering trade costs. On average, auxiliary shipping charges outweigh terminal handling charges across countries and commodities in Asia, with variation in such charges contributing significantly to variations in trade costs.

In addition, the composition of freight charges can vary significantly across countries and commodity categories. De finds that the share of total freight charges accounted for by inland freight may be less than that of ocean freight, but is frequently greater. The actual balance depends on the country, suggesting an inland focus for trade-related infrastructure priorities in those countries where the inland share is greater. From 2000 to 2005, transport costs became relatively higher and shipping distance relatively lower, and a 10 per cent rise in transport costs (expressed as an *ad valorem* tax equivalent) lowers Asia's trade by 3–4 per cent from what it would otherwise be. Differentiating among commodity groups, the weight–value ratio is found to be the major determinant of transport cost, suggesting that road, rail and sea may be in increasing order of preference for transport modes for heavier cargos. Hummels and Skiba (2004) similarly found that a 10 per cent increase in product weight–value ratio results in a 4 per cent increase in *ad valorem* shipping costs.

ISSUES IN TRADE-RELATED INFRASTRUCTURE

Cargo owners' port choice is influenced by distance and time to ports, shipping routes and intended destination(s), and total costs. Indirect trade-offs in regulatory compliance and enforcement, and between port location and security of delivery (and quality of delivered product), also influence choices of ports and modes of transportation.

Producers generally choose a port that is consistent with minimum distribution cost, including time effectiveness, regulatory requirements and unscheduled costs, as well as monetary costs. In Chapter 5, Arianto Patunru, Nanda Nurridzki and Rivayani explore exporters' assessments of seaport competitiveness in the context of the Indonesian archipelago economy, where roughly 90 per cent of external trade (and much of internal trade) passes through seaports. Competition may be in the form of inter-port, intra-port, or intra-terminal competition. Comparing Tanjung Perak Port in Surabaya and Tanjung Emas Port in Semarang, the analysis considers captive and contestable hinterlands and port-choice decision-making by exporters in the contestable hinterlands.

Traditional economies concerned with raw materials distribution are more likely to exhibit the 'trade follows the ships' principle, where exporters are attracted to use ports with shipping routes that best reach the desired markets. Regions more dominated by service sector exports generally exhibit the 'ships follow the trade' principle, in which ships are routed to serve those regions.

Seaport competitiveness may suffer from poor physical infrastructure such as inadequate channel depth, shortage of berths, and limited cargo handling equipment, storage and transit areas. It may also suffer from limitations in soft infrastructure, such as labour skills, regulation, bureaucracy and other institutional factors affecting port capacity utilization. In the case of Indonesia, soft infrastructure is found to play a vital role in constraining port efficiency, more so than hard infrastructure, although the two are linked. Lack of direct competition between ports controlled by the same government authority is also a critical factor.

While port performance is crucial to this archipelago, capitalizing on the links and complementarities between different modes of transportation can boost trade substantially. Air- and seaports can move more goods, particularly for containerized shipping, when served by efficient rail and road networks. Similarly, telecommunications and information technology infrastructure reduce search costs and border clearance costs (including time costs). Improvements in infrastructure service efficiency can lead to cost savings equivalent to those accruing from moving production to locations thousands of kilometres closer to trading partners.

Process time and its variability in fragmented production processes depend on integrated logistics infrastructure. This can be crucial in sectors such as fashion clothing or auto parts, where the use of just-in-time production and delivery processes is widespread. For example, Suzhou Park in the People's Republic of China includes free trade zones with streamlined customs procedures and dedicated transport routes to ports, and has thereby reduced both costs and waiting times (Hausman et al., 2005).

Exploiting complementarity of hard and soft infrastructure raises overall trade and economic performance. This is especially noticeable in the case of networks. Many communication and infrastructure services that are important for economic development and trade expansion exhibit network externalities. Infrastructure networks exhibiting service externalities include telephones, railways, and water supply systems (see Laffont and Tirole, 2000). In the presence of such externalities, the maximum amount that consumers are willing to pay for a good or service depends in part on the number of other consumers who also purchase the item in question. This interrelationship calls for consideration of these network systems' governance in competition policy. As one example, Korea has achieved one of the highest rates of broadband internet penetration at competitive prices by balancing the technical advantages of network infrastructure with the efficiency advantages of competition.

It is now common to hear stories of how mobile phones have benefited small farmers or fishing outfits in developing countries by enabling them to check prices in different nearby (or distant) markets before deciding where to deliver their products. The quality of communication infrastructure services is not only strongly correlated with search costs, but also with costs of entering into contracts with suppliers and monitoring implementation of those contracts. Costs related to the time elapsed between the perception of demand and subsequent supply of products to the relevant retailer(s) can also figure prominently (Nordås and Piermartini, 2004).

Fink et al. (2002) found that the cost of making a telephone call has a significant and negative impact on bilateral trade flows. In addition, the bilateral costs of telecommunications have a greater effect on trade of differentiated than of homogeneous products. This highlights the value of access to information and the importance of information technology infrastructure as well as telecommunications at the dynamic extensive margin of trade. In particular, as the number of smaller shipments of a wider variety of higher value-added products rises, ICT (information and communications technology) infrastructure services become especially valuable and more amenable to private sector financing.

The same is true as growth in trade of services outpaces that of goods. Significantly, infrastructure, especially telecommunications infrastructure, is particularly important for trade in services, where the main services traded (banking and business services, communications, etc.) are highly dependent on well-developed infrastructure in both the exporting and importing countries (Nicoletti et al., 2003). Given the huge value of ICT infrastructure demanded, it is fortunate that ICT is an infrastructure sector that the private sector is especially adept at innovating, expanding and financing.

INFRASTRUCTURE'S ROLE IN TRADE PATTERNS

Infrastructure influences not only absolute, but also comparative, advantage. Differences between countries in the quality of infrastructure services help to explain differences in total factor productivity. These impacts on productivity vary across sectors, depending on how intensively each sector uses infrastructure services and how reliant it is on good-quality infrastructure services (and the availability of technology for alternative production processes). Thus patterns of specialization and trade are determined in part by the influence of the quality of infrastructure services on comparative advantage. Moreover, limitations in factor endowments may be mitigated by infrastructure services, also affecting the dynamics of comparative advantage. In different cases, infrastructure services may serve either as complements to, or substitutes for, physical inputs. The significance of factor endowments in determining comparative advantage may thus be modified by infrastructure development (Yeaple and Golub, 2007).

Malaysia is a prime example of a country where the government has actively promoted infrastructure development in order to strengthen its competitive and comparative advantage. Since the mid-1980s, Malaysia has progressed towards a FDI-led, export-oriented development strategy, with FDI contributing to the economy's integration in global production networks. As Tham Siew Yean, Evelyn Devadason and Loke Wai Heng point out in Chapter 6, foreign firms' interest in Malaysia as a key link in global supply chains has been sharpened by the country's competitive locational advantages, which in turn are closely linked to its infrastructure development and resulting high-quality services. Institutional infrastructure at the macroeconomic level, in the form of exchange rate regime, has also played an important role.

The chapter on Malaysia illuminates the role of infrastructure in attracting export-oriented FDI through observing FDI's sectoral and locational pattern, and through interviews with managers of local subsidiaries of foreign firms involved in international trade. The location of FDI is found to be biased towards areas with relatively good infrastructure and amenities. Thus infrastructure improvements increase the chances of attracting FDI, which in Asia has frequently been directed towards export sectors, and therefore also influences patterns and quantities of imported raw materials and intermediate inputs.

Amiti and Javorcik (2008) find that market and supplier access are the most important factors affecting foreign entry, and have about four times as great an effect on choice of foreign investment location as do production costs. In particular they find that in the People's Republic of China (PRC), access to markets and suppliers within the province of entry matters more than access to the rest of the country, consistent with observed market fragmentation. An increase of one standard deviation in the number of sea berths is found to increase foreign entry by about 11 per cent, while a one standard deviation increase in the length of rail lines increases it by 7 per cent. This reinforces the observation that provinces with more developed ports, and to a lesser extent a more developed rail network, tend to attract greater FDI flows. Over time, however, such related factors as congestion, security concerns, connectivity of airports and delays in processing trade documentation may reduce the positive impact of infrastructure on lowering trade costs for foreign investors.

When growth is very rapid, congestion may result as the increase in traffic induced by the economic growth outpaces the expansion of infrastructure services. As discussed by Liqiang Ma and Jinkang Zhang in Chapter 7, this is the current situation in China. Seaport congestion results from the long neglect of access transport and port facilities infrastructure. Six per cent of the world's rail lines struggle to move one-quarter of the world's rail freight turnover, and only 2 per cent of the country's highway network is expressways.

In recent years Chinese exporters have experienced fluctuating trends in freight and insurance costs for ocean trade but a steady decrease in those for air cargo. In 2002, the *ad valorem* costs of air freight and insurance fell below those of sea freight and insurance, and have remained lower since. Over the period from 1990 to 2004, the share of air cargo was relatively constant in terms of weight but roughly tripled in terms of value. The analysis finds that relative to the country's average trade with the rest of the world, China's exports are lower and declining in terms of the weight–value ratio while imports are higher and increasing (reflecting the rise in imports of raw materials). Like Malaysia, the PRC sees port infrastructure as a means to attract FDI from potential exporters.

Congestion has been rising, most notably at Shanghai, as the physical infrastructure is overloaded and there is a lack of collaboration to achieve higher levels of supply chain efficiency among different stakeholders at the port. The drive to increase port and modal competition for greater gains in efficiency presents an opportunity to increase both hard and, increasingly, soft infrastructure. In terms of soft infrastructure, reliability of trade facilitation and administrative procedures at customs is crucial, including rationalization of the customs transit system in order to reduce customs inspection time, and simplify declarations and the documentation process. Shanghai's congestion is raising competition with nearby ports in neighbouring economies, endangering its hub status and as a premier gateway to international markets and suppliers. In recent years, the number of trans-shipped containers from Shanghai via Hong Kong accounted for as much as 20 per cent of the total container throughput of Shanghai.

The limited extent of infrastructure connections to western regions in China results in high trade costs for inland regions and hinders regionally balanced growth. As land and labour costs rise near coasts, investors are looking to locate production facilities further inland. However, they are hampered by poor infrastructure connections that raise trade costs to and from those areas. This has led to a shift in infrastructure policy emphasis, giving more weight to hinterland access. In particular, railway construction is crucial for inland provinces, where a greater share of production is of bulk commodities. At the same time, the lack of a seamless logistics management system adds to delays in the use of multimodal transportation, especially in inland areas where it may be most valuable.

Domestic infrastructure behind the border can have as much effect on the length and variability of time-to-market as freight services between countries. This is particularly true in large or landlocked countries, where the proliferation of inland dry ports has evolved partly in response to this problem. Limao and Venables (2001) found that domestic infrastructure explains about 40 per cent of transport costs for coastal countries, while domestic and transit country infrastructure together account for an estimated 60 per cent of transport costs for landlocked countries. Furthermore, they found that land transport is about seven times more costly than sea transport over similar distances, and that estimates of the elasticity of trade flows with respect to transport costs range from -2 to -3.5, suggesting that lowering a country's trade costs by 10 per cent through infrastructure development could increase its exports by over 20 per cent.

For South Asia, Prabir De finds in Chapter 8 that inland transport cost is the major component, accounting for about 88 per cent, of overall trade transportation costs. Such costs are very high across South Asian countries, with the exception of Sri Lanka, and vary across goods and countries, being even higher when countries are landlocked. Land border crossings are overcrowded, needing special policy attention to reduce delays and monetary costs. Complex requirements in cross-border trade raise the possibilities for corruption and have encouraged sharp growth in informal trade. The magnitude of border effects in South Asia argues strongly for improvements in soft infrastructure, complemented by inland transportation infrastructure to raise the competitiveness of the sub-region's exports.

TRADE-RELATED INFRASTRUCTURE AND REGIONAL COOPERATION

Regional infrastructure coordination can lower infrastructure costs and limit resulting environmental and other negative social impacts, while still contributing to trade expansion. In the case of the Greater Mekong Subregion, special forums have been established to coordinate transport, telecommunications and electric power infrastructure developments, particularly for the development of cross-country economic corridors (ADB, 2006).

The diversity of Asian economies, supported by infrastructure expansion and enhancement to lower trade costs, has helped the region to benefit as a microcosm of global patterns of production fragmentation, expanding intraregional trade, and diversification of development opportunities. The studies in this volume help to quantify these impacts, delineate emerging trends and issues, and highlight policy implications. In this context they build our knowledge infrastructure for trade.

The impacts of trade-related infrastructure can be leveraged by coordination across borders. In the international context, the role of harmonizing and strengthening soft infrastructure stands out as an essential partner of enhanced physical infrastructure. Supported by a conducive policy environment and capitalizing on regional externalities through cooperative arrangements, the expansion, improvement and maintenance of infrastructure services can reduce trade costs and facilitate trade expansion, economic growth and development, and regional integration.

REFERENCES

Amiti, B. and B.S. Javorcik (2008), 'Trade costs and location of foreign firms in China', *Journal of Development Economics*, **85**, 129–49.
Asian Development Bank (2006), 'Regional cooperation and integration strategy', Manila, the Philippines: Asian Development Bank, http://www.adb.org/documents/policies/RCI-strategy/final-RCI-strategy-paper.pdf.
Brooks, D.H. and F. Zhai (2008), 'The macroeconomic effects of infrastructure financing: a tale of two countries', *Journal of Integration and Trade*, **28**, 297–323.
Brooks, D.H., D. Roland-Holst and F. Zhai (2005), 'Asia's long-term growth and integration: reaching beyond trade policy barriers', ERD Policy Brief No. 38, Manila: Asian Development Bank.
Clark, X., D. Dollar and A. Micco (2004), 'Port efficiency, maritime transport costs and bilateral trade', NBER Working Paper 10353.
Fink, C., A. Matoo and H.C. Neagu (2002), 'Assessing the impact of telecommunication costs on international trade', World Bank Policy Research Paper 2552.
Francois, J. and M. Manchin (2006), 'Institutional quality, infrastructure, and the propensity to export', available at: http://siteresources.worldbank.org/INTTRADECOSTANDFACILITATION/Resources/InstitutionalQuality_Infrastructure&PropensityToExport.pdf.
Hausman, W.H., H.L. Lee and U. Subramanian (2005), 'Global logistics indicators, supply chain metrics, and bilateral trade patterns', World Bank Policy Research Working Paper 3773.
Hummels, D. and A. Skiba (2004), 'Shipping the good apples out: an empirical confirmation of the Alchian–Allen conjecture', *Journal of Political Economy*, **112**, 1384–1402.
Laffont, J. and J. Tirole (2000), *Competition in Telecommunications*, Cambridge, MA: MIT Press.
Limao, N. and A.J. Venables (2001), 'Infrastructure, geographical disadvantage, transport costs and trade', *World Bank Economic Review*, **15**, 451–79.
Nicoletti, G., S. Golub, D. Hajkova, D. Mirza and K.Y. Yoo (2003), 'Policies and international integration: influences on trade and foreign direct investment', OECD Economics Department Working Papers 359.

Nordås, H.K. and R. Piermartini (2004), 'Infrastructure and trade', World Trade Organization Staff Working Paper ERSD-2004-04.
Yeaple, S. and S.S. Golub (2007), 'International productivity differences, infrastructure and comparative advantage', *Review of International Economics*, **15**(2), 223–42.

2. Trends in Asian trade: implications for transport infrastructure and trade costs

David Hummels

INTRODUCTION

The Asian region has long been home to some of the world's most dynamic trading economies. The last decade has proved no exception to that rule, with China and India achieving historically unparalleled trade growth. This growth brings prosperity but also a series of challenges for both private and public sectors. Chief among these challenges is building and maintaining a trade infrastructure adequate to the new trading environment.

The purpose of this chapter is to examine the evolution of merchandise trade in Asia with a focus on how this evolution affects infrastructure needs. The starting point is an analysis of rapid growth in aggregate volumes of trade, its geographic orientation and growing cargo imbalances. The extent of trade growth carries obvious implications for infrastructure demand, as more trade requires improved infrastructural development to keep pace.

However, aggregate changes are reasonably well understood and so the primary focus of this chapter is change in the composition of Asian trade. A traditional approach to thinking about composition is to disaggregate trade by product categories, for example, manufacturing versus agriculture and mining. Instead, I focus on four types of compositional change, each of which affects the type and intensity of transportation services demanded. These include: changes in the weight–value ratio of trade; growth in air shipping and the demand for timeliness; growth in new flows and large versus small shipments; and growth in fragmentation/vertical specialization.

AGGREGATE TRADE: GROWTH AND ORIENTATION

Aggregate trade volumes are growing rapidly in Asia. Table 2.1 reports values of imports and exports (in billions of 2000 US$) for 12 Asian

Table 2.1   Trade growth, 1995–2005

Country	Exports (billion 2000$)			Imports (billion 2000$)		
	1995	2005	Annualized growth rate	1995	2005	Annualized growth rate
China	161.0	674.0	15.4	142.0	583.0	15.2
Indonesia	47.9	75.9	4.7	42.5	51.2	1.9
India	33.9	90.8	10.4	37.0	132.0	13.6
Kyrgyz Republic	0.4	0.6	2.7	0.6	1.0	5.6
Malaysia	78.1	123.0	4.6	80.1	99.8	2.2
Philippines	21.6	36.6	6.0	36.7	41.6	1.4
Thailand	60.5	96.3	4.8	74.1	104.0	3.4
Hong Kong	186.0	259.0	3.4	209.0	266.0	2.4
Japan	469.0	505.0	0.7	354.0	450.0	2.4
Korea	136.0	252.0	6.4	147.0	232.0	4.7
Singapore	126.0	196.0	4.5	134.0	176.0	2.8
Taipei,China	128.0	167.0	3.4	114.0	160.0	4.3

Note: First year of Philippines data is 1996; first year of Taipei,China data is 1997.

Source: COMTRADE database, author's calculations.

countries in 1995 and 2005 from COMTRADE. The countries are roughly grouped by level of development, with emerging markets at the top and established developed markets at the bottom.

   In this period China and India stand out prominently. Chinese exports (imports) grew at 15.4 (15.2) per cent per year, while Indian exports (imports) grew at 10.4 (13.6) per cent per year. The result was that in ten years Indian trade tripled, and Chinese trade quadrupled – with China becoming the most prolific trader in Asia. The remaining countries also experienced trade growth, but at rates comparable to or less than the world-wide average in this period of 4.9 per cent per year.

   Also noteworthy is the fact that many countries have merchandise trade imbalances that are large relative to flows: China has a merchandise surplus equal to 15.6 per cent of imports; India has a merchandise deficit of 45.4 per cent of exports. Typically trade balances are thought to be a subject of concern only in so far as they reflect problems with currency valuation or with domestic savings and investment rates. But they also matter for infrastructure and transport planning purposes. Transportation expenses are minimized when ships and planes run at full capacity in both directions. A country that runs a large trade surplus in dollar terms typically also runs a trade surplus in full relative to empty containers, and this drives up shipping costs.

With whom are the Asian countries trading? Table 2.2 reports the shares in 2005 of each major geographic region (Asia, North America, Europe, Other) as an export destination or import source for each listed country. Asia is the dominant origin and destination point for all listed countries except India and the Kyrgyz Republic.

Further, within Asia trade is growing in importance for most countries. Table 2.2 also reports the percentage point change in shares for the Asian region. For example, the share of Indonesian exports destined for Asian markets grew from 60.4 per cent in 1995 to 65.2 per cent in 2005, a growth of 4.8 percentage points. For every country here but the Kyrgyz Republic, Asia as a source of imports grew in importance in this period, by an average of 6.3 percentage points. Similarly, Asia as a destination region for exports grew in pronounced fashion for most Asian traders. Again the Kyrgyz Republic is an exception, as is China. China is especially interesting as its exports shifted in dramatic fashion away from Asia, which received nearly 60 per cent of China's exports in 1995 but only 45 per cent in 2005.

Recalling the spectacular growth in both imports and exports for China reported in Table 2.1, the changing geographic composition of China's trade paints a clear picture. The rest of Asia exports inputs (parts and components, capital machinery, raw materials) to China, which combines these inputs into final goods for sale in the rest of the world.

This raises the following question: but for China, what would trade performance look like in the rest of Asia? The first column of Table 2.3 reports the share of China in exports for each country in 2005. China as a destination represents less than 10 per cent of exports for the emerging markets, but much higher percentages for the developed economies – 13.4 per cent for Japan, just under 22 per cent for Korea and Taipei,China, and 45 per cent of Hong Kong's exports. Exports to China grew very rapidly, with rates as high as 65 per cent per year for Taipei,China. Even the modest 6.6 per cent per annum growth for Hong Kong represents a very large dollar growth given that its exports to China started from a very high base in 1995.

One way to measure the China effect is to conduct a thought-experiment. Suppose a particular exporter experienced no growth in exports to China but all other flows stayed the same. By how much would their aggregate export growth be reduced? To show this, the last two columns of Table 2.3 report annualized growth in exports to the World and to the World minus China. For the emerging markets (top half of the table) and Singapore, exports to China are growing fast but still represent a fairly small share of aggregate exports. The consequence is that eliminating China from the aggregate growth totals has a small effect – typically lowering export growth by less than one percentage point per year. For the remaining countries China is a major export destination, and so after netting growth in

Table 2.2 Geographic orientation of trade, 2005

	Export destination region (shares)					Import source region (shares)				
	Asia	North America	Europe	Other	1995–2005 change in Asia share	Asia	North America	Europe	Other	1995–2005 change in Asia share
China	44.6	23.0	21.7	10.7	−15.0	62.2	8.5	14.6	14.7	4.8
Indonesia	65.2	12.1	12.8	9.9	4.8	62.0	7.9	12.2	17.9	12.3
India	31.6	17.9	24.3	26.2	0.6	34.0	9.7	33.9	22.4	10.1
Kyrgyz Republic	31.5	3.4	35.0	30.1	−23.6	37.3	7.4	50.0	5.2	−11.8
Malaysia	58.0	20.4	12.4	9.2	1.9	65.6	13.4	13.2	7.7	6.7
Philippines	61.1	18.7	17.2	3.0	18.3	60.7	18.1	9.5	11.7	9.4
Thailand	56.7	16.4	14.6	12.3	3.8	60.9	7.7	11.9	19.5	3.4
Hong Kong	62.3	17.1	15.7	4.9	10.1	82.3	5.6	9.0	3.1	7.3
Japan	48.1	24.4	16.1	11.4	4.7	44.1	14.4	13.9	27.6	7.6
Korea	51.7	16.1	17.3	14.9	2.3	48.3	12.8	12.8	26.1	7.3
Singapore	67.4	10.9	12.4	9.4	8.0	61.5	12.1	13.3	13.2	1.8
Taipei,China	64.8	16.1	12.4	6.7	14.0	57.9	12.1	12.2	17.8	7.9

Data Source: COMTRADE data, author's calculations.

Table 2.3   Export growth to China

	Export share to China, 2005	Annual growth in exports to		
		China	World	World−China
Indonesia	7.8	12.2	4.7	4.3
India	6.6	32.5	10.4	9.7
Kyrgyz Republic	4.1	−10.9	2.7	4.1
Malaysia	6.6	14.5	4.7	4.2
Philippines	9.9	31.6	6.0	5.0
Thailand	8.4	16.3	4.8	4.2
Hong Kong	44.7	6.6	3.4	1.3
Japan	13.4	11.3	0.7	−0.2
Korea	21.8	18.7	6.4	4.6
Singapore	8.8	19.7	4.6	3.8
Taipei,China	21.7	64.9	3.4	0.4

exports to China off their overall trade growth, we see Hong Kong's and Taipei,China's exports growing at anaemic 1.3 and 0.4 per cent per year, and Japan's export growth actually going negative.

Trade of course requires two partner countries, and infrastructure problems at either end can be costly to both parties. Put another way, the importance of the Asian region as an origin/destination of trade for these countries indicates an important interdependence. As China's trade grows rapidly and suffers inevitable congestion effects, it becomes a problem not just for China and Chinese firms but for all other Asian nations that have come to rely on China as a trading partner.

THE WEIGHT–VALUE RATIO OF TRADE

Transportation specialists are accustomed to thinking of transportation costs in per unit terms, the cost of transportation services necessary to move grain a ton-km or to move one TEU (twenty-foot equivalent unit) container from Los Angeles to Hong Kong. International trade specialists who pay attention to shipping costs as an impediment to trade are accustomed to thinking of these costs in *ad valorem* terms, the cost of transportation services necessary to move a dollar of grain or microchips between two points. The distinction is important because even if the cost of moving one TEU container remains constant over time, the *ad valorem* cost and the implied impediment to trade will change as the contents of the container grow more valuable.

To see this, suppose we sell 1 kg of a good at a price per kg of p, and pay shipping costs f per kg shipped. Note that the price per kg, p, is just the value–weight ratio, that is, the inverse of the weight–value ratio. If the shipping price per kg f is independent of the goods price per kg, the ratio of destination to origin prices is

$$p^*/p = (p + f)q/pq = 1 + f/p = 1 + (weight\text{–}value)f \qquad (2.1)$$

If the container holds scrap metal, p is low (weight–value is high), and the ratio p^*/p is high. That is, shipping charges drive a large wedge between the prices at the origin and at the destination. If the container holds microchips, p is very high (weight–value is very low), the ratio p^*/p is close to 1, and shipping charges drive only a small wedge between prices at the origin and at the destination.

Of course, the shipping charge f may be increasing in the value of the container's content because higher-value goods require more careful handling and a larger insurance premium. We can then write the per kg shipping charge as $f = p^\beta X$, where X represents other costs shifters such as distance, port quality and so on. In this case we have

$$p^*/p = 1 + p^{\beta-1}X = 1 + X(weight\text{–}value)^{1-\beta} \qquad (2.2)$$

Unless $\beta = 1$, the weight–value ratio of a product will be an important determinant of the transportation expenses incurred when trading that product. Hummels and Skiba (2004) and Hummels et al. (2007) examine the dependence of shipping costs on product weight–value. They estimate that a 10 per cent increase in product weight–value leads to a 4–6 per cent increase in shipping costs measured *ad valorem*, i.e. relative to the value of the good shipped. Further, since there is tremendous variation across products in weight–value ratios, weight–value explains far more variation in observed transportation costs than do other observables, including: the distance goods are shipped; the technology with which they are shipped; the quality of port infrastructure; or the intensity of competition between carriers on a trade route.

What has happened to the weight–value ratio for Asian trade? Systematic data on product weights are not available for trade worldwide, but by combining detailed shipment characteristics from US trade data with the worldwide coverage of the COMTRADE data we can calculate the weight of the trade bundle for each country. To do this, we calculate the median weight–value ratio for each HS (Harmonized System) 6-digit product k in US imports between 1990 and 2005, ω_k.[1] We then multiply the weight–value ratio by the share of product k in the trade bundle of country

c at time t, s_{ckt}. Summing over products yields the aggregate weight–value ratio for each country's imports and exports at a point in time:

$$\omega_{ct} = \sum_k s_{ckt} \omega_k$$

This of course assumes that a dollar of some particular product, say, wooden furniture, weighs the same when shipped to the USA as when shipped to other destinations, so that variation across countries and over time is driven by differences in the trade shares of heavy and light products.

We report time series on weight–value measured in kg per constant year (2000) US dollars for each country's imports (solid line) and exports (dashed line) in Figure 2.1. Several patterns are notable. One, a dollar of exports weighs far less for the developed market economies (Japan, Korea, Taipei,China, Hong Kong, Singapore) than for the emerging market economies. Indonesia is a notable outlier in the weight of its exports, which are almost 40 times heavier per dollar than those of Singapore or Japan. Two, most of these Asian economies (with the exception of Malaysia and Indonesia) are net importers of weight; that is, their import bundles weigh far more than do their export bundles. Three, the picture of China's trade that emerged in the aggregate flows is reinforced here. China's imports are getting heavier and exports are getting lighter as China imports raw materials, transforms them, and shifts increasingly to high-value exports.

Two final points about weight–value are worth emphasizing. First, the falling weight–value ratio for Chinese exports may play an important role in its export expansion. Equation (2.2) indicates that shipping costs are a function of weight–value and other factors X such as port quality and geography. China faces cost disadvantages due to geography when shipping to the USA and European markets. However, by upgrading product quality and producing goods with lower weight–value China has been able to minimize the impact of these other disadvantages.

Second, changes in the weight–value ratio of trade have implications for how goods are shipped and for changes in competitive advantage in world trade markets. Reductions in weight–value make it easier to shift from ocean to air shipping because it reduces the *ad valorem* price differential between the two modes. Consider this example. I want to import a $16 bottle of wine from France. Air shipping costs of $8 are twice ocean shipping costs of $4. Going from ocean to air increases the delivered cost by $4, or 25 per cent. Now suppose my tastes improve and I want to import a $160 bottle of wine from France so that the weight–value ratio of the product has dropped sharply. The shipping costs are the same, but now the $4 cost to upgrade to air shipping represents just a 2.5 per cent increase in the delivered price. The consumer is much

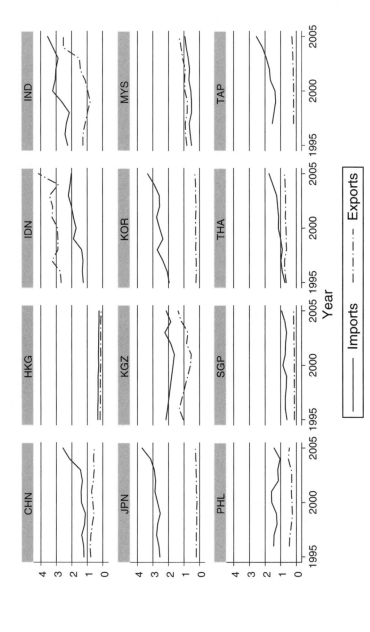

Source: COMTRADE.

Figure 2.1   Weight–value of trade by country, 1995–2005

more likely to use the more expensive shipping option when the effect on delivered price is smaller.

The broad point for transportation planning is that final consumers are sensitive to changes in the delivered price, not to changes in the transportation price. If the cost of transportation substantially affects the delivered price, as in the first example, modal choice will be driven by cost considerations. But if the transportation price is only a small fraction of the delivered price, it will probably be trumped by other factors such as timeliness or reliability. It should be noted that the same lesson is true of all cost differentials related to transportation. Port A may charge handling fees per container that are twice the handling fees for Port B, but unless these differences substantially affect delivered prices of products they will have minimal impacts on the derived demand for transportation.

AIR SHIPPING AND THE DEMANDS FOR TIMELINESS

As Hummels (2007) shows, air shipping worldwide has grown at a rate of 8.3 per cent per year since 1975, much faster than ocean shipping or trade growth as a whole. How important is air shipping for the Asian economies? Figure 2.2 reports data from the IATA World Air Transportation Statistics on the growth in air cargo between Asian and other major regions between 1980 and 2004, with cargo measured in terms of freight tons carried. Air cargo involving Asian nations has grown much faster than in the world as a whole, with especially rapid growth involving intra-Asian international flights.

Despite this very rapid growth in air cargo measured in terms of cargo weight shipped, the vast majority of trade by weight takes place via ocean cargo. To measure the importance of air cargos in value terms we must rely on US import data.

Table 2.4 reports on the share of air transport in export value to the USA from each Asian exporter in 1995 and 2005. Air shipping constitutes a small share of trade for Indonesia (14 per cent) and the Kyrgyz Republic (12.9 per cent) at the low end up to a remarkably high share of trade for Malaysia (71.6 per cent) and Singapore (79 per cent). These differences closely reflect differences in the weight–value of the export bundles for each exporter, as well as the importance of electronics. Air shipping has slightly declined in importance since 1995 for the developed market economies, but has significantly increased for both China and Malaysia.

What is driving the rapid growth in Asian air cargo? As argued above, declining weight–value ratios play a large role, as do the steep

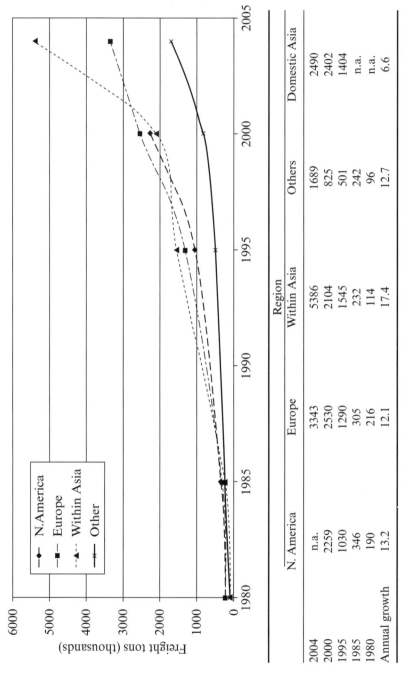

	N. America	Europe	Region Within Asia	Others	Domestic Asia
2004	n.a.	3343	5386	1689	2490
2000	2259	2530	2104	825	2402
1995	1030	1290	1545	501	1404
1985	346	305	232	242	n.a.
1980	190	216	114	96	n.a.
Annual growth	13.2	12.1	17.4	12.7	6.6

Figure 2.2 Air cargo in Asian trade (thousand freight tons)

Table 2.4 Time sensitivity of trade

	Air share in exports to USA		Per day time sensitivity	
	1995	2005	Imports	Exports
China	10.6	23.3	0.69	0.77
Indonesia	8.3	14.0	1.00	0.56
India	47.1	41.4	1.50	0.76
Kyrgyz Republic	1.6	12.9	1.22	5.92
Malaysia	48.2	71.6	0.87	0.62
Philippines	44.8	48.0	0.65	0.51
Thailand	29.4	41.3	0.87	0.84
Hong Kong	41.4	38.5	0.74	0.81
Japan	27.8	25.6	0.57	1.14
Korea	48.2	34.2	0.58	1.03
Singapore	78.2	79.0	0.75	0.82
Taipei,China	31.1	37.1	0.69	0.91

Note: Per day time costs based on Hummels and Schaur (2007).

Sources: COMTRADE, US Imports of Merchandise; author's calculations.

declines in the price of air cargo documented in Hummels (2007). In addition, four factors seem especially important: rising incomes; vertical specialization/fragmentation; testing new markets; and trade between geographically remote locations.

First, high-income households buy higher-quality goods and higher-income countries import higher-quality goods.[2] Rising incomes affect demand for air transport in three ways. One, higher-quality goods have higher prices and therefore a lower *ad valorem* transportation cost for reasons just discussed. Two, as consumers grow richer, so does their willingness to pay for precise product characteristics.[3] That in turn puts pressure on manufacturers to produce to those specifications, and be rapidly adaptable. Three, delivery speed is itself an important characteristic of product quality, and will be in greater demand as income grows.

The second factor of importance in recent trade growth is the fragmentation of international production processes, also known as vertical specialization.[4] Multi-stage production may be especially sensitive to lags and variability in timely delivery, and both are reduced by using airplanes. Of course, airplanes move people in addition to cargo. Multinational firms with foreign production plants rely heavily on the ability to fly executives and engineers for consultations with their foreign counterparts. For all the wonder of information technology, there is not yet a good substitute for face-to-face communication, especially when new products and production processes are being introduced. Below, I provide evidence that growth in vertical specialization/fragmentation has been especially important in East Asia.

The third factor, testing new markets, finds that airplanes are ideal and so are especially important for firms who are expanding trade by selling new goods for the first time. The use of air shipping is about a trade-off: speed and flexibility versus unit costs. Speed and flexibility are more important when markets are a large distance away, and when there is uncertainty in quantity demanded, product quality, or desired product characteristics. Unit cost advantages for ocean shipping are greatest when the goods have low value–weight ratios, when market demand is certain and when the scale of trade is large.

In the next section I show that much of the growth in Asian trade is along the extensive margin, meaning that nations are growing their exports by shipping new goods to new markets, not by increasing the quantities sold of existing exports. What are the characteristics of these new markets? Most firms begin producing only for a local market, slowly expand sales within their own country, and some small fraction of these gradually expand sales abroad. Of those that go abroad, most look initially to neighbouring countries. Because of this, new and unexploited markets tend to be further away. When serving these distant markets, firms face tremendous uncertainty about demand, quantities sold are likely to be very low initially, and most trading relationships fail in a few years. All of these characteristics, initially small quantities of uncertain demand in distant markets, are precisely those that make air shipping particularly attractive. This suggests that airplanes may be an especially effective tool for firms wishing to test new markets.[5]

Fourth, geographic remoteness of two kinds can be overcome by using airplanes. Ocean port cities act as entrepôts for interior regions of their own countries. These entrepôt cities can be a bottleneck choking off trade, especially for geographically large countries with economically important interior regions. This becomes more pronounced in cases where ports vie for land and coastal access that retain significant value for housing and public amenities. Trucks arriving at and departing from these facilities also compete with other users of roadways, leading to major highway congestion and significant pollution effects. Air cargo that overflies congested ports can be an effective way to reach remote interior regions. This can be seen clearly in US data, where the share of coastal facilities is shrinking in favour of direct transport into the US interior.[6]

Airplanes are also relatively more useful at reaching distant foreign markets. Suppose I am trying to decide between air and ocean shipping in reaching two foreign markets, the first proximate to and the second distant from my exporter. How does the distance affect my calculation of the appropriate mode to use? Exporters consider two costs, both rising with distance. The first is the direct cost of transport; the second is the time cost.

Time costs are unimportant for some goods, and in these cases exporters can focus more narrowly on direct transport cost considerations. In most instances, such considerations will favour ocean transport, whether the foreign destination is distant or proximate. For some goods time costs are important, and more subtle calculation is required. For the nearby export destination, direct costs favour ocean shipment, and the time difference between ocean and air is small enough that time costs can be ignored in the calculation. For the distant export destination, however, the time difference between ocean and air can loom large indeed. In short, the further away the market, the greater the time advantages provided by air shipping.

More generally, we can calculate the importance of timeliness by combining estimates of the time value of trade by product with data on trade shares. Hummels and Schaur (2007) estimate the value of time saving using US import data that report the price and quantity of air shipping relative to ocean shipping as well as time delays associated with ocean shipping. The idea is that a firm's willingness to pay for more expensive air shipping is increasing in the number of days saved with airplanes, and decreasing in the premium paid for air shipment. The sensitivity of air shipment to these factors can then be used to calculate a per day valuation for time savings that is product specific. Call this per day valuation for an HS-4 product k, τ_k. As with the weight–value ratio we can then calculate the aggregate time sensitivity of a country's trade bundle by multiplying the product-specific time cost by the share of that product k in the trade bundle:

$$\tau_{ct} = \sum_k S_{ckt} \tau_k.$$

The last two columns of Table 2.4 report the time sensitivity of the import and export bundle for each country. The values are written in *ad valorem* equivalents per day. A value of 0.77 for Chinese exports means that each day of delay in transit is equivalent to a tariff of 0.77 per cent, so that a four-day delay is equivalent to a tariff of just over 3 per cent *ad valorem*. Two things are notable about these figures. First, time sensitivity is much more important for the developed compared to the emerging market economies. Second, the time sensitivity of the import and export bundles are considerably different – developed markets export goods that are more time sensitive than those they import, while the emerging market do the reverse. Note that the import bundles of India and Indonesia are twice as time sensitive as their exports. Of course, the numbers on time sensitivity in the last two columns of Table 2.4 are intended to capture aggregate tendencies, and do not reflect the sensitivity of particular sectors. Malaysia, for example, ships extremely time-sensitive products to the USA, as demonstrated by the very high share of air shipping shown in the first two columns of Table 2.4.

NEW FLOWS AND LARGE/SMALL FLOWS

Recent theoretical and empirical research in international trade has begun to emphasize the importance of extensive and intensive margins of trade expansion. A country can expand exports by trading larger quantities of a given set of goods (the intensive margin), or by expanding the set of goods that are traded (the extensive margin). Higher trade costs can affect both margins.[7]

Suppose that exporting firms must pay a fixed cost of trade (for example, the cost of collecting information about foreign markets or setting up distribution networks) and marginal costs of trade (proportional to quantities traded). In this case, firms must sell a sufficiently high volume of exports to justify paying the fixed costs. A fall in marginal costs of trade lowers delivered prices and expands quantities demanded abroad. This has two effects: existing exporters can sell larger quantities (an increase in the intensive margin); and more firms can now cover their fixed costs of trade and begin exporting for the first time (an increase in the extensive margin). In contrast, a drop in fixed costs of trade leads to trade expansion only along the extensive margin.

Which of these is most important? In order to decompose trade growth in this manner, write the aggregate value of a country c's exports at time t as

$$X_t^c = N_{jkt}^c \overline{X}_{jkt}^c, \qquad (2.3)$$

where N_{jkt}^c is the number of unique shipments of products k (measured at the 6-digit HS level) to destinations j from exporter c at time t, and $\overline{X}_{jkt}^c$ is the average value per unique shipment. If c ships ten distinct products apiece to each of five destination markets, the number of unique shipments is 50.[8] Exports could increase over time because country c ships more goods, has more export destinations per good or higher average value per shipment. (Note that it is also possible to separate N into the number of products and number of destinations per product. However, at this 6-digit HS level of aggregation we see very little growth in number of products traded in this period. As a result, changes in the number of unique shipments for these countries and this time period are driven almost entirely by expansions in the number of markets with which trade occurs.)

We can then express the log percentage change in total exports over time as the sum of the log changes in the components:

$$\ln\frac{X^c_{t+1}}{X^c_t} = \ln\frac{N^c_{jkt+1}}{N^c_{jkt}} + \ln\frac{\overline{X}^c_{jkt+1}}{\overline{X}^c_{jkt}}.$$

This is useful because we can then assess the percentage contribution of each component to the total change. Table 2.5 provides such a decomposition separately for imports and exports of each country. For simplicity we report only the log change in each variable. For example, using the values from Table 2.1, the log change in Chinese exports between 1995 and 2005 is ln(674/161) = 1.43. Of this 1.43, 0.80 came from an increase in the number of unique shipments, and 0.63 came from an increase in average value per shipment. Contrast this mixed growth with Thailand and Malaysia, where almost all growth came via an increase in the number of shipments rather than an increase in the average shipment. Conversely, almost all the growth for Hong Kong and Japan came through an increase in average shipment size rather than an increase in the number of unique shipments.

The calculation of the changes in average shipment size can be misleading – the average can rise because all existing shipments get larger, or it could be that shipment size grows differentially at different points in the size distribution. To show this distinction, Table 2.5 also reports growth in the size of the median and 90th percentile shipment. By comparing these with growth in the mean shipment, we can understand where trade growth is occurring.

Consider Chinese exports, where the number of shipments and mean shipment size are growing rapidly, as are 90th percentile shipments, but median shipment sizes are falling. This indicates that China has experienced a tremendous growth in new shipments, but these tend to be very small, pushing down the median shipment size. At the same time, established flows that were already large (90th percentile) in 1995 have grown larger still, and this increased the mean shipment size. The pattern across all reported countries is similar – median shipment sizes are falling while mean shipment sizes are rising (or, in some cases, both are falling but medians are falling faster).

What do we learn from this exercise? For most of these countries we have export expansion occurring in two very different ways: there are large and existing flows that are the principal drivers of aggregate trade growth; but there is also a very large number of new entrants that do not, to date, represent a large fraction of overall trade. This distinction matters for several reasons. One, the infrastructure needs of small and medium-sized firms

Table 2.5   Decomposing trade growth, 1995–2005

	Log change in export				
	Value	Number of shipments	Shipment value		
			Mean	Median	90th pctile
China	1.43	0.80	0.63	−0.09	0.38
Indonesia	0.46	0.65	−0.19	−0.91	−0.47
India	0.99	0.80	0.19	−0.32	−0.02
Kyrgyz Republic	0.26	0.61	−0.35	−1.84	−1.25
Malaysia	0.46	0.42	0.03	−0.12	−0.04
Philippines	0.53	0.35	0.18	−0.65	−0.43
Thailand	0.46	0.51	−0.04	−0.85	−0.24
Hong Kong	0.33	0.04	0.29	−0.61	−0.14
Japan	0.07	−0.06	0.13	−0.18	0.01
Korea	0.62	0.29	0.33	−0.33	−0.05
Singapore	0.45	0.10	0.35	−0.29	0.07
Taipei,China	0.27	0.10	0.17	−0.37	−0.12

	Log change in import				
	Value	Number of shipments	Shipment value		
			Mean	Median	90th pctile
China	1.42	0.39	1.03	−0.27	0.44
Indonesia	0.19	0.19	−0.01	−0.57	−0.38
India	1.27	0.64	0.63	−0.45	0.09
Kyrgyz Republic	0.55	1.81	−1.26	−2.35	−1.66
Malaysia	0.22	0.12	0.10	−0.29	−0.07
Philippines	0.12	0.09	0.03	−0.56	−0.49
Thailand	0.34	0.34	0.00	−0.85	−0.38
Hong Kong	0.24	0.11	0.13	−0.63	−0.35
Japan	0.24	0.12	0.12	−0.37	−0.13
Korea	0.46	0.30	0.16	−0.70	−0.23
Singapore	0.27	0.11	0.16	−0.58	−0.22
Taipei,China	0.34	0.13	0.20	−0.62	−0.19

Note: First year of Philippines data is 1996; first year of Taipei,China data is 1997.

Sources: COMTRADE database; author's calculations.

may be considerably different from those of large firms. They typically lack the internal capacity for facilitating trade and must work through trade intermediaries to gather information about foreign market opportunities, and to handle trade finance, transportation and distribution functions. Two, small firms face higher shipment costs because they are unable to negotiate bulk discounts. Three, if we take the fixed versus marginal cost view of trade costs, these new flows associated with small and medium-sized firms are highly tenuous. Small increases in trade costs could quickly kill off many exporting firms. Now, one could view this as a minor concern: these flows are small and their loss could be absorbed with little impact on aggregate numbers, but this ignores the dynamic nature of new flows. Besedes and Prusa (2003, 2004) use survival analysis to show that new trade flows suffer high failure rates, but those that do survive go on to ever-larger trade shares. That is, today's success story was yesterday's fragile newborn.

FRAGMENTATION AND VERTICAL SPECIALIZATION

Rather than producing final goods in their entirety, countries are increasingly specializing in stages of production. This is true to a much greater degree in Asia than in any other region of the world and is largely responsible for the large fraction of intra-Asian flows shown above. Fragmentation puts a much greater strain on transport and trade infrastructure than other types of production arrangements. Because products engage in 'round tripping', the impact of higher transportation expenditures is multiplied by the number of times a component is shipped. Further, timeliness in delivery and information tracking matters to a greater extent as entire factories can be shuttered by the absence of key components.

How important is this phenomenon in Asian trade? One way to measure the fragmentation process is to look at the share of trade that occurs in goods labelled 'parts and components'. This approach has been widely employed and is useful, but it also leaves out intermediate goods (e.g. chemicals) that do not contain the 'parts and components' label. An alternative approach introduced in Hummels et al. (2001) is to employ input–output tables that track use of imported intermediate inputs. One can measure the contribution of imported inputs into gross output and the portion of gross output that is exported. This provides us with the value of goods that are traded twice – once as an imported input, and again embodied in an exported final good.

Uchida (2007) employs this technique in conjunction with Asian input–output data produced by JETRO–IDE to measure vertical specialization in

Table 2.6   Vertical specialization in Asia

	Millions of 2000$			Percentage of total exports				
	1990	1995	2000	1975	1985	1990	1995	2000
China	966	5 373	13 932	n.a.	2.2	4.3	7.2	9.5
India	584	1 583	2 873	1.4	1.9	3.0	4.9	6.9
Japan	5 742	11 451	14 939	3.8	4.1	3.6	4.1	5.1
Korea	5 710	11 819	19 673	20.6	18.5	16.1	17.6	19.8
Malaysia	2 906	11 303	25 606	7.2	12.7	15.1	23.5	37.2
Taipei,China	7 938	14 420	24 368	n.a.	15.5	19.7	25.0	26.4
Philippines	990	2 623	7 687	4.3	10.4	15.7	18.8	30.6
Singapore	8 281	19 354	17 811	20.9	36.1	35.8	42.6	35.5
Thailand	2 326	7 690	10 815	3.0	8.2	19.0	24.4	26.5
USA	2 107	6 431	7 438	0.9	1.7	2.1	3.8	4.3

Note: The dollar or percentage content of exports composed of imported inputs equals (share of imported inputs in gross output) * value of exports.

Source: Uchida (2007).

Asia. Summary results are reported in Table 2.6. Consider China, for example. Roughly 9.5 per cent of China's exports in 2000 consisted of imported inputs, up from 2.2 per cent in 1985. The importance of vertical specialization is greatest for Malaysia, the Philippines, Singapore, Taipei,China and Thailand, whose exports include from 26 to 37 per cent foreign content. The numbers are smaller for Japan, Indonesia and the USA because these countries engage in one but not both sides of vertical specialization. Indonesia provides inputs in large quantities but engages in less processing. Japan and the USA import inputs in large quantities, but do not combine these with domestic value-added to export goods.

CONCLUSION

It is well known that Asian trade has grown very rapidly in the past decade, and this growth has put infrastructure under considerable strain. The aim of this chapter has been to highlight the particular nature of that trade growth, its changing composition, and the particular demands compositional change places on infrastructure. The key points are these: trade is growing and growing lighter; exports are expanding primarily by reaching new markets with smaller flows; and fragmented production networks are becoming the norm. All of these changes put a premium on speed, flexibility and information. Infrastructure improvements targeted on these points will be more likely to pay off in the form of increasingly efficient integration into the global economy.

NOTES

1. Weight variables in the data are subject to significant measurement error; in particular, extreme outliers that make simple or trade-weighted averages a misleading measure of central tendency. Medians do not suffer this problem and, moreover, exhibit a very high degree of over time correlation for a given product.
2. Hallak (2006); Choi et al. (2007).
3. Hummels and Lugovskyy (2005).
4. See Yi (2003) and Hummels et al. (2001).
5. Aizenman (2004) and Schaur (2006) examine the use of airplanes in hedging demand volatility. Evans and Harrigan (2005) and Harrigan and Venables (2004) discuss the importance of demand volatility in determining comparative advantage and industrial agglomerations.
6. Haveman and Hummels (2004).
7. See Hummels and Klenow (2005) on extensive and intensive margin expansion, and Hillberry and Hummels (2008) and Eaton et al. (2004) on the role of geographic frictions.
8. One could further decompose this into the number of products multiplied by the average number of destinations per product.

REFERENCES

Aizenman, J. (2004), 'Endogenous pricing to market and financing cost', *Journal of Monetary Economics*, **51**(4), 691–712.
Besedes, Tibor and Thomas Prusa (2003), 'On the Duration of Trade', NBER Working Paper 9936.
Besedes, Tibor and Thomas Prusa (2004), 'Surviving the US import market: the role of product differentiation', NBER Working Paper 10319.
Choi, Yo Chul, David Hummels and Chong Xiang (2007), 'Explaining import variety and quality, the role of the income distribution', NBER Working Paper 12531.
Eaton, Jonathan, Samuel Kortum and Francis Kramarz (2004), 'Dissecting trade: firms, industries and export destinations', NBER Working Paper 10344.
Evans, Carolyn and James Harrigan (2005), 'Distance, time, and specialization: lean retailing in general equilibrium', *American Economic Review*, **95**(1) March, 292–313.
Hallak, J.C. (2006), 'Product quality and the direction of trade', *Journal of International Economics*, **68**(1), 238–65.
Harrigan, James and Anthony Venables (2004), 'Timeliness, trade and agglomeration', NBER Working Paper 10404.
Haveman, Jon and David Hummels (2004), *California's Global Gateways, Trends and Issues*, San Francisco, CA: Public Policy Institute of California.
Hillberry, Russell and David Hummels (2008), 'Trade responses to geographic frictions: a decomposition using microdata', *European Economic Review*, **52**, 527–50.

Hummels, David (2007), 'Transportation costs and international trade in the second era of globalization', *Journal of Economic Perspectives*, **21**(3), 131–54.

Hummels, D. and P.J. Klenow (2005), 'The variety and quality of a nation's trade', *American Economic Review*, **95**(3), 704–23.

Hummels, David and Volodymyr Lugovskyy (2005),' 'Trade in ideal varieties: theory and evidence', NBER Working Paper 11828.

Hummels, David and Georg Schaur (2007), 'Time as a trade barrier', mimeo, Purdue University.

Hummels, David and Alexandre Skiba (2004), 'Shipping the good apples out? An empirical confirmation of the Alchian–Allen conjecture', *Journal of Political Economy*, **112**, 1384–402.

Hummels, David, Jun Ishii and Yi Kei-Mu (2001), 'The nature and growth of vertical specialization in world trade', *Journal of International Economics*, **54**, 75–96.

Hummels, David, Volodymyr Lugovskyy and Alexandre Skiba (2007), 'The trade reducing effects of market power in international shipping', NBER Working Paper 12914.

International Air Transport Association, *World Air Transport Statistics*, various years.

Schaur, Georg (2006), 'Hedging volatility with fast transport', mimeo, Purdue University.

Uchida, Yoko (2007), 'Trade growth and vertical specialization in East Asia', JETRO-IDE mimeo.

Yi Kei-Mu (2003), 'Can vertical specialization explain the growth in world trade', *Journal of Political Economy*, **111**, 52–102.

3. Trade infrastructure and trade costs: a study of selected Asian ports

Jon Haveman, Adina Ardelean and Christopher Thornberg

1. INTRODUCTION

For many years, research in international trade focused primarily on environments without costs to trade. Recently, trade costs have become increasingly important in explaining the rapid growth of world trade. A growing literature on trade costs has focused on lower tariffs, declining ocean and air transport costs, and the revolution in information technology as potential explanations for the rise in international trade over the last five decades. Transport costs are an important part of trade costs, being at least as large as or even larger than tariffs.[1]

Transport costs typically include the costs of loading/unloading, insuring and moving the goods from the origin to the destination. These explicit costs are typically expressed in *ad valorem* terms: a percentage change in the delivered price after paying for freight and insurance. Goods move across borders by various modes of transportation. Trade between neighbouring countries represents 23 per cent of world trade and mostly takes place through surface modes such as rail, truck, or pipeline. The rest of world trade takes place by air or by ocean (Hummels, 2007).

The technological developments in ocean and air shipping have been the focus of research that tries to understand their impact on the size and pattern of international trade in the last five decades. The introduction of containerization in ocean shipping has been thought to be the most significant innovation in this area in the last century because it generates cost savings by allowing goods to be packed once and transported over large distances.

Levinson (2006) qualitatively documents that the associated productivity gains of using container ships led to lower ocean shipping prices. Surprisingly the benefits of containerization do not appear in the historical ocean shipping price series,[2] as they should, mostly because of increases in oil prices during the adoption period of container ships (Hummels, 2007). Countries also differ in their ability to adopt container shipping, with developing countries having started to adapt their port infrastructure only from the late 1970s onward. As a result, some countries and routes have only recently started to fully take advantage of the potential benefits of containerization.

No doubt containerization remains an important technological innovation in transportation, but the technological change in air shipping has had a critical impact on international trade, especially in the postwar period. Despite larger and faster ships and lower loading and unloading times, ocean shipping remains many times slower than air shipping. The development of jet aircraft engines has significantly reduced the cost of speed. If timeliness matters, the falling air transportation costs can explain trade growth, especially for fresh or time-sensitive products (Evans and Harrigan, 2005). Also air transportation can improve the ability to cope with demand uncertainty in foreign markets and hence increase trade (Aizenman, 2004; Schaur, 2006).

Another non-pecuniary cost is the uncertainty involved in transporting goods over large distances. Part of this uncertainty can be eliminated through insurance, another pecuniary cost, but much cannot.[3] In particular, variability in the time it takes to transport goods from point A to point B plays a role in not only whether or not trade occurs, but with whom. Ocean shipping remains the most used mode of transporting goods across borders, especially for heavyweight products and bulk commodities.[4] Thus further improvements in efficiency at moving goods across oceans can reap greater benefits and significantly affect the volume of international trade. These improvements could be investments in port infrastructure to take full advantage of the benefits of the developments in ocean shipping in the last half of the century such as bigger ships, deeper channels, specialized cranes and terminals for container ships or refinements to communications and tracking systems.

It is these investments in trade infrastructure that are the focus of this chapter. In particular, we are looking for evidence that infrastructure developments in a set of ports in three Asian countries have served to reduce the cost with which they process exports to the USA.[5]

We have been generously supplied with two different types of evidence of infrastructure improvements by authors of other chapters in this volume. First, we have evidence of the introduction of specific infrastructure enhancements for a group of the largest ports in China and Malaysia. The enhancements include the expansion of port operating facilities, construction of new berths, procurement of all types of new cranes, and deepening of port channels. Port facilities include the construction of new harbours, transshipment terminals, container terminals and wharfs. Malaysian ports have also implemented new modern management systems for handling port operations. Shanghai deepened its navigation channel by 1.5 metres in 2002 and 2005 consecutively (from 7 metres to 10 metres).

Second, for the top five ports in India, we have detailed annual investment data. Rather than showing particular 'events' at the ports, these data allow an assessment of the extent to which differences in investment across these ports have cost-reducing effects. The detail in the data also permits an evaluation of different types of investment. In particular, we have aggregated the data into the following categories: dock facilities, channel deepening, and loading and unloading equipment. The first category includes the development of new dock facilities and the modernization of old docks. The second is reasonably self-explanatory and includes dredging and deepening operations. The final category includes the installation of new cranes, new rubber-tyred gantries, and similar equipment for loading and unloading.

We measure changes in the port costs by assessing changes in the relative contribution of Asian ports to 'c.i.f.' (cost, insurance, freight) charges on shipments to the USA. The charges levied at Asian ports, the charges levied by shippers for the ocean voyage, and the charges levied by US ports all contribute to the level of charges. Improved infrastructure at the Asian port should reduce port handling charges.

We find that investments in infrastructure and the procurement of new cranes have a significant impact on a port's measured costs, and hence on its efficiency. Some investments, such as the addition of new berths and channel deepening, however, may well have more important implications for overall port capacity than for port costs. Also, our results show that different kinds of investment matter for different goods: the introduction of new cranes used mainly to load and unload container ships matters more for commodities with a high percentage of containerized trade.

The chapter proceeds as follows. In the next section, we introduce our Asian ports for which we have infrastructure investment data. Section 3 outlines the methodology employed and links it back to previous literature. Section 4 discusses recent changes in measured port costs, while Sections 5 and 6 present results on the effect of infrastructure investments in terms of discrete investment events and dollars spent, respectively. A final section presents concluding observations.

2.   ASIAN PORTS

The ports included here are from three of the four countries included in this study. Table 3.1 lists these ports. Most of the ports are the source of significant amounts of exports to the USA. We have also included smaller ports in the hope of generating a more broadly useful set of results.

Table 3.2 provides greater background into the 12 ports and their trading relationship with the USA. For most of the ports, there has been a dramatic increase in the value of the flow of goods to US ports. At one extreme, the

Table 3.1   Asian ports

China	India	Malaysia
Shanghai	Mumbai	Johore
Ning Bo	Jawaharlal Nehru	Kelang
Yantian	Madras	Penang
Xiamen	Tuticorin	
	Calcutta	

Chinese port of Yantian increased its exports to the USA from just $1 million in 1991 to just over $45 billion in 2005. More common among Chinese ports is growth by a factor of 5, 10 or even 40.

Although the Chinese ports are largely outliers, and their growth should not be highly surprising, the vast majority of the other ports in this study also experienced very rapid growth. Indeed, several of India's ports increased exports by a factor of 10 to 20. The ports in Malaysia did not achieve these lofty rates, but none the less greatly outpaced growth that could be explained by increases in US import prices. Between 1991 and 2005, there was an increase in the import price index of the USA of approximately 15 per cent.[6] The index rose from 97.0 in January of 1991 to 112.3 in 2005. The increase in price pales in comparison with the growth of trade from these ports to the USA. The growth is part and parcel of the rapid growth of world trade during the last 30 years, which is well documented elsewhere.[7]

The vast majority of these ports ship goods to the USA primarily in containers. By 2005, all but six of these ports sent more than 90 per cent of their goods by container – one of these six shipped 88 per cent in containers. With four exceptions, all of these ports increased their use of containers significantly between 1991 and 2005. Of these exceptions, Jawaharlal Nehru in India reduced its percentage containerized by less than 1 per cent and still averaged close to 100 per cent.

The number of observations reported in the table reflects the diversity of goods shipped and the number of destinations in the USA to which the ports ship. As observations in our data are at the US port/commodity level, we are not able to observe individual shipments, but this is a good proxy for diversity. As did the overall volume of flows between the Asian ports and US ports, the diversity of this trade also increased substantially.

3.   METHODOLOGY

The primary goal of this chapter is to evaluate the effect of port infrastructure investments on port-related trade costs. This is accomplished in a two-

Table 3.2   Key statistics for Asian ports

Port	Value of exports to the USA (millions $)	Percentage containerized	Number of observations	Year in dataset (earliest & latest)
China				
Shanghai	1 090	91	4 280	1991
	40 986	96	41 779	2005
Yantian	1	100	16	1991
	45 778	98	28 276	2005
Ning Bo	5	94	105	1991
	4 835	98	17 950	2005
Xiamen	25	91	188	1995
	3 963	97	8 833	2005
India				
Jawaharlal Nehru	30	99	288	1995
	2 622	98	8 077	2005
Mumbai	763	72	3 086	1991
	2 300	78	8 374	2005
Madras	278	65	1 102	1991
	1 060	95	3 247	2005
Calcutta	86	79	540	1991
	233	97	1 410	2005
New Tuticorin	41	96	126	1991
	982	97	2 342	2005
Malaysia				
Penang	1 051	59	1 666	1991
	1 919	98	3 067	2005
Kelang	601	62	1 286	1991
	1 949	91	3 687	2005
Johore	52	75	86	1991
	1 401	88	1 217	2005

stage procedure that first estimates a time series of relative port costs for our Asian ports and then correlates cost changes with infrastructure investments.

Estimation of the Asian Port Costs (First Stage)

The first stage is carried out by utilizing a methodology recently developed by Blonigen and Wilson (2006). In their article, they provide a framework for estimating the relative productivity of the world's ports.[8] The framework makes use of highly detailed US trade data and the information collected on the costs of moving goods from foreign ports to the US ports. The charges are generally referred to as c.i.f.

C.i.f. charges include fees for services at the foreign port, fees for the transportation of goods between ports, and fees for services at the US port. Isolating the relative costs of the foreign port involves teasing out the relative contributions of each of the three segments to the total cost of the shipment of a good between a pair of ports. Only the first of the contributions to the c.i.f. charges is related to the costs of using a foreign port.

We rely on US trade data jointly produced by the US Army Corps of Engineers and the US Maritime Administration Office in the Department of Transportation to separate the contribution of the payment for services at the foreign port.[9] The data are known as the Waterborne Trade Databanks, and provide detail on trade between each US port and thousands of foreign ports. This detail includes the percentage containerized, the trade value and volume, and the commodity type aggregated to the 6-digit HS level.[10] Fortunately, the US government makes available the c.i.f. charge data at the same detailed level as it makes available the other information on waterborne trade, such as value, volume and the extent of containerization.

Exploiting these data, Blonigen and Wilson (2006) develop a fixed effects, or elaborate dummy variables approach, that distinguishes between the three pieces of waterborne costs. Their methods incorporate a comprehensive set of foreign (exporting) port dummies, a measure of distance between the ports, and a comprehensive set of US (importing) port dummies. Other bilateral measures included indicate differences in the relative costs of distance. In particular, there is a measure of the density of trade, a measure of the bilateral trade deficit between the two ports, and a measure of the extent of containerization. All these factors are important determinants of the cost of distance.

We rely heavily on Blonigen and Wilson's (2006) methodology and estimate the following regression to tease out the foreign port's costs:[11]

$$CIF_{ijk} = \alpha + \beta_1 Dist_{ij} + \beta_2 Wgt_{ijk} + \beta_3 Valwgt_{ijk} + \beta_4 Cont_{ijk}$$
$$+ \beta_5 Cont_{ijk} \times Wgt_{ijk} + \beta_6 Cont_{ijk} \times Valwgt_{ijk} + \beta_7 Im\_Imbal_{ij}$$
$$+ \beta_8 Ex\_Imbal_{ij} + \eta_i + \theta_j + \gamma_k + \varepsilon_{ijk} \qquad (3.1)$$

where (i) indexes US ports, (j) indexes foreign ports and (k) indexes 6-digit HS products; *CIF* denotes c.i.f. charges, *Dist* is the bilateral great circle distance between a pair of ports, *wgt* is the weight of a traded product, *Valwgt* is the US dollar value per kg of a traded product, *Cont* is the percentage of the trade value transported in a container ship, *Im_Imbal* and *Ex_Imbal* is the import and export imbalance between the pair of ports. All variables are expressed in logarithmic form.

These regressions are run separately for each year between 1991 and 2005. In addition, we run the regressions separately for specific commodity groupings, each of the 1-digit SITC categories from 1 through 9; category 0, 'food and live animals', is excluded because of data limitations. The first-stage regressions are estimated with three years of combined data. For example, the 1992 coefficients would be based on data from 1991, 1992 and 1993. In this way, we smooth out the coefficients and present an average coefficient for the three years centred on the year for which the estimated port costs are reported. For 1991 and 2005, we report coefficients based on only two years of data, combining them with 1992 and 2004, respectively.

The fixed effects, θ_j and η_i, identify the first and third components of the c.i.f. charges, yielding measures of the relative costs of individual ports, both in the exporting country and in the USA. It is possible to measure exporting port costs because a single foreign port ships a variety of goods to multiple US ports. The catch, however, is that the foreign port's costs are measured relative to some other foreign port. That is, the set of dummy variables in the regression is necessarily incomplete. The dummy for one particular exporting port is omitted. Similarly, fixed effects for US ports are included in the analysis to separate their cost changes from those of the exporting ports in the c.i.f. cost data.

The choice of a reference port is a key element in estimating fixed effect coefficients that are conducive to our subsequent analysis. The results presented here are for the port of Tokyo. While Blonigen and Wilson (2006) use the port of Rotterdam, we have elected to go with a major port in Asia that is not primarily a transshipment port, such as Hong Kong or Singapore.[12] Blonigen and Wilson (2006) identified the port of Tokyo as being in the top quartile of exporting ports, in terms of their costs relative to the port of Rotterdam. It also had a relatively small, 7 per cent, change in costs between 1991 and 2003. This small change is important as it suggests that the changes that we observe for our target ports are indeed due to circumstances at the target port and not at the reference port.

Another issue that we deal with is distance. Although Blonigen and Wilson (2006) use very detailed information on shipping distances between US and foreign ports, these data are no longer available. They are maintained by the US Maritime Administration, which is in the process of updating and improving them, and is not willing to release the old version of the data. So we have implemented an alternative. For a minority of the ports, we have information on the minimum shipping distance between them.[13] For the remaining ports, we have used the great-circle distance between the foreign port and the US port. While the latter measure is clearly imperfect, it may not be of great importance. We have estimated the relative cost coefficients both with and without the specific shipping distance data and the resulting estimates are highly correlated.

It is at this point that the established methodology stops. Our purpose in this chapter, however, is to attribute changes in the relative costs of our Asian ports to infrastructure developments. In other words, we proceed in an attempt to explain changes in the estimated relative costs of our 12 Asian ports over time.

Asian Port Costs and Infrastructure Developments (Second Stage)

Having assembled a set of cost measures for the 12 Asian ports in our study, we endeavour to explain some of the variation over time with measures of ports' infrastructure improvements. Our cost measures span the period 1991–2005, the only years for which c.i.f. data are available for US waterborne trade data. In principle, this gives us a set of 15 coefficients for each port; there is not always a sufficient number of commodities shipped to the USA for each port. As this is a very small number of observations, and different products rely on different types of port infrastructure, we also estimate cost measures for different commodities at the Asian ports. It is these commodity- and year-specific measures that form the basis of our analysis.[14]

The approach is similar in each case, and involves regressions attempting to explain variation in the Asian port fixed effects coefficients in the first stage of the analysis. The coefficient estimates of the first stage are the dependent variables in the second stage. As these coefficients are measured with varying degrees of precision, the regressions are weighted by the standard errors of the first-stage estimates. This reduces issues of heteroscedasticity, effectively giving more emphasis to relative cost coefficients that are measured with more precision.

The evidence on infrastructure is entered as an explanatory variable in each of the specifications. For China and Malaysia, we have evidence on specific infrastructure developments for the period between 1991 and 2005, but not on the costs of these investments, and thus we include a dummy variable. The dummy variable indicates the year in which the investment became operative. For India, we have evidence on the dollar value of the investments taken place at Indian ports between 1991 and 2005.

We are conscious of the fact that there are other determinants of port costs, and we include other variables that attempt to control for these effects. In particular, we include controls for labour costs and exchange rate changes. Port tariffs are surely influenced by the labour costs at the ports. Accordingly, we include a measure of the country's wages. As the data report c.i.f. charges in US dollars, there are likely to be residual effects of changes in exchange rates that lead to variability in reported charges. These effects will be country and year specific, and we control for them by including the exchange rate between the Asian currency and the US dollar. Additionally we include 1-digit SITC commodity and port fixed effects. In this way we use time variation to identify the impact of the infrastructure developments on the estimated port costs. We also include country fixed effects when pooling across Chinese and Malaysian ports.

More precisely, for China and Malaysia, we estimate the following specification:

$$\hat{\theta}_{jst} = \delta_1 + \delta_2 t + \delta_{3l}\hat{\theta}_{jst-l} + \delta_4 Port_{jt-1} + \delta_5 Berths_{jt-1} + \delta_6 Cranes_{jt-1}$$
$$+ \delta_7 Channel_{jt-1} + \delta_8 Ex\_rate_{ct} + \delta_9 Wages_{ct} + \varphi_s + \varphi_j + \varphi_c + \varepsilon_{jst} \quad (3.2)$$

where (j) indexes the Asian ports, (s) indexes the 1-digit SITC commodities, (t) indexes the year and (c) indexes the country. *Port* denotes improvements in port facilities, *Berths* and *Cranes* denote the introduction of new berths and new cranes, respectively, and *Channel* denotes channel deepening.[15]

For India, we run two sets of regressions. First we use total dollar value of investments and then group dollar investments in four categories: dock facilities (*Dock*), loading/unloading (*Load/Unload*), other schemes (*Other*) and channel deepening (*Channel*):[16]

$$\hat{\theta}_{jst} = \delta_1 + \delta_2 t + \delta_{3l}\hat{\theta}_{jst-l} + \delta_4 Dock_{jt-1} + \delta_5 Load/Unload_{jt-1} \quad (3.3)$$
$$+ \delta_6 Channel_{jt-1} + \delta_7 Other_{jt-1} + \delta_8 Ex\_rate_t + \delta_9 Wages_t + \varphi_s + \varphi_j + \varepsilon_{jst}$$

Besides the data we employ for port infrastructure developments, the difference between (3.2) and (3.3) lies in the type of fixed effects included. We include port, commodity and country fixed effects when pooling across Malaysian and Chinese ports, but only port and commodity fixed effects for Indian regressions. In both specifications we include lags of the dependent variable and a time trend. The right-hand-side variables capturing the port infrastructure developments, exchange rates and wages are in levels. The estimated port costs ($\hat{\theta}$) are in logarithmic form since they are the dummies from the first-stage regression estimated in logarithms. As a result the estimates of the impact of ports' developments on costs should be interpreted as semi-elasticities.

To sum up, the methodology employed here boils down to a two-stage process. In the first stage, we estimate cost parameters for our 12 Asian ports. In the second stage, we attempt to explain the variation over time in the estimated cost parameters. In the first stage, we include a subset of all foreign ports and a subset of the US ports. In particular, we include our 12 Asian ports along with the top 30 exporting ports to the USA. We also include the top 35 US ports, which accounted for 86 per cent of the value of all US waterborne imports in 1991 and 81 per cent in 2005.

4.   TRENDS IN ASIAN PORT COSTS

In the first stage of our analysis, we generate estimates of the costs of our Asian ports relative to the port of Tokyo. A value greater than one reveals that a port has higher costs than the port of Tokyo. This is characteristic of most of the ports in our dataset. Figure 3.1 depicts the results for one port in each of the three countries (India, Malaysia and China, respectively). Of the three ports, only Penang has consistently rivalled the low costs of the port of Tokyo over the period from 1991 to 2005. Its relative costs started out below zero in 1991, have stayed there for most of the period, but experienced a temporary and inexplicable decrease in costs for two years early this decade.

The other two ports have started the period as substantially more costly than the port of Tokyo. Most of our observations on these ports are in the 10 to 20 per cent range, with Shanghai reaching a high of 23 per cent in the early 1990s. Since then the relative costs of the Shanghai port have decreased significantly, as have the relative costs of the port of Mumbai.

The port of Mumbai has experienced perhaps the most profound improvements in relative costs, falling from just under 20 per cent (0.2 in Figure 3.1) in 1997 to less than zero in 2005. As such, it is a useful port to use in thinking about differences across goods in trends in relative costs.

Figure 3.2 depicts the trends in port costs for eight of the ten 1-digit SITC Revision 3 categories from 1 to 8.[17] ('SITC all products' replicates the chart in Figure 3.1 for Mumbai.) From these charts, it is evident that costs can vary significantly within a given port from good to good. The cost differences can arise from the way in which the various commodities are handled at the ports. Some commodities are handled similarly in Mumbai to the way that they are handled in Tokyo; others may be handled in a less efficient manner.

Most of the goods at the port of Mumbai have experienced the same downward trend as the port as a whole. Notable exceptions include SITC 1, Beverages and Tobacco, SITC 2, Crude Materials, Inedible, except Fuels, SITC 3, Mineral Fuels, Lubricants, and Related Materials, and SITC 4, Animal and Vegetable Oils, Fats and Waxes. Each of these goods experienced significant volatility in costs over the years.

5.   THE IMPACT OF SPECIFIC INVESTMENTS

For ports in Malaysia and China, we have been fortunate enough to obtain evidence of the implementation of specific infrastructure investments. As described in Appendix 3A.3, these infrastructure developments pertain to the introduction of new berths, new cranes for manipulating containers, and channel deepening. We have incorporated this information into

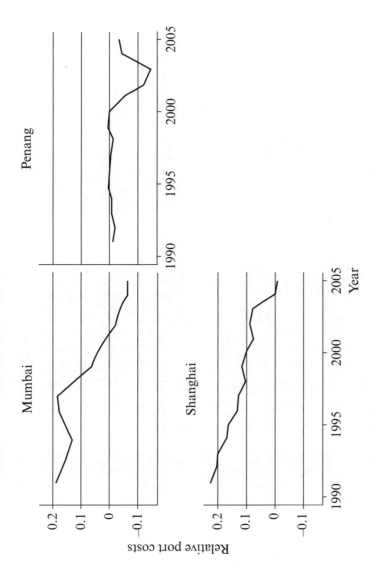

Note: Graphs by port name.

Figure 3.1 Trends in Asian port costs

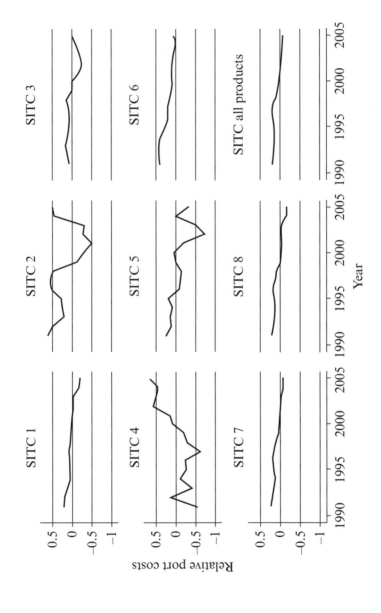

Note: Graphs by product.

Figure 3.2 Product grouping costs changes at Mumbai

48

regression (3.2), which seeks to explain changes in the measured costs of Chinese and Malaysian ports. Table 3.3 presents the regression results estimated by pooling across all 1-digit SITC commodities from three separate specifications. The three specifications differ only in the number of lags of the dependent variable that are included.

As discussed in Section 3, we have also included the relevant exchange rate to control for changes in measured costs that are not necessarily tied to specific changes in port tariffs, but that come about as a byproduct of the way that these data are reported. That is, a weaker Asian currency can reduce the Asian port tariffs set in local currency but reported in US dollars. Thus the exchange rate is likely to be negatively correlated to the estimated port costs. We also control for Chinese and Malaysian wages as labour costs are likely to be positively correlated with port tariffs. We employ data on Chinese provincial wages from the *China Statistical Yearbook, 1991–2005*, and Malaysian wages at the country level from *World Development Indicators*, spanning 1991–2003. Since we lack data on Malaysian wages for 2004 and 2005, we restrict the sample to 1991–2003.

The results clearly indicate that infrastructure investments play a role in reducing measured port costs. Both the enhancements in port facilities and the introduction of new cranes reduce port costs in a statistically significant way. Opening operations in a new harbour, wharf, transshipment or container terminal and the procurement of a new crane reduces port costs by 2 per cent and 1 per cent, respectively. Increasing the number of berths available results in coefficient estimates of the right sign, but they are not close to being statistically significant at conventional levels. Channel deepening performs even less well, with insignificant coefficients of the wrong sign. The exchange rate appears to play no role in explaining port costs, and wages have, contrary to our priors, a negative and statistically significant effect on estimated port tariffs.

Since most of the investments aim to improve the port infrastructure to make it more suitable for handling container ships, we expect different types of enhancements to have different impacts on port costs, depending on whether the commodities are shipped in containers or not. Thus we split our sample into two groups: commodities with a high percentage of containerized trade and commodities with a high percentage of non-containerized trade.[18] Tables 3.4 and 3.5 present the estimation results. Improvements in port facilities remain statistically significant in both specifications but they have a lower impact on port costs for commodities mostly shipped in containers and a higher effect for the non-containerized trade. The procurement of new cranes, probably used to load and unload container ships, has a slightly larger impact on port tariffs of containerized commodities and seems to have no effect in the case of non-containerized trade.

*Table 3.3   The determinants of relative Chinese and Malaysian port costs
             (pooled across all 1-digit SITC commodities)*

	(1)	(2)	(3)
Relative port costs (1st lag)	0.75***	0.80***	0.79***
	(0.01)	(0.01)	(0.01)
Relative port costs (2nd lag)		−0.076***	−0.01
		(0.01)	(0.01)
Relative port costs (3rd lag)			−0.1***
			(0.01)
Port facilities	−0.02***	−0.02***	−0.02***
	(0.00)	(0.00)	(0.00)
Number of new berths	−0.00	−0.00	−0.00
	(0.00)	(0.00)	(0.00)
Number of cranes	−0.01***	−0.01***	−0.01***
	(0.00)	(0.00)	(0.00)
Channel deepening	0.02	0.01	0.01
	(0.01)	(0.01)	(0.01)
Exchange rate	0.00	0.01*	0.00
	(0.00)	(0.00)	(0.00)
Wage rate	−0.00001***	−0.00001***	−0.00001**
	(0.00000)	(0.00000)	(0.00000)
Adj. R-squared	0.62	0.61	0.60
N	14 303	13 596	12 820

Note: ***, **, *: significant at 1 per cent, 5 per cent and 10 per cent respectively.

Most of the port infrastructure developments documented in our data can potentially reduce costs through increases in the percentage of trade shipped in containers. In the first-stage regression, we control for the percentage of containerization trade shipped from the Asian ports to the USA and thus our port cost estimates are netted out of the cost-reducing effect of adopting containerships. As a result, the impact of infrastructure developments at the Asian ports is likely to be much lower on the estimated port costs.

Tables 3A4.4, 3A4.5 and 3A4.6 in Appendix 3A4 provide estimation results for the impact of improving port facilities, of procuring additional cranes and the introduction of new berths on the port costs estimated without controlling for per cent of containerization. When we pool across all 1-digit SITC, all coefficients remain qualitatively unchanged.

Table 3.4 The determinants of relative Chinese and Malaysian port costs
(pooled across 1-digit SITC commodities with containerized trade)

	(1)	(2)	(3)
Relative port costs (1st lag)	0.79***	0.81***	0.80***
	(0.01)	(0.01)	(0.01)
Relative port costs (2nd lag)		−0.02	0.04**
		(0.01)	(0.01)
Relative port costs (3rd lag)			−0.1***
			(0.01)
Port facilities	−0.01**	−0.01**	−0.01***
	(0.00)	(0.00)	(0.00)
Number of new berths	−0.00	−0.00	−0.00
	(0.00)	(0.00)	(0.00)
Number of cranes	−0.02***	−0.02***	−0.02***
	(0.00)	(0.00)	(0.00)
Channel deepening	0.03*	0.03*	0.03*
	(0.01)	(0.01)	(0.01)
Exchange rate	0.01*	0.01***	0.01
	(0.00)	(0.00)	(0.01)
Wage rate	−0.00002***	−0.00001***	−0.00002***
	(0.00000)	(0.00000)	(0.00000)
Adj. R-squared	0.63	0.62	0.61
N	9 303	8 847	8 345

Note: As for Table 3.3.

6. THE EFFICACY OF INDIAN PORT INVESTMENTS

For five major ports in India, Mumbai, Calcutta, Madras (Chennai), Jawaharlal Nehru and New Tuticorin, we have obtained annual data on the dollar value of investments made at the ports.[19] These investments fall into four broad categories: dock facilities, loading and unloading, channel deepening, and other.

Dock facilities include the construction of new terminals or berths, the installation of navigational aids, or the modernization of existing dock facilities; channel deepening includes both the costs of dredging and the purchase of new equipment; loading and unloading involves the replacement or addition of new cranes, the replacement of mobile equipment, and the procurement of new tugs.[20]

Appendix 3A2 presents charts with the total investment amounts in each port and year as well as by investment type. Several characteristics of these

Table 3.5   *The determinants of relative Chinese and Malaysian port costs (pooled across 1-digit SITC commodities with non-containerized trade)*

	(1)	(2)	(3)
Relative port costs (1st lag)	0.58***	0.70***	0.65***
	(0.02)	(0.03)	(0.03)
Relative port costs (2nd lag)		−0.24***	−0.11**
		(0.03)	(0.04)
Relative port costs (3rd lag)			−0.20***
			(0.03)
Port facilities	−0.03*	−0.04**	−0.04**
	(0.01)	(0.01)	(0.02)
Number of new berths	−0.01	−0.01	−0.01
	(0.01)	(0.01)	(0.01)
Number of cranes	0.01	0.02	0.01
	(0.01)	(0.01)	(0.01)
Channel deepening	−0.04	−0.09	−0.07
	(0.06)	(0.06)	(0.06)
Exchange rate	0.02	0.04**	0.04
	(0.01)	(0.01)	(0.02)
Wage rate	0.00007***	0.00008***	0.00007***
	(0.00001)	(0.00002)	(0.00002)
Adj. R-squared	0.43	0.45	0.48
N	1 112	1 046	979

Note: As for Table 3.3.

investments are immediately obvious. First, they tend to be lumpy. Investments in new terminals, dredging projects, and the purchase of new cranes are not regular occurrences, but rather occur in large amounts and with relatively low frequency. Second, they are biased towards the latter part of the time period. For the four ports other than Jawaharlal Nehru, these investments tended to occur with greater frequency in the late 1990s and early part of this decade. It was clearly determined in roughly 1995 that Jawaharlal Nehru was of some importance and, for the next several years, tremendous investments were made in the port. These investments have permitted traffic to increase from 6.9 tons in 1995 to 44.8 tons in 2006 of largely containerized exports.

The results from our second-stage regressions for Indian ports are quite striking. Table 3.6 presents the results from six separate specifications. There are two groups of three specifications. The first group presents level regressions, with aggregate investment expenditures included as an explanatory variable. The second group disaggregates these expenditures into the four categories. Within the two groups, the three specifications differ only in the number of lags of the dependent variable that are included.

As can be seen in Table 3.6, investment dollars, the exchange rate and local wages all appear with the expected signs. For investment dollars in the aggregate, these results indicate that each $1 million reduces relative costs by 0.03 per cent. Therefore it takes about $33 million to reduce costs by 1 per cent. The fact that the investment appears with the correct sign is comforting, but not of great economic significance. The exchange rate is also an important determinant, with a higher exchange rate (weaker rupee) leading to lower measured port costs evaluated in US dollars. This is not a cost effect, but merely due to the translation of port tariffs and other charges from rupees into dollars. Wage rates are our final explanatory variable and they act predictably. Higher wages translate into higher port costs.

The results are less clear when investments are broken down into their separate categories. Of the four categories, three regression coefficients remain negative, but only two are significant. Other schemes enters positively and is startlingly significant.

When we split the sample into containerized and non-containerized trade (Tables 3.7 and 3.8), total investment does not appear to affect port costs for non-containerized commodities. Dock facilities and loading/ unloading have a slightly higher effect on port costs for the group of SITC categories shipped in containers and no or positive impact in the case of non-containerized trade.

As for China and Malaysia, we estimate all the second-stage specifications using port cost estimates without netting out the cost-reducing effects of adopting containerships. Tables 3A4.1, 3A4.2 and 3A4.3 in Appendix 3A4 provide the estimation results. When we pool across all 1-digit SITC commodities, all coefficients remain roughly unchanged except for the impact of the loading and unloading investments on port costs, which increases slightly. Moreover, the increase becomes even stronger for the specification pools across 1-digit SITC with a high percentage of containerized trade. The results provide further evidence that different types of investment matter differently across goods, and in this case loading and unloading dollar investment seems to affect the handling costs of containerized trade more.

7.   CONCLUSIONS

In this chapter, we have provided evidence of the influence of port infrastructure developments in three countries on the relative costs of using those ports. The results for China and Malaysia are based on the implementation

Table 3.6   The determinants of relative Indian port costs (pooled across all 1-digit SITC commodities)

	(1)	(2)	(3)
Relative port costs (1st lag)	0.7743***	0.9000***	0.9027***
	(0.0072)	(0.0127)	(0.0131)
Relative port costs (2nd lag)		−0.1541***	−0.1268***
		(0.0128)	(0.0170)
Relative port costs (3rd lag)			−0.0368**
			(0.0125)
Total investment	−0.0003***	−0.0002***	−0.0002***
	(0.0001)	(0.0001)	(0.0001)
Exchange rate	−0.0045***	−0.0043***	−0.0048***
	(0.0006)	(0.0006)	(0.0006)
Wage rate	0.0043***	0.0040***	0.0031***
	(0.0008)	(0.0008)	(0.0008)
Adj. R-squared	0.77	0.76	0.76
N	7 447	7 015	6 538

	Detailed port investments		
	(1)	(2)	(3)
Relative port costs (1st lag)	0.7745***	0.9022***	0.9039***
	(0.0072)	(0.0127)	(0.0130)
Relative port costs (2nd lag)		−0.1552***	−0.1208***
		(0.0129)	(0.0169)
Relative port costs (3rd lag)			−0.0449***
			(0.0125)
Dock facilities	−0.0002***	−0.0002***	−0.0002**
	(0.0001)	(0.0001)	(0.0001)
Loading/unloading	−0.0016***	−0.0018***	−0.0019***
	(0.0003)	(0.0003)	(0.0003)
Other schemes	0.0013***	0.0019***	0.0019***
	(0.0004)	(0.0004)	(0.0004)
Channel deepening	−0.0003	−0.0007	−0.0006
	(0.0004)	(0.0004)	(0.0004)
Exchange rate	−0.0059***	−0.0060***	−0.0066***
	(0.0006)	(0.0006)	(0.0006)
Wage rate	0.0043***	0.0039***	0.0030***
	(0.0008)	(0.0008)	(0.0008)
Adj. R-squared	0.77	0.76	0.76
N	7 447	7 015	6 538

Note: As for Table 3.3.

Table 3.7   The determinants of relative Indian port costs (pooled across 1-digit SITC commodities with containerized trade)

	(1)	(2)	(3)
Relative port costs (1st lag)	0.7596***	0.8770***	0.8879***
	(0.0081)	(0.0135)	(0.0138)
Relative port costs (2nd lag)		−0.1461***	−0.1451***
		(0.0136)	(0.0176)
Relative port costs (3rd lag)			−0.0175
			(0.0132)
Total investment	−0.0003***	−0.0002***	−0.0002***
	(0.0000)	(0.0000)	(0.0000)
Exchange rate	−0.0023***	−0.0022***	−0.0025***
	(0.0005)	(0.0005)	(0.0005)
Wage rate	0.0033***	0.0030***	0.0025***
	(0.0007)	(0.0007)	(0.0007)
Adj. R-squared	0.78	0.77	0.77
N	6 513	6 147	5 741

	Detailed port investments		
	(1)	(2)	(3)
Relative port costs (1st lag)	0.7583***	0.8801***	0.8906***
	(0.0080)	(0.0135)	(0.0137)
Relative port costs (2nd lag)		−0.1493***	−0.1430***
		(0.0136)	(0.0175)
Relative port costs (3rd lag)			−0.0240
			(0.0131)
Dock facilities	−0.0003***	−0.0002***	−0.0002***
	(0.0001)	(0.0001)	(0.0001)
Loading/unloading	−0.0021***	−0.0024***	−0.0025***
	(0.0003)	(0.0003)	(0.0003)
Other schemes	0.0012***	0.0020***	0.0021***
	(0.0003)	(0.0004)	(0.0004)
Channel deepening	0.0002	−0.0003	−0.0001
	(0.0004)	(0.0004)	(0.0004)
Exchange rate	−0.0043***	−0.0045***	−0.0049***
	(0.0006)	(0.0006)	(0.0006)
Wage rate	0.0032***	0.0029***	0.0023***
	(0.0007)	(0.0007)	(0.0007)
Adj. R-squared	0.78	0.77	0.77
N	6 513	6 147	5 741

Note: As for Table 3.3.

Table 3.8   The determinants of relative Indian port costs (pooled across 1-digit SITC commodities with non-containerized trade)

	(1)	(2)	(3)
Relative port costs (1st lag)	0.6062***	0.7294***	0.6439***
	(0.0263)	(0.0358)	(0.0355)
Relative port costs (2nd lag)		−0.2161***	0.0100
		(0.0376)	(0.0434)
Relative port costs (3rd lag)			−0.3535***
			(0.0370)
Total investment	0.0002	−0.0000	−0.0005*
	(0.0002)	(0.0002)	(0.0002)
Exchange rate	−0.0152***	−0.0126***	−0.0119***
	(0.0025)	(0.0026)	(0.0025)
Wage rate	0.0181***	0.0202***	0.0166***
	(0.0034)	(0.0035)	(0.0033)
Adj. R-squared	0.74	0.75	0.79
N	934	868	797

	Detailed port investments		
	(1)	(2)	(3)
Relative port costs (1st lag)	0.6040***	0.7352***	0.6521***
	(0.0261)	(0.0357)	(0.0354)
Relative port costs (2nd lag)		−0.2327***	−0.0016
		(0.0378)	(0.0448)
Relative port costs (3rd lag)			−0.3559***
			(0.0381)
Dock facilities	−0.0001	−0.0002	−0.0008**
	(0.0003)	(0.0003)	(0.0003)
Loading/unloading	0.0033**	0.0038**	0.0028*
	(0.0012)	(0.0012)	(0.0012)
Other schemes	0.0021	−0.0010	0.0006
	(0.0014)	(0.0016)	(0.0016)
Channel deepening	−0.0025	−0.0014	−0.0021
	(0.0015)	(0.0016)	(0.0016)
Exchange rate	−0.0125***	−0.0085**	−0.0085**
	(0.0027)	(0.0029)	(0.0028)
Wage rate	0.0191***	0.0206***	0.0169***
	(0.0034)	(0.0035)	(0.0033)
Adj. R-squared	0.74	0.75	0.79
N	934	868	797

Note: As for Table 3.3.

of specific port investments, such as the introduction of new berths into operation, channel deepening projects, and the purchase of new cranes for processing containers. For India, we have information on the level of annual port expenditures on infrastructure. These are detailed at the project level and we have provided evidence of the effect of aggregate expenditures in addition to narrower categories of expenditures.

Taken together, the results provide broad support for the notion that infrastructure developments at the Asian ports in our study do lower trade costs by lowering the cost of moving goods through the ports. The evidence is not uniform across types of investment, however; nor do we find that the effects are large. From both types of analysis, we find support for the notion that general investments in dock facilities and specific investments in container processing and procurement of new cranes lead to statistically significant increases in efficiency. However, the impact of $1 million in investment leads to a relatively small 0.03 percentage point increase in efficiency. Whether or not this makes the investment ultimately worthwhile, from a strict efficiency perspective, is as yet undetermined. These investments have the ability to increase capacity at the ports, beyond their cost effects, probably making them worthwhile, even in the short term, and the cumulative cost-reducing effects of each investment can potentially make them worthwhile in the long run.

From a pure cost perspective, it does not appear as though channel deepening and the expansion of the number of berths at the ports have consistent cost-reducing effects. The regressions do not yield significant effects of these investments. None the less, both types of investments can be crucial to the expansion of the ports, which, from a financial perspective, increases the likelihood that they are sound investments.

That we do not find cost benefits for all types of investments is not surprising. Some investments are more likely to reduce costs than others. For instance, the introduction of additional cranes enables existing berths to function more quickly and efficiently. While the deepening of channels in principle allows ships to move more smoothly into and out of ports, it is likely that this investment is more productive from an expansion perspective, allowing larger vessels to call. Whether larger vessel calls lead to lower costs at ports is an open question. They most certainly enhance a port's ability to attract a larger proportion of the ever-expanding flow of world trade. Similarly, the introduction of more berths may also provide a capacity effect without a strong measurable effect on costs.

Although we have borrowed heavily from Blonigen and Wilson (2006) in developing our methodology, we have taken things one step further to reveal not only changes in relative trade costs, but the relationship between infrastructure developments and relative trade costs. In addition, the results presented here benefit from the use of very detailed data in terms of both infrastructure investments and trade flows. By focusing on these specific aspects, we are more able to highlight particular relationships between infrastructure investments and trade costs than is done in the literature that precedes this work. Furthermore, because we have incorporated the fixed effects methodology, the results presented here are more clearly devoid of noise arising from the incomplete control for other variables that influence measured trade costs, including exchange rates, changes in efficiency at partner ports, and commodity-specific means of shipment (container, break-bulk, or bulk).

Finally, we find significant support for the notion that port infrastructure investments have implications for trade costs. Given that transportation costs play a significant role in the overall costs of moving goods across the world's oceans, there is undoubtedly an impact on overall trade flows. However, the effect that we find is not necessarily of great economic significance; these investments may have a more significant effect in that they certainly increase the capacity of the ports in question to process waterborne trade flows.

NOTES

1. The cost of US imports transportation represents 85 per cent of total costs faced by an exporter (Hummels et al., 2007).
2. Blonigen and Wilson (2006) estimate that an increase of containerized trade by 1 per cent lowers shipping rates by only 0.05 per cent. Hummels (2007) employs a different methodology and finds a much bigger impact of containerization on shipping costs: a 1 per cent change in container usage lowers costs by 0.134 per cent after controlling for composition of trade, fuel costs and cross-country differences.
3. A reduction in theft at seaports worldwide is likely to be an important positive side effect of the anti-terrorism security measures being implemented not only in the USA, but at ports worldwide. See Haveman and Shatz (2006).
4. A total of 99 per cent of world trade by weight and a majority of world trade by value – see Hummels (2007).
5. The USA was chosen as destination port due to data availability.
6. http://www.bls.gov/mxp/. The producer price index rose from 114.4 to 154.5 during this same period, or by about 35 per cent. Economic Report of the President, February 2007.
7. Hummels et al. (2001); Baier and Bergstrand (2001).
8. See the *Global Competitiveness Report* for a survey attempt to identify port efficiency. Clark et al. (2004), Wilson et al. (2004) and Sanchez et al. (2003) make use of this measure to assess efficiencies effect on trade. They find a positive correlation.
9. http://marad.dot.gov/MARAD_statistics/index.html.
10. http://www.usitc.gov/tata/hts/index.htm.
11. The results from our estimation are broadly consistent with those presented by Blonigen and Wilson (2006).
12. As a robustness check, we compared the coefficient estimates resulting from the use of Tokyo as a reference port to those resulting from the use of Hong Kong and Singapore, and found that they are highly correlated.
13. NIMA Publication 151.

14. The first-stage regressions are carried out separately for each of the nine 1-digit SITC commodities.
15. See Appendix 3A.3 for a more detailed description of the Chinese and Malaysian port infrastructure enhancements.
16. See Appendix 3A.3 for a more detailed discussion of the type of investments taken place at Indian ports in our study.
17. SITC 0 and SITC 9 were dropped because of a lack of data. It is also not likely to be relevant to the current analysis. SITC 9 is Commodities and Transactions not elsewhere classified (n.e.c.).
18. Containerized: Beverages and Tobacco; Animal and Vegetable Oils, Fats and Waxes; Chemicals and Related Products, n.e.s. (not elsewhere specified); Manufactured Goods classified chiefly by material; Machinery and Transportation Equipment; and Miscellaneous Manufactured Articles. Non-containerized include: Crude Materials, Inedible, except Fuels; Mineral Fuels, Lubricants and Related Materials.
19. Prabir De kindly provided these data for us.
20. See Appendix 3A.3 for more on specific investment projects.

REFERENCES

Aizenman, J. (2004), 'Endogenous pricing to market and financing costs', *Journal of Monetary Economics*, **51**(4), May, 691–712.

Baier, S. and J. Bergstrand (2001), 'The growth of world trade: tariffs, transport costs, and income similarity', *Journal of International Economics*, **53**(1), February, 1–27.

Blonigen, Bruce A. and Wesley Wilson (2006), 'New measures of port efficiency using international trade data', NBER Working Paper 12052.

Clark, X., D. Dollar and A. Micco (2004), 'Port efficiency, maritime transport costs and bilateral trade', NBER Working Paper 10353.

Evans, C. and J. Harrigan (2005), 'Distance, time, and specialization: lean retailing in general equilibrium', *American Economic Review*, **95**(1), March, 292–313.

Global Competitiveness Report (1996–2000), Cambridge, MA: Harvard University and Geneva, Switzerland: World Economic Forum.

Haveman, Jon D. and Howard Shatz (eds) (2006), *Protecting the Nation's Seaports: Balancing Security and Cost*, San Francisco, CA: Public Policy Institute of California.

Hummels, D. (2007), 'Transportation costs and international trade in the second era of globalization', *Journal of Economic Perspectives*, **21**(3), 131–54.

Hummels, D., J. Ishii and K. Yi (2001), 'The nature and growth of vertical specialization in world trade', *Journal of International Economics*, **54**(1), June, 75–96.

Hummels, D., V. Lugovskyy and Alexandre Skiba (2007), 'The trade reducing effects of international shipping', NBER Working Paper 12914.

Levinson, M. (2006), *The Big Box: How the Shipping Container Made the World Smaller and the World Economy Bigger*, Princeton, NJ: Princeton University Press.

Sanchez, R.J., J. Hoffmann, A. Micco, G.V. Pizzolitto, M. Sgut and G. Wilmsmeier (2003), 'Port efficiency and international trade: port efficiency as a determinant of maritime transport costs', *Maritime Economics and Logistics*, **5**, 199–218.

Schaur, G. (2006), 'Hedging price volatility using fast transport', mimeo, Purdue University.

Wilson, T., K. Cullinane and D.W. Song (2004), 'Container port production efficiency: a comparative study of DEA and FDH approaches', *Journal of Eastern Asian Society for Transportation Studies*, **5**, 698–713.

APPENDIX 3A1

China

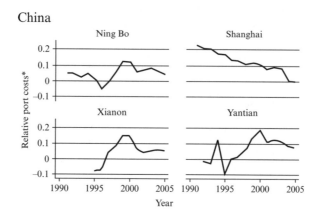

India

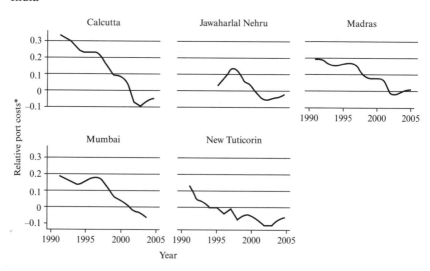

Note: Graphs by port name. *Relative to Tokyo.

Figure 3A1.1   Productivity changes in all sample ports

Malaysia

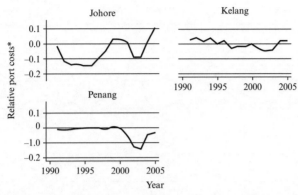

Note: Graphs by port name. *Relative to Tokyo.

Figure 3A1.1   (continued)

APPENDIX 3A2

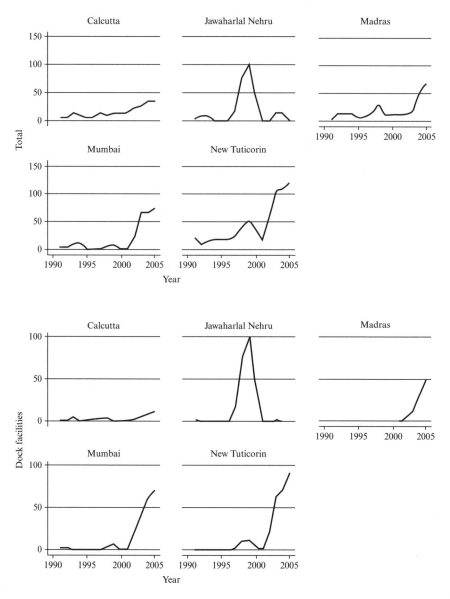

Note: Graphs by port name.

Figure 3A2.1   Investment at Indian ports ($ millions)

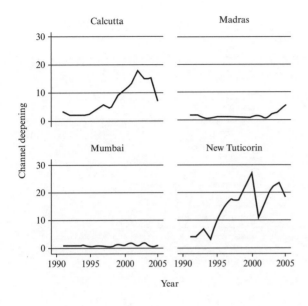

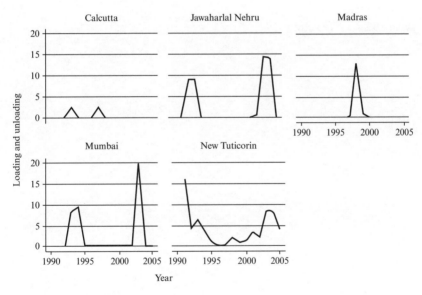

Note: Graphs by port name.

Figure 3A2.1 (continued)

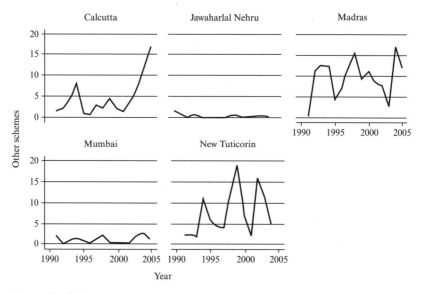

Note: Graphs by port name.

Figure 3A2.1 (continued)

APPENDIX 3A3   DATA SOURCES

First-stage Analysis

Waterborne trade databanks
This dataset can be obtained from the US Maritime Administration (Marad) and provides highly detailed information about both US imports and US exports. The records in this dataset are bilateral to the port level, including thousands of foreign ports and nearly 400 US ports. The data are aggregated over shipments so that the greatest detail available is at the 6-digit HS level on a port-to-port basis. Individual shipment records are not available in this dataset. The data provide detail on the value of shipments of goods in 6-digit HS categories between ports in addition to the weight, the percentage of both weight and value that are containerized, and on the c.i.f. charges associated with those shipments.

Distance
The waterborne data do not include information on the distance between ports. This information was assembled from a variety of sources as we are not aware of an available dataset that includes the distances along common shipping routes, which is the ideal measure. Instead, we take a three-pronged approach to the problem. First, we have information on great circle distances between the capital cities of countries. This is the coarsest measure of distance. Second, we have measures of the great circle distance between ports. These data have been collected for each of the target ports and all the US ports included in the data. Finally, for a select group of ports, we have the shortest shipping distance. The distance between capital cities was taken from the Macalaster website (accessible through www.freit.org) of concordances and other useful trade data. The port latitude and longitude were obtained from various issues of Lloyd's *Ports of the World* (previously *Atlas of World Ports*). Specific shipping distances were taken from NIMA Publication 151: Distances between ports (http://www.landfallnavigation.com/pd151.html). Dummy variables were included in the regression to indicate instances where the first and second measures were used.

Second-stage Analysis

Exchange rates
International Financial Statistics.

Wages
World Development Indicators (for India and Malaysia); *China Statistical Yearbook* 1991–2005.

Indian investment data
These data were kindly provided by Prabir De. They were painstakingly acquired through the inspection of annual port reports. We are indebted to him for his efforts. As discussed in the text, the data were provided for individual infrastructure improvements within the gates of the five ports. For the sake of analysis, we have

Table 3A3.1   Level of detail in Indian investment data

---

1. Dock facilities
    – Construction of container terminal (P&O)
    – Construction of container berth
    – Navigational aids
    – Revamping of old dock
    – Extension of Jawar Dock by 220 m towards south
    – Extension of Outer Jawar Dock by 220 RMQCs at container terminal
    – Construction of breakwater and groynes at Sagar Island
    – Modernization/upgrading of VTMS
    – Terminal for handling of LPG at Budge Budge
    – Construction of outer harbour 1st phase

2. Channel deepening
    – Channel deepening
    – Procurement of one trailing suction Hooper Dredger
    – Capital dredging

3. Loading and unloading
    – Purchase of RMGCs
    – Replacement of existing 8 nos of RTGCs at container terminal
    – Replacement of existing 2 nos of RMQCs with super Post Panamax
      RMOCs at container terminal
    – Replacement of 2 QGCs
    – Procurement of 2 nos 32-ton tugs
    – Construction of edible oil jetty
    – Replacement of tug
    – Purchase of 3 nos 20 MT cranes

4. Other schemes

---

aggregated these investments into four categories. These categories are detailed in
Table 3A3.1.

Other evidence of infrastructure implementation
Researchers participating in this study from Malaysia and China have provided us
with information on the relevant infrastructure developments at seaports in these
countries. Information was also provided for Indonesia, but was not suitable for
inclusion in this analysis.

   These infrastructure developments include expanding operating port facilities, construction of new berths, procurement of all types of new cranes and deepening of port
channels. Port facilities include the construction of new harbours, transshipment terminals, container terminals and wharfs. Malaysian ports have also implemented new
modern management systems for handling port operations. Shanghai deepened its navigation channel by 1.5 metres in 2002 and 2005 consecutively (from 7 metres to 10
metres).

APPENDIX 3A4   OTHER REGRESSION RESULTS

Table 3A4.1   *The determinants of relative Indian port costs (pooled across all 1-digit SITC commodities)*

	(1)	(2)	(3)
Relative port costs (1st lag)	0.7777***	0.9013***	0.9038***
	(0.0072)	(0.0127)	(0.0130)
Relative port costs (2nd lag)		−0.1517***	−0.1288***
		(0.0128)	(0.0169)
Relative port costs (3rd lag)			0.0309*
			(0.0124)
Total investment	−0.0002***	−0.0002***	−0.0002***
	(0.0001)	(0.0001)	(0.0001)
Exchange rate	−0.0045***	−0.0042***	−0.0047***
	(0.0006)	(0.0006)	(0.0006)
Wage rate	0.0036***	0.0034***	0.0026***
	(0.0008)	(0.0008)	(0.0008)
Adj. R-squared	0.77	0.76	0.76
N	7 445	7 012	6 536

	Detailed port investments		
	(1)	(2)	(3)
Relative port costs (1st lag)	0.7779***	0.9032***	0.9046***
	(0.0071)	(0.0127)	(0.0130)
Relative port costs (2nd lag)		−0.1523***	−0.1218***
		(0.0128)	(0.0169)
Relative port costs (3rd lag)			−0.0394**
			(0.0124)
Dock facilities	−0.0002***	−0.0002**	−0.0002**
	(0.0001)	(0.0001)	(0.0001)
Loading/unloading	−0.0017***	−0.0020***	−0.0020***
	(0.0003)	(0.0003)	(0.0003)
Other schemes	0.0014***	0.0019***	0.0019***
	(0.0004)	(0.0004)	(0.0004)
Channel deepening	−0.0003	−0.0007	−0.0007
	(0.0004)	(0.0004)	(0.0004)
Exchange rate	−0.0061***	−0.0061***	−0.0067***
	(0.0006)	(0.0006)	(0.0006)
Wage rate	0.0036***	0.0033***	0.0024**
	(0.0008)	(0.0008)	(0.0008)
Adj. R-squared	0.77	0.76	0.76
N	7 445	7 012	6 536

Notes: The estimated port costs include the cost-reducing effect of containerization.
***, **, *: significant at 1 per cent, 5 per cent and 10 per cent respectively.

Table 3A4.2   *The determinants of relative Indian port costs (pooled across 1-digit SITC commodities with containerized trade)*

	(1)	(2)	(3)
Relative port costs (1st lag)	0.7639***	0.8743***	0.8825***
	(0.0080)	(0.0135)	(0.0137)
Relative port costs (2nd lag)		−0.1377***	−0.1321***
		(0.0134)	(0.0175)
Relative port costs (3rd lag)			−0.0189
			(0.0130)
Total investment	−0.0003***	−0.0002***	−0.0002***
	(0.0000)	(0.0000)	(0.0000)
Exchange rate	−0.0023***	−0.0022***	−0.0024***
	(0.0005)	(0.0005)	(0.0005)
Wage rate	0.0027***	0.0025***	0.0020**
	(0.0007)	(0.0007)	(0.0007)
Adj. R-squared	0.78	0.77	0.77
N	6 511	6 145	5 739

	Detailed port investments		
	(1)	(2)	(3)
Relative port costs (1st lag)	0.7625***	0.8771***	0.8848***
	(0.0080)	(0.0134)	(0.0136)
Relative port costs (2nd lag)		−0.1405***	−0.1291***
		(0.0135)	(0.0174)
Relative port costs (3rd lag)			−0.0255*
			(0.0130)
Dock facilities	−0.0003***	−0.0002***	−0.0002**
	(0.0001)	(0.0001)	(0.0001)
Loading/unloading	−0.0023***	−0.0025***	−0.0026***
	(0.0003)	(0.0003)	(0.0003)
Other schemes	0.0013***	0.0021***	0.0022***
	(0.0003)	(0.0004)	(0.0004)
Channel deepening	0.0002	−0.0003	−0.0001
	(0.0004)	(0.0004)	(0.0004)
Exchange rate	−0.0044***	−0.0046***	−0.0050***
	(0.0006)	(0.0006)	(0.0006)
Wage rate	0.0026***	0.0024***	0.0018**
	(0.0007)	(0.0007)	(0.0007)
Adj. R-squared	0.78	0.77	0.77
N	6 511	6 145	5 739

Notes: As for Table 3A4.1.

Table 3A4.3   The determinants of relative Indian port costs (pooled across 1-digit SITC commodities with non-containerized trade)

	(1)	(2)	(3)
Relative port costs (1st lag)	0.6029***	0.7411***	0.6557***
	(0.0263)	(0.0356)	(0.0356)
Relative port costs (2nd lag)		−0.2381***	−0.0201
		(0.0376)	(0.0437)
Relative port costs (3rd lag)			−0.3483***
			(0.0373)
Total investment	0.0001	−0.0001	−0.0005*
	(0.0003)	(0.0003)	(0.0003)
Exchange rate	−0.0155***	−0.0125***	−0.0118***
	(0.0025)	(0.0026)	(0.0025)
Wage rate	0.0170***	0.0186***	0.0153***
	(0.0034)	(0.0035)	(0.0034)
Adj. R-squared	0.74	0.75	0.78
N	933	867	796

	Detailed port investments		
	(1)	(2)	(3)
Relative port costs (1st lag)	0.6005***	0.7465***	0.6635***
	(0.0262)	(0.0355)	(0.0356)
Relative port costs (2nd lag)		−0.2545***	−0.0330
		(0.0378)	(0.0451)
Relative port costs (3rd lag)			−0.3486***
			(0.0384)
Dock facilities	−0.0001	−0.0002	−0.0008**
	(0.0003)	(0.0003)	(0.0003)
Loading/unloading	0.0031**	0.0037**	0.0027*
	(0.0012)	(0.0012)	(0.0012)
Other schemes	0.0019	−0.0011	0.0004
	(0.0014)	(0.0016)	(0.0016)
Channel deepening	−0.0022	−0.0014	−0.0021
	(0.0015)	(0.0016)	(0.0016)
Exchange rate	−0.0130***	−0.0085**	−0.0085**
	(0.0027)	(0.0029)	(0.0028)
Wage rate	0.0179***	0.0189***	0.0156***
	(0.0034)	(0.0035)	(0.0034)
Adj. R-squared	0.74	0.75	0.79
N	933	867	796

Notes: As for Table 3A4.1.

Table 3A4.4   The determinants of relative Chinese and Malaysian port costs (pooled across all 1-digit SITC commodities)

	(1)	(2)	(3)
Relative port costs (1st lag)	0.75***	0.81***	0.80***
	(0.01)	(0.01)	(0.01)
Relative port costs (2nd lag)		−0.1***	−0.03**
		(0.01)	(0.01)
Relative port costs (3rd lag)			−0.1***
			(0.01)
Port facilities	−0.02***	−0.02***	−0.02***
	(0.00)	(0.00)	(0.00)
Number of new berths	−0.00	0.00	0.00
	(0.00)	(0.00)	(0.00)
Number of cranes	−0.01***	−0.01***	−0.01***
	(0.00)	(0.00)	(0.00)
Channel deepening	0.02	0.01	0.01
	(0.01)	(0.01)	(0.01)
Exchange rate	0.00	0.01*	0.00
	(0.00)	(0.00)	(0.00)
Wage rate	−0.00001***	−0.00001***	−0.00001***
	(0.00000)	(0.00000)	(0.00000)
Adj. R-squared	0.62	0.61	0.61
N	14 303	13 595	12 819

Notes: As for Table 3A4.1.

Table 3A4.5   *The determinants of relative Chinese and Malaysian port costs (pooled across all 1-digit SITC commodities with containerized trade)*

	(1)	(2)	(3)
Relative port costs (1st lag)	0.79***	0.83***	0.81***
	(0.01)	(0.01)	(0.01)
Relative port costs (2nd lag)		−0.05***	0.02
		(0.01)	(0.01)
Relative port costs (3rd lag)			−0.10***
			(0.01)
Port facilities	−0.01**	−0.01***	−0.01***
	(0.00)	(0.00)	(0.00)
Number of new berths	−0.00	0.00	−0.00
	(0.00)	(0.00)	(0.00)
Number of cranes	−0.02***	−0.02***	−0.02***
	(0.00)	(0.00)	(0.00)
Channel deepening	0.03*	0.03*	0.03*
	(0.01)	(0.01)	(0.01)
Exchange rate	0.01*	0.01***	0.01
	(0.00)	(0.00)	(0.01)
Wage rate	−0.00002***	−0.00001***	−0.00002***
	(0.00000)	(0.00000)	(0.00000)
Adj. R-squared	0.64	0.63	0.62
N	9 304	8 847	8 345

Notes: As for Table 3A4.1.

Table 3A4.6   The determinants of relative Chinese and Malaysian port costs (pooled across all 1-digit SITC commodities with non-containerized trade)

	(1)	(2)	(3)
Relative port costs (1st lag)	0.57***	0.70***	0.64***
	(0.02)	(0.03)	(0.03)
Relative port costs (2nd lag)		−0.24***	−0.11**
		(0.03)	(0.04)
Relative port costs (3rd lag)			−0.20***
			(0.03)
Port facilities	−0.03*	−0.04*	−0.04*
	(0.01)	(0.01)	(0.02)
Number of new berths	−0.00	−0.00	−0.01
	(0.00)	(0.01)	(0.01)
Number of cranes	0.01	0.02	0.01
	(0.01)	(0.01)	(0.01)
Channel deepening	−0.03	−0.09	−0.08
	(0.06)	(0.06)	(0.06)
Exchange rate	0.02	0.04**	0.04
	(0.01)	(0.01)	(0.02)
Wage rate	0.00006***	0.00008***	0.00007**
	(0.00001)	(0.00002)	(0.00002)
Adj. R-squared	0.43	0.45	0.47
N	1 113	1 046	978

Notes: As for Table 3A4.1.

4. Empirical estimates of transportation costs: options for enhancing Asia's trade[*]

Prabir De

1. INTRODUCTION

The last few decades have seen significant changes in international economic integration. A growing number of researchers have started to reveal a long list of trade cost barriers that affect international economic integration. According to Anderson and van Wincoop, 'The 170 per cent of "representative" trade costs in industrialized countries breaks down into 21 per cent transportation costs, 44 per cent border related trade barriers and 55 per cent retail and wholesale distribution costs' (Anderson and van Wincoop, 2004, p. 692). What makes any study of trade costs in Asia significant is that the price of the vast majority of traded goods depends on many exogenous factors. On the one hand, Asia conducts increasingly higher trade, where higher trade costs push up the landed price of imports, and, on the other, Asia's trade covers an increasingly large volume of intermediate goods, where expensive imports, resulting from higher trade costs, escalate the cost of production.

The present chapter attempts to contribute to the empirical literature on the dynamics of Asia's trade. By using direct and indirect evidence on trade barriers, it seeks to enhance understanding of trade costs in Asia.[1] How are the Asian countries performing in reducing trade costs? Which barriers matter most – tariff or transport costs? Do inland transportation costs influence Asian trade much more significantly than international transportation costs? What do the estimates of freight rates look like across Asian countries? This chapter provides empirical evidence to show that an important impediment to trade expansion in Asia is high transportation costs. We report evidence that lower transportation costs are not only crucial for expanding Asia's trade but also a decisive instrument in integrating the economies in the region. The remaining part of the chapter is organized as follows.

Section 2 provides an illustration of gains from reduction in transportation costs. It is important to understand how and why transport cost reduction leads trade volume to rise. Some stylized literature on transport cost reduction and its impact on trade are briefly discussed in this section. Since international transportation costs depend, to a great extent, on ocean freight rates, our next task is to understand the relative importance of these rates in Asia. Section 3 is devoted to this topic. Section 4 provides an illustration of the composition of transportation costs in selected Asian countries, where we estimate the *ad valorem* transportation costs prevailing across countries and commodities. The aforesaid discussion is finally summarized with a formal assessment of the relationship between trade cost elements and trade flows in Section 5. We attempt to measure the movement of Asian countries on a tariff–freight plane in a comparative static framework. Econometric results are presented and discussed in this section, followed by conclusions in Section 6.

2.   DEFINITION AND SIGNIFICANCE OF TRADE COSTS

In general, an exporter or importer incurs trade costs at all phases of the export or import process, starting from obtaining information about market conditions in any given foreign market to receipt of the final payment. One part of trade costs is trader specific and depends upon a trader's operational efficiency. The magnitude of trade cost elements diminishes with an increase in the efficiency level of the trader, under the prevailing framework of any economy. The other part of trade costs is specific to the trading environment and is incurred by the traders due to in-built inefficiencies in the trading environment. It includes institutional bottlenecks (transport, regulatory and other logistics infrastructure), information asymmetry and administrative power, which give rise to rent-seeking activities by government and other officials at various stages of the transaction. This may cost traders (or their country) time and money, making transactions more expensive.

In broad terms, trade costs include all costs incurred in getting merchandise to a final user other than the cost of producing the good itself, such as transportation costs (both freight costs and time costs), policy barriers (tariff and non-tariff barriers – NTBs), information costs, contract enforcement costs, costs associated with the use of different currencies, legal and regulatory costs, local distribution costs (wholesale and retail) and so forth.[2] This means two things. First, trade cost is measured as a mark-up between export and import prices, where this mark-up roughly indicates the relative costs of transfer of goods from one country to another. Second, trade costs are reported in terms of their *ad valorem* tax equivalent.

Trade costs are generally quite large, even aside from trade policy barriers and even between apparently highly integrated economies. In explaining trade costs, Anderson and van Wincoop (2004) cited the example of Mattel's Barbie doll, as discussed in Feenstra (1998). Feenstra indicated that the production costs for the doll were US\$1, whereas it sold for about US\$10 in the USA. The cost of transportation, marketing, wholesaling and retailing represent an *ad valorem* tax equivalent of 900 per cent. Anderson and van Wincoop (2004, p. 69) commented:

> Tax equivalent of representative trade costs for rich countries is 170 per cent. This includes all transport, border-related and local distribution costs from foreign producer to final user in the domestic country. Trade costs are richly linked to economic policy. Direct policy instruments (tariffs, the tariff equivalents of quotas and trade barriers associated with the exchange rate system) are less important than other policies (transport infrastructure investment, law enforcement and related property rights institutions, informational institutions, regulation, language).

Direct evidence on border costs shows that tariff barriers are now low in most countries, on average (trade-weighted) less than 5 per cent for rich countries, and with a few exceptions are on average between 10 and 20 per cent for developing countries.[3] While the world has witnessed a drastic fall in tariffs over the last two decades, many barriers remain that penalize trade. Some among them are termed 'soft' barriers and others 'hard' barriers. One set of such 'soft' barriers is dealt with by trade and business facilitation measures, and the 'hard' set of barriers, often cited as physical or infrastructure barriers, are dealt with by transport facilitation measures. To aid understanding, the costs appearing from these barriers may be termed trade costs.

Trade costs are often cited as an important determinant of the volume of trade. High trade costs are an obstacle to trade and impede the realization of gains from trade liberalization.[4] Most of the studies on trade costs show that integration is the result of reduced costs of transportation in particular and other infrastructure services in general. The supply constraints are the primary factors that have limited the ability of many developing countries and LDCs to exploit trade opportunities arising from trade liberalization. Realization of optimal gains from trade, therefore, depends not only on tariff liberalization but also on the quality of infrastructure and related services associated with trading across borders.

The cost of international transportation is a crucial determinant of a country's trade competitiveness. Doubling of a country's transportation costs leads to a drop in its trade by 80 per cent or even more (Limao and Venables, 2001). Shipping costs, the major element of transportation costs, represent a greater burden than tariffs.[5] The effective rate of protection provided by the international transport costs was in many cases found to be higher than that provided by tariffs.[6] Therefore shipping costs represent a more binding constraint to greater participation in international trade than tariffs and other trade barriers. Complementary trade policies focusing on inland and international transport costs have, therefore, gained immense importance in enhancing international trade and integration.

Gains from Reduction in Transportation Costs

Of all the components of trade costs, transportation costs have been studied most extensively. Transport costs depend on a mixture of geographic and economic circumstances. Adverse geographical locations, landlocked and island countries, and low income levels, with poor infrastructure and low transport volumes, pose an inherent challenge for many countries' trade and development prospects. Improved infrastructural and logistical services play an important role in the flow of international trade. On the one hand, they generate enormous wealth by reducing costs of trade across borders because of its non-discriminatory and non-rival characteristics, and, on the other, they integrate production and trade across countries.

Direct transport costs include freight charge and insurance, which is customarily added to the freight charge. Indirect transport costs include holding costs for the goods in transit, inventory costs due to buffering the variability of delivery dates, preparation costs associated with shipment size (full container load versus partial container load) and the like. Indirect costs have to be inferred. Alongside tariffs and NTBs, transport costs appear to be comparable in average magnitude and in variability across countries, commodities and time.

Gains from reduction in transport costs are illustrated in Figure 4.1. The importing country takes the world price of the good (P_w) as given and DM is the demand for imports. Assuming transport cost (T_1), the price facing the importing country will be $P_w + T_1$. If as a result of the improvement of international transport services, the transport cost falls to T_2, then the import price drops to $P_w + T_2$. The area ($b+c$) represents welfare gains to the importing country due to an increase in consumer surplus, consisting of not only the triangle c (formerly a deadweight loss), but also the rectangle b of gains from reduced transport costs.

In traditional trade theory, it is assumed that trade takes place between countries that have no spatial dimensions.[7] Neoclassical trade theory

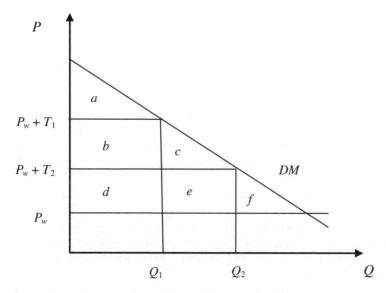

Figure 4.1 Gains from reduction in transportation costs

completely ignores transport costs, and considers some assumptions that have comparatively less relevance in today's complex trade environment. For example, in the factor abundance model, popularly known as the Heckscher, Ohlin and Samuelson (HOS) model, comparative advantage is determined by cross-country differences in relative abundance of factor endowments. The HOS model uses some assumptions such as perfect competition, homogeneous goods, production with constant returns to scale, no transport costs, and mobility of factors between industries and not between countries. In new trade theory, transport cost is incorporated as a determining factor, where trade is analysed in models in a world of increasing returns to scale and monopolistic competition (Dixit and Stiglitz, 1977).[8] One of the implications of new trade theory is growing interdependence between countries through increased trade and/or increased factor mobility, where transportation cost plays a pivotal role in integrating the economies and/or factors.

Current literature on the subject suggests two approaches to transport modelling in trade: (i) where transport is modelled implicitly with the traded goods; and (ii) where explicit transport sector modelling is done. The 'iceberg' model (Samuelson, 1954), where transport cost is implicit, is the most widely used in the literature.[9] While some studies have explicitly modelled transport costs (interchangeably, trade transaction costs), as in Steininger (2001), those influenced by new trade theory – Bergstrand (1985,

1989), Davis (1998), Deardorff (1998), Limao and Venables (2001), Fink et al. (2002), Clark et al. (2004), Redding and Venables (2004), Hummels (1999, 2001), among others – considered transport costs more explicitly.

However, Samuelson (1954) in effect laid the foundation of new trade theory when he introduced the concept of 'iceberg' transport costs. The literature on new trade theory introduces the importance of transport costs in explaining cross-country trade and movement of factors, especially Krugman and Venables (1990) and Krugman (1991). They show how an increase in the degree of economic integration (using a fall in transport costs as a proxy) affects the countries engaged in trade. In a two-country model, Krugman and Venables show that in autarky (when high transportation costs prohibit trade) both countries have a share in the manufacturing sector equal to their share in world endowments.[10] There is thus a non-linear relationship between a country's share in world industry and transport costs in which the shares always sum to one. In other words, it can be argued that gains from reduction in transport costs are always a positive-sum game.

Trade costs have large welfare implications. Current policy-related trade costs are often worth more than 10 per cent of national income (Anderson and van Wincoop, 2002). Obstfeld and Rogoff (2000) commented that all the major puzzles of international macroeconomics hang on trade costs. Some of the studies, such as that by Francois et al. (2005), estimated that for each 1 per cent reduction in trade transaction costs, world income could increase by US$30 to 40 billion.[11] Some studies have indicated that the cost of trade facilitation, specifically trade documentation and procedures, is high, between 4 to 7 per cent of the value of goods shipped.[12] For example, the gains from streamlining customs procedures exceeded those resulting from trade liberalization, such as tariff reduction. Gains from effective trade facilitation accounted for about 0.26 per cent of the real GDP of APEC members (about US$45 billion), while the gains from trade liberalization would be 0.14 per cent of real GDP (about US$23 billion).[13]

For a firm, high transport costs have several implications. Trade costs and firm's exports are theoretically found to be inversely related. According to Bernard et al. (2004), firm reactions to trade liberalization generate endogenous (Ricardian-type) productivity responses at the industry level that magnify countries' comparative advantages (Bernard et al., 2004). As trade costs fall, firms in comparative advantage industries are more likely to export, so that relative firm size, the relative number of firms and the relative employment increase more in comparative advantage industries than in comparative disadvantage industries (Bernard et al., 2004). Trade cost components also influence the entry of foreign firms into an economy.[14]

Higher transport costs at firm level reduce profits and wages, and thereby penalize a country's exports. The efficiency of transport services greatly determines the ability of firms to compete in foreign markets. For a small economy – for which world prices of traded goods are largely exogenous – higher costs of transportation show up in import and export prices. To remain competitive in such a situation, exporting firms that face higher shipping costs must pay lower wages to workers, accept lower returns on capital, or have to be more productive.

The pressure on factor prices and productivity is even higher for industries with a high share of imported inputs. In these cases, even small differences in transport costs come to determine whether or not export ventures are at all profitable. In developing countries, for labour-intensive manufacturing industries such as textiles, high transport costs are most likely to translate into lower wages, thus directly affecting the standard of living of workers and their dependants.

Trading over long distances has a negative effect on profitability. It leads to additional losses in terms of a product's shortened lifetime in the export market.[15] It was estimated that doubling the distance increases overall freight rates by 20 to 30 per cent (Hummels, 1999). Hummels (2007) noted that transportation costs are larger, tend to co-vary with distance, and exhibit much greater variability across exporters than do tariffs.

Time delays also strongly affect international trade. For example, on average, each additional day that a product is delayed before being shipped reduces trade by at least 1 per cent (Djankov et al., 2006). Delivery time is found to have a more pronounced effect for imports of intermediate products (Hummels, 2001), suggesting that fast delivery of goods is crucial for maintaining multinational vertical product chains. Quality aspects of transportation are thus likely to be an important factor in the location decisions of multinational companies.

Poor institutions and poor infrastructure also act as impediments to trade differentially across countries. While dealing with barriers to trade, some studies have emphasized the quality of infrastructure (as a proxy of trade costs) associated with cross-country trade. A country's infrastructure plays a vital role in carrying trade. By incorporating transport infrastructure in a two-country Ricardian framework, Bougheas et al. (1999) indicated the circumstances under which it affects trade volumes. According to Francois and Manchin (2006), transport and communication infrastructure and institutional quality are significant determinants not only for a country's export levels but also for the likelihood of exports. Nordås and Piermartini (2004) found that quality of infrastructure is an important determinant of trade performance, and port efficiency alone has the largest impact on trade among all the indicators of infrastructure. While dealing with Asia's trade, De (2005, 2006b) provided evidence that port efficiency and infrastructure quality are two important determinants of trade costs – the higher the transport costs, the lower is the volume of trade.[16]

The infrastructure variables have explanatory power in predicting trade volume. Limao and Venables (2001) emphasized the dependence of trade costs on infrastructure, where infrastructure is measured as an average of the density of the road network, the paved road network, the rail network and the number of telephone main lines per person. A deterioration of infrastructure from the median to the 75th percentile of destinations raises transport costs by 12 per cent. A median landlocked country has transport costs around 55 per cent higher than the median coastal economy.[17]

A country's comparative advantage also depends upon quality of infrastructure. Yeaple and Golub (2002) found that differences in the quality of public infrastructure between countries can explain differences in total factor productivity.

The point is that trade costs are shaped by the nature of trade (requirements of firms) and by policy actions. Transportation costs, therefore, play an important role in integrating firms (and economies). Understanding the trade costs and their role in determining international trade volumes must therefore incorporate the internal geography of countries and the associated interior trade costs. With these building blocks in place, we now turn to a discussion of trade cost elements.

3.   RELATIVE IMPORTANCE OF OCEAN FREIGHT RATES IN ASIA

Containerization in ocean transportation has changed the composition of freight rates where freight (ocean) cost is one of the major components of international transportation costs.[18] It has an impact on trade similar to customs tariffs.[19] Freight costs vary across regions, where inefficient transport services could be the potential element for freight cost differentials resulting in a longer time for delivery. Inefficient transport services in Asia are reflected in higher freight costs and a longer time for delivery. Table 4.1 compares levels of freight rates across countries for the year 2005 and the growth rates for the first half of the ongoing decade.[20] The following two observations are worth noting.

First, among the seven Asian countries reported in Table 4.1, India appears to be most expensive in terms of ocean freight rates on both legs of the journey. In 2005, the ocean freight rate for importing a container to India was about 67 per cent higher than for exporting a container from the country. The average ocean freight per TEU was about US$1447 in 2005

Table 4.1   Ocean freight rates in selected Asian countries in 2005

Origin	Destination							
	China	India	Indonesia	Japan	Malaysia	Thailand	Korea	Average*
China		2289.22 (25.58)	874.92 (10.82)	1101.02 (4.35)	762.35 (5.82)	705.52 (8.75)	819.82 (1.00)	1092.14
India	1503.16 (10.34)		1423.47 (11.96)	1798.45 (10.20)	1324.26 (10.92)	1240.70 (11.78)	1392.35 (9.93)	1447.07
Indonesia	840.95 (4.77)	2545.64 (22.06)		1376.53 (10.99)	954.26 (8.12)	827.89 (8.05)	865.00 (4.34)	1235.05
Japan	501.51 (2.26)	2067.96 (13.61)	835.44 (4.91)		706.20 (3.92)	641.04 (10.48)	608.67 (3.37)	893.47
Malaysia	572.46 (9.29)	1877.37 (30.71)	820.55 (4.46)	1786.42 (33.26)		556.23 (8.46)	695.01 (13.89)	1051.34
Thailand	829.48 (7.18)	1881.34 (17.22)	1142.83 (13.08)	1050.22 (10.94)	889.80 (5.03)		874.06 (11.20)	1111.29
Korea	587.65 (10.07)	2310.44 (19.21)	884.32 (11.53)	876.38 (0.13)	888.71 (8.66)	671.39 (7.39)		1036.48
Average**	805.87	2162.00	996.92	1331.50	920.93	773.80	875.82	

Notes:

1. Rates are collected for shipment of a 20-foot container (TEU) between the major container ports of origin and destination countries. Rates are quarterly averaged for 2005.
2. Rates include container handling charges, documentation fees, government taxes and levies, etc. of both the trading partners. For details of ocean freight components, see De (2007a).
3. Numbers in parentheses are average annual growth rate (in per cent) for the years 2000 and 2005.
* Average across destination countries for each origin country.
** Average across origin countries for each destination country.

Source: Calculated based on Maersk Sealand (2007).

for export shipment of a container from India to six Asian countries, while for import from six Asian countries to India it was about US$2162. That made India the most expensive import destination among the countries reported here. In the case of China, it was just the opposite. For example, in the same year, the ocean freight rate for importing a container from six Asian countries to China was about 74 per cent lower than for exporting a container from that country.

Second, ocean freight rates have been rising almost across the board, but especially fast for India. The growth in these rates varies from country to country. When a longer period is considered, as between 2000 and 2005, the ocean freight rates for exporting a container from India to six Asian countries increased by an average of 10–12 per cent per annum, while for China, India, Malaysia and Japan the rates were about 26 and 33 per cent, respectively. In general, the growth in ocean freight rates for importing a container to India from each bilateral pair are higher than for the others except Malaysia and Japan. We also found that ocean freight rates grew at a very low rate for shipment between China, Japan and Korea, compared to other countries. Interestingly, growth in ocean freight rates is comparatively low in the case of adjacent countries such as Malaysia and Thailand, or Malaysia and Indonesia.

Table 4.2 provides the composition and structure of ocean freight in seven Asian countries for 2005. About 66 per cent of total shipping costs for movement of cargo between origin and destination countries was charged by shipping lines as base ocean freight, and 34 per cent as auxiliary shipping charges,[21] such as container handling charges and government duties, among others (Table 4.3). The extent of auxiliary shipping charges is very wide and covers several components, such as peak season surcharge, congestion surcharge, bunker adjustment factor (BAF), yen appreciation surcharge (YAS), fuel adjustment factor (FAF), and delivery order, among others. All these make shipping between countries quite costly. For example, an exporter had to pay on an average US$39 per TEU for BAF in 2005, which was imposed by the shipping lines as a fuel surcharge, and US$34 per TEU on average as YAS for cargoes going to Japan. In many cases auxiliary shipping charges often overtake base ocean freight rates. Table 4.2 shows the overall situation. Cargo originating from Japan going to Thailand had to pay on average US$366 per TEU towards auxiliary shipping charges in 2005, where the base ocean freight rate was only US$275, thus making container transportation between the two countries effectively costlier. The ocean trade between Japan and Korea follows the same pattern. Because of the close proximity and the availability of advanced port and shipping facilities, the auxiliary charges would be low, one would have thought, but that is not the case. It has been found that the

Table 4.2   Average ocean freight rates in 2005

Origin	Destination	Base ocean freight (US$/TEU)	Auxiliary charges* (US$/TEU)	Total ocean freight (US$/TEU)	Share of auxiliary charges** (%)
China	India	2000.00	289.22	2289.22	12.63
China	Indonesia	500.00	374.92	874.92	42.85
China	Japan	800.00	301.02	1101.02	27.34
China	Korea	500.00	319.82	819.82	39.01
China	Malaysia	600.00	162.35	762.35	21.30
China	Thailand	600.00	105.52	705.52	14.96
Japan	China	275.00	226.51	501.51	45.17
Japan	India	1600.00	467.96	2067.96	22.63
Japan	Indonesia	425.00	410.44	835.44	49.13
Japan	Korea	275.00	333.67	608.67	54.82
Japan	Malaysia	375.00	331.20	706.20	46.90
Japan	Thailand	275.00	366.04	641.04	57.10
India	China	837.00	666.16	1503.16	44.32
India	Japan	945.00	853.45	1798.45	47.45
India	Indonesia	810.00	613.47	1423.47	43.10
India	Korea	856.00	536.35	1392.35	38.52
India	Malaysia	690.00	634.26	1324.26	47.90
India	Thailand	627.00	613.70	1240.70	49.46
Indonesia	China	483.00	357.95	840.95	42.56
Indonesia	India	2025.00	520.64	2545.64	20.45
Indonesia	Japan	925.00	451.53	1376.53	32.80
Indonesia	Korea	381.00	484.00	865	55.95
Indonesia	Malaysia	367.00	587.26	954.26	61.54
Indonesia	Thailand	427.00	400.89	827.89	48.42
Korea	China	350.00	237.65	587.65	40.44
Korea	India	1950.00	360.44	2310.44	15.60
Korea	Indonesia	500.00	384.32	884.32	43.46
Korea	Japan	400.00	476.38	876.38	54.36
Korea	Malaysia	400.00	488.71	888.71	54.99
Korea	Thailand	400.00	271.39	671.39	40.42
Malaysia	China	350.00	222.46	572.46	38.86
Malaysia	India	1600.00	277.37	1877.37	14.77
Malaysia	Indonesia	400.00	420.55	820.55	51.25
Malaysia	Japan	1350.00	436.42	1786.42	24.43
Malaysia	Korea	350.00	345.01	695.01	49.64
Malaysia	Thailand	300.00	256.23	556.23	46.07
Thailand	China	650.00	179.48	829.48	21.64
Thailand	India	1650.00	231.34	1881.34	12.30
Thailand	Indonesia	700.00	442.83	1142.83	38.75

Table 4.2   (continued)

Origin	Destination	Base ocean freight (US$/TEU)	Auxiliary charges* (US$/TEU)	Total ocean freight (US$/TEU)	Share of auxiliary charges** (%)
Thailand	Japan	750.00	300.22	1050.22	28.59
Thailand	Korea	600.00	274.06	874.06	31.35
Thailand	Malaysia	650.00	239.80	889.8	26.95

Notes:
1. Rates are collected for shipment of a 20-foot container (TEU) among countries' major ports. Rates are quarterly average for 2005.
* Including container handling charges, documentation fees, government taxes and levies, etc. of both the trading partners.
** As a percentage of total ocean freight.

Source: Calculated based on freight rates provided by Maersk Sealand (2007).

auxiliary charges between the two countries were higher than the base ocean freight rate. Ports serving the coast of Japan impose comparatively higher auxiliary shipping charges, and the volume of average auxiliary shipping charges in India compared to its six Asian partners is found to be very high. One obvious reason is that India's major container ports are highly congested, so that the port authorities find it easy to impose a peak season surcharge and a congestion surcharge on the serving shipping lines and thus net short-term gains. Their bottom lines improve, but Indian ports appear very expensive.[22]

The auxiliary shipping charges are becoming increasingly critical to trade in Asia. These high charges are presumably offsetting the gains arising from trade liberalization, and making merchandise trade costlier in Asia. A major part of these charges, such as documentation fees, government taxes and levies etc., are the 'soft' barriers to trade. Traders (exporters and importers) have little control over them. While some of these charges, such as the terminal handling charges, are market driven, government duties and levies (similar to tariffs) are very much *ad hoc*. And these charges are relatively high among ports in India and Japan, and also in most of the countries in Northeast and Southeast Asia, where the volume of two-way trade is also very high. The depressing part is that despite technological advances, costs of moving goods across countries in Asia have not come down. Venables (2006, p. 64) observed: 'Technical change in shipping is no longer faster than technical change in goods shipped, so freight rates relative to shipment value are no longer falling.' The net result is that

Table 4.3   Components of total ocean freight in Asia in 2005

Freight components	Collected by	Rate (%)*
(a) Mandatory charges		
Base ocean freight rate between origin and destination	Shipping company	65.67
Container handling charge at origin	Terminal or port operator	12.00
Container handling charge at destination	Terminal or port operator	11.00
Carrier security charge	Shipping company	0.82
Documentation fee at origin	Shipping company	2.11
Documentation fee at destination	Shipping company	1.42
Government and port duties	Terminal or port operator	2.04
(b) Optional charges		
Wharfage	Terminal or port operator	0.53
Container cleaning charge	Shipping company	0.16
Peak season surcharge	Shipping company	0.69
Congestion surcharge	Shipping company	0.89
Bunker Adjustment Factor (BAF)	Shipping company	0.58
Yen Appreciation Surcharge (YAS)	Shipping company	0.63
Fuel Adjustment Factors (FAF)	Shipping company	0.58
Delivery order	Shipping company	0.64
EDI charge	Terminal or port operator	0.24
	Total	100.00

Note: * Average charges, calculated based on shipping rates provided by Maersk Sealand for the year 2005 for movement of a container vessel among seven Asian countries as listed in this chapter.

differences across countries and regions in ocean freight rates affect the trade in very much the same way as high tariffs.

4.   RELATIVE IMPORTANCE OF TRANSPORTATION COSTS IN ASIA

We have argued in the previous section that ocean freight rates, a major component of international transportation costs, are quite varied and uneven in Asia. In this section we examine the level and variation of freight rates at disaggregated commodity levels for seven Asian countries: China, India, Indonesia, Japan, Korea, Malaysia and Thailand. We deal with this analysis as follows: first, we aggregate the freight rates and their composition; and second, we estimate the transportation costs in order to understand their relative importance in trade flows.

The trade volume in Asia has been rising very rapidly. Intra-Asian trade in manufactures is quite large. Unlike exports in agriculture or fuel and minerals, exports in manufactures are mostly concentrated in Asia. The majority of intra-Asian trade in goods goes as intermediate goods, feeding a country's production or import demand when variations in trade costs could be crucial for the region's competitiveness in manufactures (Kuroiwa, 2006). Reduction in trade costs is therefore likely to help the Asian countries get their goods to market more quickly and cheaply.

However, the problem is exacerbated when one attempts to measure 'price' and 'non-price' barriers to trade in Asia.[23] Hummels (1999) commented:

> With tariffs, international and domestic transportation costs, time, and information cost, it is not difficult to understand a credible impact of trade costs on international trade. However, the difficulty lies in directly measuring acceptable indicators of cross-country differentials in 'price' and 'non-price' factors in general, which are traditionally seen as two major determinants of cross-country variations in trade costs.

The absence of compatible quantitative information on elements of trade costs for Asian countries restricts researchers from venturing into trade and transportation costs study for the continent. Asian countries do not compile information on import and export by transport modes and commodity groups as is done in the USA.[24] As a result, researchers rely on a proxy of transport costs, and sometimes on indirectly measured non-price factors when assessing barriers to trade flows for Asian countries.

Aggregated Freight Rates

The cost of transportation of merchandise from one country to another is a combination of two major components: inland and international transportation costs. Understanding the unit freight rate on two legs of the journey – inland and international – will help us to discover the variation in cost of transportation across commodities in Asia.

We first derive the country-wise freight rate, which is a weighted average of all commodity groups across all trading partners for both international and inland shipments of a container from one country to another. We use equations (4.1) and (4.2) to estimate the country-wise freight rate (weighted average) per container for both inland and international shipment.

$$F_{ij} = \frac{\sum_k Q_{ij}^k f_{ij}^k}{\sum_k Q_{ij}^k} \qquad (4.1)$$

$$F_i = \frac{1}{n}(F_{ij}) \qquad (4.2)$$

where F_i represents the weighted-average freight rate per container for country i, which is averaged over all commodity groups across all trading partners of country i, F_{ij} denotes the weighted-average freight rate per container for country i for import of commodity k from country j, Q_{ij}^k stands for import of commodity k in TEU by country i from country j, F_{ij}^k represents the freight rate per TEU of import of commodity k by country i from country j, k is the commodity group traded (at the 4-digit HS level) between partners i and j, and n is number of bilateral trading partners of i. We collect F_{ij}^k for inland and international shipment separately. F_i is estimated from the 4-digit HS level for imports of country i from its partner for the years 2000 and 2005.[25] Here, commodity-wise freight rates for inland and international shipment were collected from Maersk Sealand (2007),[26] whereas countries' imports by weight at the 4-digit HS level were collected from COMTRADE (UN, 2007).[27] Table 4.4 provides estimated freight rate (F_i) per container for selected Asian countries for the year 2005. The following are the major observations.

First, we have found that the estimated freight rate varies across countries. The total freight rate per container is highest (US$3488 per TEU 2005) in India, and lowest in Malaysia (US$1284 per TEU). With US$1409 per TEU, China comes next to Malaysia. India has the highest rate in both inland and international freight. In contrast, China and Thailand have the lowest inland (US$395 per TEU in 2005) and international (US$704 per TEU in 2005) freight rate respectively in this group, much lower than that of other Asian countries (Figure 4.2(a)).

Second, while the costs of inland and international freight in Thailand and Korea appear pretty similar, they are more or less the same for the other five Asian countries. The aggregated inland freight rates in Korea and Thailand are comparatively higher than their comparable international freight rates. However, the other Asian countries show an opposite scenario: their international freight rate is higher than their inland freight rate. Taking the total transportation leg, the cost of inland transportation takes the major share in Thailand and Korea, compared to other Asian countries. For others, it is the international freight rate that matters most.

Third, the share of inland freight in total freight varies across countries. Asian countries witnessed an absolute rise in both inland and international freight rate per container between 2000 and 2005, whereas the changes in

Table 4.4   Estimated freight rates in 2005

Importer	Exporter	Total freight rate (US$/TEU)	Inland freight		International freight	
			Rate (US$/TEU)	Share** (%)	Rate (US$/TEU)	Share** (%)
China	India	2933	795	27	2138	73
	Indonesia	1160	390	34	770	66
	Japan	1409	321	23	1088	77
	Malaysia	1062	386	36	676	64
	Korea	979	206	21	773	79
	Thailand	908	256	28	652	72
	Total*	1409	395	28	1014	72
India	China	3960	1505	38	2455	62
	Indonesia	3538	1309	37	2229	63
	Japan	3596	1187	33	2409	67
	Malaysia	3299	1287	39	2012	61
	Korea	3394	1425	42	1969	58
	Thailand	3142	974	31	2168	69
	Total*	3488	1284	37	2204	63
Indonesia	China	1520	701	46	819	54
	India	2724	984	36	1740	64
	Japan	1529	642	42	887	58
	Malaysia	1133	573	51	560	49
	Korea	1651	688	42	963	58
	Thailand	1243	520	42	723	58
	Total*	1633	685	42	949	58
Japan	China	1758	765	44	993	56
	India	3933	1640	42	2293	58
	Indonesia	1890	905	48	985	52
	Malaysia	1806	710	39	1096	61
	Korea	1356	489	36	867	64
	Thailand	2144	630	29	1514	71
	Total*	2148	857	40	1291	60
Malaysia	China	1201	602	50	599	50
	India	1938	762	39	1176	61
	Indonesia	1242	422	34	820	66
	Japan	1352	288	21	1064	79
	Korea	1048	240	23	808	77
	Thailand	924	292	32	632	68
	Total*	1284	434	34	850	66
Korea	China	1475	879	60	596	40
	India	3420	1866	55	1554	45

Table 4.4   (continued)

Importer	Exporter	Total freight rate (US$/TEU)	Inland freight		International freight	
			Rate (US$/TEU)	Share** (%)	Rate (US$/TEU)	Share** (%)
	Indonesia	1862	1162	62	700	38
	Japan	1247	369	30	878	70
	Malaysia	1594	1063	67	531	33
	Thailand	1534	955	62	579	38
	Total*	1855	1049	57	806	43
Thailand	China	1824	1042	57	782	43
	India	2894	1844	64	1050	36
	Indonesia	1276	740	58	536	42
	Japan	1538	920	60	618	40
	Malaysia	1492	923	62	569	38
	Korea	1482	810	55	672	45
	Total*	1751	1047	60	705	40

Notes:
* Weighted average over all partners.
** Share in total freight rate.

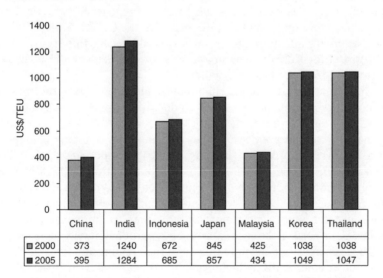

	China	India	Indonesia	Japan	Malaysia	Korea	Thailand
2000	373	1240	672	845	425	1038	1038
2005	395	1284	685	857	434	1049	1047

Figure 4.2(a)   Inland freight rate (weighted average) per container

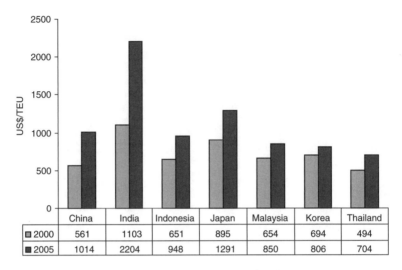

	China	India	Indonesia	Japan	Malaysia	Korea	Thailand
■ 2000	561	1103	651	895	654	694	494
■ 2005	1014	2204	948	1291	850	806	704

Figure 4.2(b)   International freight rate (weighted average) per container

the weighted-average freight rate are prominent across countries. It is interesting that the rise in the inland freight rate per container is marginal, compared to the international freight rate. In contrast, the change in the international freight rate is dispersed across countries and also high. For example, India has witnessed a steep rise in its international freight rate, which has gone up from US$1103 per TEU to US$2204 per TEU, the highest among all the Asian countries considered in this study (Figure 4.2(b)). But for Korea it is comparatively low (US$806 per TEU in 2005, up from US$694 per TEU in 2000).

Fourth, the variation in international freight rates across countries and commodities presumably has much to do with terminal handling charges (THC) and auxiliary shipping charges. Tables 4.5(a) and 4.5(b) provide the estimated weighted average of THC and auxiliary shipping charges for 2005. On average, auxiliary shipping charges are much higher than THC across commodities and countries. They are exceptionally high in India. Quite naturally, imports of manufactures such as electronics, and office and telecom equipment, which come in containers and have relatively high shares in total imports, cost more in India than traditional commodities. Malaysia imports a large quantity of traditional items such as food products, chemicals, paper and pulp, and fuel, mining and forest products, which incur comparatively high ocean freight charges. Why is the international freight rate per container so expensive in the case of India? Perhaps it is due to the high THC, US$795 per TEU, and auxiliary shipping charges, US$1408 per TEU,[28] at ports.

Table 4.5(a) Terminal handling charge (weighted average) in 2005 (US$/TEU)

Commodity groups	China	India	Indonesia	Japan	Malaysia	Korea	Thailand	Commodity total (weighted average)
Electronic integrated circuits	238	768	316	459	316	252	240	626
Office and telecom equipment	231	720	298	412	278	251	243	510
Fuels, mining and forest products	542	817	360	550	370	316	308	468
Food products	422	986	476	408	386	363	386	409
Electrical and electronics	228	734	303	364	276	247	232	384
Chemicals	272	824	357	425	402	249	267	368
Textiles and clothing	249	785	361	360	322	264	248	349
Paper and pulp	245	1010	351	471	380	327	258	325
Pharmaceuticals	260	784	341	361	353	243	249	324
Leather	311	775	312	336	369	255	262	321
Rubber and plastics	274	885	360	452	274	270	253	320
Metal	214	795	303	380	299	251	272	298
Automobiles and components	212	906	325	381	313	244	238	296
Machinery and mechanical appliances	205	750	303	366	270	238	242	282
Iron and steel	245	839	324	371	279	235	236	279
Transport equipment	187	793	318	340	283	225	233	228
Country total (weighted average)	437	795	358	521	337	295	279	403

Table 4.5(b) Auxiliary shipping charges (weighted average) in 2005 (US$/TEU)

Commodity groups	China	India	Indonesia	Japan	Malaysia	Korea	Thailand	Commodity total (weighted average)
Electronic integrated circuits	336	1419	565	557	514	466	398	1126
Office and telecom equipment	337	1541	592	731	486	530	412	1034
Electrical and electronics	346	1422	600	726	511	537	428	737
Fuels, mining and forest products	697	1263	567	793	537	518	409	665
Food products	569	1359	701	717	573	573	552	646
Textiles and clothing	355	1451	601	744	507	545	456	646
Leather	404	1535	611	763	586	565	436	622
Pharmaceuticals	392	1371	543	722	550	458	482	587
Chemicals	377	1341	606	676	535	485	425	523
Metal	341	1436	599	735	496	558	455	517
Machinery and mechanical appliances	333	1484	587	672	491	491	432	516
Automobiles and components	329	1328	593	694	502	497	427	510
Rubber and plastics	383	1322	563	675	478	474	405	485
Iron and steel	368	1379	586	557	482	478	445	485
Paper and pulp	373	1386	590	674	528	477	411	477
Transport equipment	326	1481	597	733	539	460	401	437
Country total (weighted average)	577	1408	590	770	512	511	425	602

92

Fifth, the combined incidence of THC and auxiliary shipping charges is higher in the case of high-value manufactures such as electronic integrated circuits, office and telecom equipment, and electrical and electronics items than for traditional commodities and mining and forest products.

Estimated *Ad Valorem* Transportation Costs

In order to evaluate the extent of trade cost barriers and the impact on trade flow, we now attempt to measure *ad valorem* transportation costs for the shipment of a container from one country to another.[29] The *ad valorem* (trade-weighted) transportation costs give us the US\$ transport cost per US\$ of import. We use equation (4.3) to estimate the commodity distribution of *ad valorem* transportation cost (*AdvTC*) for import of commodity k to country i from country j.

$$AdvTC_i^k = \frac{\sum_l Q_{ij}^k f_{ij}^k}{\sum_l M_{ij}^k} * 100 \tag{4.3}$$

where $AdvTC_i^k$ represents *ad valorem* transportation costs respectively for country i for commodity k, Q_{ij}^k stands for import of commodity group k in weight (here, in TEU) by country i from country j, f_{ij}^k represents the inland freight rate per TEU for import of commodity k by country i from country j, M_{ij}^k stands for import of commodity group k in value (here, in US\$) by country i from country j, and k is the commodity group traded at the 4-digit HS level. The transport costs are estimated for k commodity group for imports of country i from its partner for the years 2000 and 2005. Commodity composition of *ad valorem* transportation costs are estimated as percentage of total import.

The following are the sources of data. Inland and international freight rates were collected from Maersk Sealand (2007), whereas countries' imports at the 4-digit HS level were collected from COMTRADE (UN, 2007). Table 4.6 provides evidence on the level and distribution of *ad valorem* transportation cost for each importer by commodity across seven Asian countries for the year 2005.[30] The following broad features emerge.

First, the *ad valorem* transportation cost for all goods is lowest in the case of Japan (10.4 per cent in 2005) and highest in the case of India (22.8 per cent in 2005).

Second, transportation costs are lower for manufactured goods than for traditional commodities. Fuels, minerals and forest products incur the highest transportation costs in all the countries.

Third, the transportation costs for imports of high-end manufactures such as electrical and electronics, office and telecom equipment, and electronic integrated circuits in India appear to be very high.

Table 4.6　Ad valorem *transportation costs (trade-weighted) in 2005*

Commodity groups	China	India	Indonesia	Japan	Malaysia	Korea	Thailand
Transport equipment	8.50	8.10	11.10	7.20	9.40	11.80	11.90
Automobiles and components	16.90	22.90	22.70	3.10	11.50	6.70	12.10
Chemicals	8.30	19.00	12.50	10.50	14.80	10.80	15.30
Electrical and electronics	9.20	12.40	13.10	3.70	9.40	6.60	8.60
Electronic integrated circuits	4.50	28.90	9.30	2.00	9.10	8.24	9.90
Food products	25.10	48.50	14.40	12.00	22.00	17.90	12.70
Fuels, mining and forest products	41.80	59.00	27.30	34.60	41.76	40.21	27.62
Iron and steel	8.70	30.90	18.50	9.20	17.50	12.50	17.20
Leather	8.10	15.60	9.00	1.10	9.20	2.20	12.10
Machinery and mechanical appliances	9.80	12.20	12.80	3.10	11.60	8.30	11.60
Metal	14.20	16.00	14.60	9.50	16.10	12.00	15.50
Office and telecom equipment	6.20	20.80	2.80	1.60	1.80	6.40	8.70
Paper and pulp	9.50	24.20	12.60	9.60	15.60	13.90	12.60
Pharmaceuticals	8.10	12.30	11.80	7.50	12.70	7.00	11.40
Rubber and plastics	8.20	16.80	8.60	7.20	8.50	4.30	4.00
Textiles and clothing	8.80	15.60	5.60	1.30	3.30	2.90	3.90
Country total	16.90	22.80	17.20	10.40	18.40	14.90	15.60

Fourth, Malaysia stands out as having an exceptionally high transport cost in the case of traditional commodities. However, the costs of transportation there are relatively much lower in the case of manufactures.

Fifth, the *ad valorem* transportation costs vary across commodities and countries. For example, transportation costs for imports of chemicals, fuels, mining and forest products, iron and steel and metal are comparatively very expensive in Malaysia. Similarly, India witnesses relatively high transportation costs for import of food products, electronic integrated circuits, electrical and electronics, office and telecom equipment, textiles and clothing, and paper and pulp. The international transportation cost for import of transport equipment is higher in Indonesia than in other Asian countries.

Finally, we conclude that the Asian countries have a comparatively high incidence of transportation costs (the exception being Japan) where variation across countries and commodities is driven by differences in ocean freight rates. The higher the ocean freight rate, the higher the transportation cost.

The Weight–Value Ratio of Trade and Transport Cost

In the context of the spectacular growth in trade in Asia, the changing composition of Asia's trade becomes a very important issue. Asia presently accounts for about one-third of world exports in manufacturers, and, except for pharmaceuticals, Asia's share in world exports in other manufactures varies between the lowest 18 per cent (chemicals) and the highest 66 per cent (integrated circuits). Intra-Asian trade in manufactures is conducted more in machinery and transport equipment (48.6 per cent) and less in personal and household goods, and scientific and controlling instruments, respectively. Intra-Asian exports in agriculture, fuel and mining products are even less than their exports to the world. Driven by China, Asian countries are gradually specializing in trade in intermediate and finished goods, which beef up their production or import demand.

However, to evaluate the transportation needs, it is useful to compare trade growth in relation to transport cost. We calculate the weight–value ratio for Asian countries for their regional trade with the help of equation (4.4).[31]

$$w_{it} = \sum_k S_{ikt} w_k \qquad (4.4)$$

where w_k is the median weight–value ratio for each HS 4-digit commodity k in imports (exports) for the year 2005, S_{ikt} is the share of product k in the trade bundle of country i at time t, and w_{it} is the aggregate weight–value ratio for country i's imports for the year t. We report the weight–value ratio (measured in TEU per US$10 000) for each country's imports in Table 4.7. The following patterns are worth noting.

First, Asian countries have higher trade in automobiles and transport equipment. As a result, transport equipment across all the Asian countries has a high weight–value ratio. Japan is a notable case.

Second, China's imports are comparatively heavy in transport equipment, electrical and electronics, automobiles and components, food products, and leather, which are basically heavier raw materials and intermediate products used as inputs for high-value production and exports by China. In contrast, except for transport equipment, automobiles and components,

Table 4.7 Estimated weight–value ratio (TEU/US$10000) in 2005

Commodity groups	China	India	Indonesia	Japan	Malaysia	Korea	Thailand
Transport equipment	417.436	12.086	192.917	1301.104	246.684	148.328	130.887
Automobiles and components	1.957	2.330	1.443	2.330	19.922	11.318	2.266
Chemicals	0.815	0.557	1.066	0.693	18.682	0.611	0.882
Electrical and electronics	2.216	0.458	7.098	3.202	4.164	4.244	1.848
Electronic integrated circuits	0.092	1.732	9.523	0.508	4.636	0.592	0.195
Food products	20.728	8.964	0.975	0.349	5.676	0.916	1.957
Fuels, mining and forest products	0.049	0.052	0.435	0.143	1.926	0.190	0.156
Iron and steel	0.365	0.206	0.055	0.142	0.523	0.090	0.072
Leather	2.217	3.799	13.233	0.541	7.087	1.433	4.656
Machinery and mechanical appliances	0.031	0.967	0.039	0.081	0.136	0.035	0.046
Metal	0.118	1.063	0.444	0.207	0.158	0.082	0.112
Office and telecom equipment	0.020	0.010	0.428	0.017	0.039	0.009	0.047
Paper and pulp	0.406	1.419	0.770	1.097	0.261	0.674	0.482
Pharmaceuticals	0.449	0.375	0.033	0.051	0.476	0.031	0.097
Rubber and plastics	0.019	0.003	0.057	0.006	0.009	0.120	0.052
Textiles and clothing	0.000	0.000	0.008	0.001	0.022	0.002	0.008

and electrical and electronics, Japan's imports are mostly low-weight finished products.

Third, all the Asian economies considered here (except Japan) are net importers of weight in semi-finished capital goods and raw materials.

The cost of transportation of heavier goods will certainly be higher than for lighter goods. In other words, the weight–value ratio of a product is the major determinant of the transport cost. Hummels and Skiba (2004) commented that a 10 per cent increase in the product weight–value ratio leads to a 4 per cent increase in *ad valorem* shipping cost. Since most of the Asian countries are net importers of weight, where two of them are geographically large (China and India), it would be important to understand the relationship between transport cost and weight–value ratio. This will help us to evaluate the transportation needs in Asian countries more precisely. What we found is that the heavier the good, the larger is the transportation cost, except in Japan. Japan, as a developed country, imports far less weight, implying less transport congestion and subsequently less *ad valorem* transportation costs due to its relatively superior transport infrastructure.

Further evidence on the transport barrier is provided in Figure 4.3, which plots countries' trade-weighted applied tariff and transportation cost in a cross-section pooled framework for the years 2000 and 2005. There has been an upward, even though marginal, shift of the countries' loci in a northwestern direction in the tariff–freight plane over time. This upward movement of countries has changed the trajectory representing the locus in Figure 4.3. The changes in 2005, in terms of both slope and intercept, are evident. This suggests a relatively higher incidence of transport cost on the one hand, and the reduction of relative distances among the countries in the tariff–freight plane on the other.[32] At the same time, this also indicates that tariffs as a barrier are not yet dead. This leads us to further analyse how tariff and transport costs impede trade. This is dealt with in the next section.

5. ASSESSING BARRIERS TO TRADE IN SELECTED ASIAN COUNTRIES

We now turn to assess the impact of trade costs (barriers to trade) on trade flows. We are interested in finding out how changes in trade cost components affect changes in import demand. Here, we first estimate the impact of transport costs and other barriers to trade flows, controlling for other variables. We deal only with those barriers (components of trade costs) that are imposed by policy (e.g. freight and tariff rates).

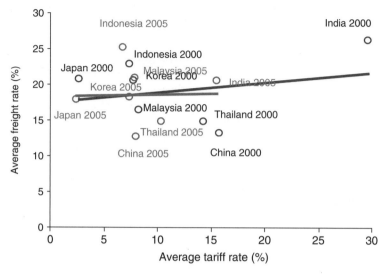

Figure 4.3   Countries in tariff–freight plane: 2000 and 2005

The Model

In order to explore the impact of trade costs on trade flows, the following constant elasticity of substitution (CES) equation is considered.

$$U_i = \left(\sum_j \lambda_j x^{\frac{1}{\theta}} \right)^{\theta} \tag{4.5}$$

where i and j are importing and exporting countries, respectively, $\theta = \sigma / (1-\sigma)$. We treat λ as a quality shifter specific to exporter j, or, in other words, it represents the number of unique varieties being produced by exporter j.

We write the import demand for a product as follows.

$$q_{ij} = E_i \left(\frac{\lambda_j}{p_j} \right)^{\sigma} t_{ij}^{-\sigma} \tag{4.6}$$

where q_{ij} is value of import of i from j, t is trade cost component, E is real expenditures on a product (expenditures divided by the price level), which we do not observe but proxy it by a country's GDP.[33] Similarly, λ/p are not really observable due to poor quality of measures of p, and also contaminated by quality differences.[34] We want prices net of quality differences and quality itself, but we cannot observe those. We want to control for a demand shifter that is exporter-specific – China is different from Malaysia, certainly in its size and probably in the quality of the products it makes, so we want to omit that. Therefore we have to omit those things that we cannot observe. We deal with this in the following ways.

First, we take a log and use a vector of importer and exporter fixed effects, which yields equation (4.7).

$$\ln q_{ij} = \ln E_i + \sigma\ln\left(\frac{\lambda_j}{P_j}\right) - \sigma\ln t_{ij} \tag{4.7}$$

Second, we replace t_{ij} by *ad valorem* transportation cost. We write the trade cost vector as follows:

$$\begin{aligned} t_{ij} &= TAR_{ij}f_{ij} \\ &= TAR_{ij}(F_{ij}/V_{ij}) \end{aligned} \tag{4.8}$$

where f_{ij} is the *ad valorem* equivalent of the transport cost, F_{ij} is the freight cost in TEU and V_{ij} is the import value per TEU. Since our purpose is to assess the impact of trade cost components on trade over time, we consider two cross-section years, namely 2000 and 2005. We rewrite equation (4.6) as follows.

$$\frac{q_{ij2005}}{q_{ij2000}} = \frac{E_{i2005}\left(\dfrac{\lambda_{j2005}}{P_{j2005}}\right)^{\sigma} t_{ij2005}^{-\sigma}}{E_{i2000}\left(\dfrac{\lambda_{j2000}}{P_{j2000}}\right)^{\sigma} t_{ij2000}^{-\sigma}} \tag{4.9}$$

By taking logs, we get

$$\ln\frac{q_{ij2005}}{q_{ij2000}} = \ln\left(\frac{E_{i2005}}{E_{i2000}}\right) + \sigma\ln\left(\frac{\dfrac{\lambda_{j2005}}{P_{j2005}}}{\dfrac{\lambda_{j2000}}{P_{j2000}}}\right) - \sigma\ln\left(\frac{t_{ij2005}}{t_{ij2000}}\right) \tag{4.10}$$

We incorporate importer and exporter fixed effects to take care of expenditures, or quality or price parameters, and rewrite (4.10) as follows.

$$\ln\frac{q_{ij2005}}{q_{ij2000}} = A_i + A_j - \sigma\ln\left(\frac{t_{ij2005}}{t_{ij2000}}\right) \tag{4.11}$$

Now, we substitute the trade cost elements by tariff (TAR_{ij}) and transport cost (TC_{ij}), and rewrite (4.10) as follows.

$$\ln\frac{q_{ij2005}}{q_{ij2000}} = A_i + A_j - \sigma\ln\left(\frac{TAR_{ij2005}}{TAR_{ij2000}}\right) - \sigma\ln\left(\frac{TC_{ij2005}}{TC_{ij2000}}\right) + \varepsilon_{ij} \tag{4.12}$$

where *i* and *j* are importing and exporting countries. Tariff represents weighted applied rate and transport cost is taken at *ad valorem* equivalent. We replace TC_{ij} by inland transportation cost and international transportation cost interchangeably in equation (4.12). We use country dummy ($=1$ when *i* is importer, and 0 otherwise). The parameters to be estimated are denoted by σ, and $ε_{ij}$ is the error term.

The model considered here uses data for the years 2000 and 2005 at the 4-digit HS level for imports of seven Asian countries: China, India, Indonesia, Japan, Korea, Malaysia and Thailand. The model considers data at the bilateral level for all the variables for their individual partners. By taking tariffs and transport costs, we cover a major portion of trade costs. Bilateral trade, transport costs and tariffs are estimated from the 4-digit HS level for the years 2000 and 2005.[35] We have about 652 observations for 16 identical commodity groups for each year and seven countries overall. Before estimating the models, we obtained a matrix of correlation coefficients to rule out any possibility of multicollinearity problems.[36]

Results

Table 4.8 reports OLS estimates of equation (4.12). We expect that the tariff and *ad valorem* transport cost variables are negatively correlated with the volume of imports. As variables are in natural logarithms, estimated coefficients show CES. The elasticity is useful as an indicator of the effect of trade barriers on trade volumes. The model performs well as most of the variables have the expected sign. Given the large cross-sectional nature of the data, the estimated model explains about 33 per cent of the variations in direction of trade flows. The most interesting result is the strong influence that changes in *ad valorem* transportation cost, both inland and international, had on changes in trade: the higher the transportation cost between each pair of partners, the less they trade. In other words, the estimated elasticity indicates that a 10 per cent rise in *ad valorem* transportation cost lowers trade by 3 to 4 per cent in Asia.

International transportation cost, when seen separately in Model 7 in Table 4.8, comes with a significant coefficient and a negative sign. The estimated elasticity indicates that a 10 per cent fall in *ad valorem* international transportation cost increases trade by 3 per cent. The same applies in the case of inland transportation cost. Considering these *ad valorem* rates separately in Model 8, we find that the inland transportation cost is the important determinant of trade flows in Asia.

The estimated models also indicate that tariff does not influence trade flow since all its estimated coefficients have appeared as statistically

Table 4.8 Non-linear least squares estimates of import demand

	Model 1	Model 2	Model 3	Model 4	Model 5	Model 6	Model 7	Model 8
Tariff (weighted applied)	0.003 (0.050)	0.002 (0.040)	0.003 (0.050)	0.004 (0.060)				
Transport cost (inland + international) (*ad valorem* equivalent)	−0.284* (−2.450)				−0.383* (−2.420)			
Inland transport cost (*ad valorem* equivalent)		−0.282* (−2.420)	−0.389* (−2.570)	−0.252* (−1.370)		−0.287* (−2.540)		−0.251* (−1.170)
International transport cost (*ad valorem* equivalent)				−0.166 (−1.002)			−0.281* (−2.390)	−0.165 (−1.001)
No. of observations	651	651	651	651	652	652	652	652
Adjusted R^2	0.326	0.326	0.338	0.327	0.328	0.329	0.328	0.328

Notes:
* Significant at the 10 per cent level.
** Significant at the 5 per cent level.
*** Significant at the 1 per cent level.
Numbers in parentheses are t-values.

insignificant. Perhaps there were few significant changes in applied tariffs between 2000 and 2005.

From the estimated elasticities and their significance level, it can also be said that inland transport cost is more important than international transportation cost in enhancing Asia's trade flows. This also directly indicates that there is a huge infrastructure bottleneck inside these countries (barring perhaps Japan). This calls for immediate attention in order to enhance trade flows in Asia.

The estimates also seem to show that the size of the effects does not vary widely. The usual caveat is that the R^2 reported in Table 4.8 indicates that equation (4.12) explains only a small part (one-third or less) of the variation in trade flows. Perhaps the inappropriateness of the structural model or omitted variable bias could be plausible reasons for the poor fit.

6.   CONCLUSION

The analysis carried out in this chapter provides sufficient evidence to emphasize that variations in transport costs have a significant influence on regional trade flows in Asia. Costlier transportation prohibits trade and taxes it in the same way as tariffs. This chapter also offers evidence on the effect of inland and international transport cost on trade flows. Two major advances are evident in this study: first, we introduce bilateral inland and international freight rates between two trading partners that we believe have an impact on trade. Second, we introduce *ad valorem* equivalent of inland and international transportation costs at the bilateral level, which are largely ignored in the empirical literature in the context of Asia.

Barriers reduce trade. This is the conclusion of a series of studies, including this one, that examine the trade-reducing effects of trade costs. The purpose of this study is to examine and explain the magnitude of barrier effects for a set of Asian countries. The following are the major findings of this study.

1.   Asia has been witnessing a sharp rise in merchandise trade and is showing greater trade interdependence in a large variety of goods, particularly intermediate and capital goods. However, rising transport costs continue to impede trade in Asia. The analysis carried out in this chapter provides sufficient evidence to ascertain how variations in transport costs influence regional trade flows in Asia.
2.   Freight (ocean) cost is one of the major components of international transportation cost. Freight costs vary across countries, where inefficient transport services could be the potential element for freight cost

differentials. These result in a longer time for delivery. The freight rate per container is highest in India, and lowest in Malaysia. China comes next to Malaysia. India witnesses the highest rate in both inland and international freights. In contrast, China and Thailand offer the lowest inland and international freight rates respectively in this group, much lower than other Asian countries. The high terminal handling charges and other expenses at Indian ports make the international leg of a journey very expensive in India.

3. While the costs of inland and international transport in Thailand and Korea are fairly similar, they are the same in the other five Asian countries. Taking the entire transportation leg, the cost of inland transportation (weighted average across all commodity groups) takes the major share in Thailand and Korea, compared to other Asian countries. For others, it is the international transport cost that matters most in the entire journey.

4. The *ad valorem* transportation cost varies across commodities and countries. Thailand and China offer the lowest *ad valorem* international and inland transportation costs for all goods, whereas Malaysia shows the highest rate in both cases. Except for Thailand, where the *ad valorem* inland transport cost exceeds the *ad valorem* international transportation cost, others show the opposite scenario. The *ad valorem* transportation costs are lower for manufactured goods than for traditional commodities. Fuels, minerals and forest products witness the highest transportation costs. Contrary to popular belief, international and inland transportation costs for imports of high-end manufactures such as electrical and electronics, office and telecom equipment, and electronic and integrated circuits in India are very high. Malaysia stands out as having exceptionally high freight rates in the case of traditional commodities. However, the costs of inland and international transportation in Malaysia are relatively low in the case of manufactures.

5. The variation in *ad valorem* international transportation costs across countries and commodities depends on terminal handling charges (THC) and auxiliary shipping charges. On average, auxiliary shipping charges are much higher than THC – across commodities and countries in Asia, of which India has exceptionally high THC and auxiliary shipping charges. Naturally, imports of manufactures such as electronics, office and telecom equipment, which have higher shares in total imports, are costlier in India than traditional commodities.

6. Since Asian countries have higher trade in automobiles and transport equipment, trade in transport equipment across all the Asian countries has a high weight–value ratio. China's imports are comparatively heavy in transport equipment, electrical and electronics, automobiles and

components, food products, and leather, which are basically heavier raw materials and intermediate products used as inputs to high-value production and exports in China. In contrast, except for transport equipment, automobiles and components, and electrical and electronics, Japan's imports are mostly low-weight finished products. Therefore all the Asian economies considered here (except Japan) are net importers of weight in semi-finished capital goods and raw materials.

7. The cost of transportation of heavier goods will certainly be higher than for lighter goods. In other words, the weight–value ratio of a product is the major determinant of its transport cost. We find that the heavier the good, the higher the transportation cost, except in Japan. Japan, as a developed country, imports much less weight, implying less transport congestion and subsequently less transport cost due to its relatively superior transport infrastructure.

8. There has been a fall in absolute tariffs between 2000 and 2005. Most Asian countries have been successful in reducing the average applied tariffs, showing an upward shift of the countries' loci, even though marginal, to northwestern direction in the tariff–freight plane over time. It suggests a relatively higher incidence of freight in Asia, on the one hand, and the reduction of relative distances among the Asian countries in the tariff–freight plane, on the other.

9. The most interesting result is the strong influence that changes in *ad valorem* transportation cost, both inland and international, had on changes in trade: the higher the transportation cost between each pair of partners, the less they trade. A 10 per cent increase in *ad valorem* transportation cost lowers trade by 3 to 4 per cent. The inland transportation cost is more important than international transportation cost in enhancing Asia's trade flows. This also directly indicates that there is a huge infrastructure bottleneck inside the countries in Asia (barring perhaps Japan), which calls for immediate attention in order to enhance trade flows in Asia.

Given these broad findings, any attempt towards deeper integration of the economies of the region holds high promise if accompanied by initiatives that help improve trade efficiency and reduce trade costs. Reduction in inland transportation costs should get priority attention, while formulating policy for Asia's infrastructure development since the fall in transportation costs, as an outcome of improved infrastructure, will stimulate trade. The challenge for Asian countries is thus to identify improvements in logistics services and related infrastructure that can be achieved in the short to medium term and that would have a significant impact on competitiveness of these countries.

NOTES

*   An earlier version of this chapter was presented at the Asian Development Bank Institute (ADBI) Conference on 'Trade Costs in Asia', held in Tokyo, 25–26 June 2007. The author acknowledges the insightful comments and guidance provided by David Hummels, and thanks Douglas Brooks, Jayant Menon, Biswa Bhattacharyay, Ajitava Raychaudhury, Prema-Chandra Athukorala, Yann Duval, Jayanta Sarkar and conference participants for comments and suggestions. Bhisma Raout provided excellent research assistance. The author sincerely acknowledges the research grant provided by the ADBI for carrying out this study. The views expressed by the author are his personal views. The usual disclaimers apply.
1. This chapter builds on previous literature on this subject, in particular De (2006a, 2007, 2008a, 2008b). It has two distinct methodological improvements over De (2006a, 2007). First, we have estimated the *ad valorem* transportation costs for trade in selected Asian countries. Second, the model is tested on a large cross-section of pooled data for the years 2000 and 2005, taken at the 4-digit HS level.
2. See Anderson and van Wincoop (2004) for a detailed discussion on trade costs.
3. Based on WTO (2006a, 2007).
4. A growing literature in this regard has documented the impact of trade costs on the volume of trade. Some seminal studies carried out on this topic in recent years are Hummels (1999; 2007), Limao and Venables (2001) and Anderson and van Wincoop (2004).
5. For a shipment of goods across borders, transport costs refer to two major elements – international transport costs, which include costs associated with the shipment of goods from one country to another, and the inland (domestic) transport costs, which consider costs of inland transportation of merchandise in both exporting and importing countries.
6. According to the World Bank (2001), for 168 out of 216 US trading partners, transport cost barriers outweighed tariff barriers. For the majority of Sub-Saharan African countries, Latin America and the Caribbean, and a large part of Asia, transport cost incidence for exports is five times higher than tariff cost incidence.
7. Correspondingly, locational problems have also been neglected in the theory of customs unions (see Balassa, 1961).
8. See, e.g., Krugman (1980), Krugman and Venables (1990).
9. Samuelson's iceberg model assumes that a part of the transported good is consumed in transportation. The iceberg assumption is $Q^d < Q^s$, and can be expressed as $(1+\alpha) Q^d \equiv Q^s$, where $\alpha > 0$.
10. The basic assumptions of Krugman and Venables (1990) are as follows: country i is larger than country j in terms of factor endowments (capital and labour) and market size. In both countries there are two sectors, both producing tradable goods; one perfectly competitive and the other producing manufactures, imperfectly competitive. Country i has a larger number of firms in the manufacturing sector. This sector produces differentiated products under increasing returns to scale and monopolistic competition. The relative factor endowments are the same for both the countries, so there is no comparative advantage and trade is of the intra-industry type.
11. See APEC (2002); OECD (2003).
12. See APEC (2002).
13. Similar indications were obtained for countries in APEC (Cernat, 2001; World Bank, 2002; Wilson et al., 2003). According to the World Bank, raising performance across the region to halfway up to the level of the APEC average could result in a 10 per cent increase in intra-APEC exports, worth roughly US$280 billion (World Bank, 2002).
14. See, e.g., Amiti and Javorcik (2008).
15. For instance, products that are perishable, such as food, or subject to frequent changes in consumer preferences, such as high-fashion textiles.

16. For instance, De (2006b) found a negative non-linear relationship between transport costs and imports in the context of 15 Asian economies. This relationship clearly points to the fact that transport costs do influence trade.

17. For example, Bougheas et al. (1999) estimated gravity equations for a sample limited to nine European countries. They included the product of the partner's kilometres of motorway in one specification and that of public capital stock in another, and found that these have a positive particle correlation with bilateral exports.

18. According to UNCTAD, freight costs in developing Asia are on average 116 per cent higher than those in developed countries, and this difference is mainly attributable to global trade structures, regional infrastructure facilities, logistics systems, and the more influential distribution strategies of shippers of developed countries (UNCTAD, 2006).

19. The advent of fast transport (air shipping and faster ocean vessels) is equivalent to reducing tariffs on manufactured goods from 32 to 9 per cent between 1950 and 1998 (Hummels, 2001).

20. The rates are spot rates and collected for shipment of a twenty-foot equivalent unit (TEU) between the major container ports of origin and destination countries from the historical freight rate database. Rates are quarterly averaged for the years 2000 and 2005, and include container handling charges, documentation fees, government taxes and levies, etc. of both the trading partners. For details of ocean freight components, see De (2007, 2008a).

21. By auxiliary shipping charges we mean all those other than the basic ocean freight rate. Auxiliary shipping charges include container handling charge, government duties and miscellaneous charges.

22. Interestingly, ports in India impose two notorious charges: (i) peak season surcharge, and (ii) congestion surcharge to the serving shipping lines, which normally do not exist elsewhere.

23. In the literature, 'non-price' was also used as an infrastructure variable to facilitate appreciation of the importance or the scope of trade costs.

24. For example, the US Census Bureau periodically provides US import data at the 10-digit HS level by originating countries. The US Department of Transportation supplies US imports by HS, transport modes and originating countries and destination provinces, besides information on value and volume of imports.

25. See Appendix Table 4A.1, which provides the commodity classification for k commodity groups adopted in this chapter. In general, COMTRADE does not provide trade in weight at the 2-digit HS level, but from the 4-digit HS level only. So we have to classify the commodity groups at the 4-digit HS level. This classification of commodity groups follows the WTO's classification, which was reported in its *Annual Report 2006*. We exclude trade in agriculture.

26. The usual caveat is that the freight rates offered in Maersk Sealand (2007), which we have considered in this chapter, are the gross rates and not the negotiated rates that the shipping line entered into. Negotiated rates happen to be lower than the gross rates.

27. Systematic data on Asia's import by origin and commodity are not available. The problem becomes more acute when one searches trade in weight in TEUs. As a result, we had to rely on Maersk Sealand for freight rates of commodities at the bilateral level. Since COMTRADE does not provide trade in weight in TEUs, we had to convert the weight in kg into weight in TEU. This was done based on the author's personal communication with Mr S Ghosh, formerly Sr Vice President, International Navigation Association (PIANC), Brussels, and the Managing Director, Consulting Engineering Services Pvt Ltd (CES), New Delhi. The conversion rate we used here was 12 000 kg ≡ 1 TEU to get a loaded 20-foot container (popularly known as FCL) sourced from PIANC.

28. Auxiliary shipping charges represent several explicit and implicit fees. For example, they cover all shipping charges other than basic ocean freight, such as peak season surcharge, congestion surcharge, bunker adjustment factor (BAF), yen appreciation surcharge (YAS), fuel adjustment factor (FAF), and delivery order, etc. which often make shipping between the countries more expensive. For example, exporters had to pay on average US$35 per 20-foot container towards BAF in 2004, which was imposed by the shipping lines as fuel surcharge, and on average US$30 per 20-foot container as YAS for cargoes going to Japan (De, 2007, 2008a).

29. Given the formula applied here, this terminology is also used interchangeably with *ad valorem* freight in the literature.
30. Since there is not much change between 2000 and 2005, we restrict ourselves to discussing the broad features of transport cost for 2005 only.
31. Here, the methodology follows Brooks and Hummels (2007).
32. This is also further confirmed from the estimated coefficient of variation (CV), which declined in both tariff and freight rates. The CV of the tariff reduced from 0.69 in 2000 to 0.48 in 2005, whereas in the case of freight it declined to 0.25 in 2000 from 0.22 in 2005.
33. The assumption is that if all goods are consumed as a constant fraction of GDP and price levels do not vary, we do not see the change in expenditure shares or the price levels. In particular, the main way that international production sharing shows up here is that E varies a great deal across countries as a function of what they are producing – a country that makes a large amount of cars demands an unusually large amount of car parts and components.
34. For example, a high price for a product may reflect higher production costs, or it may just reflect quality differences.
35. Total pooled observations (for trade bundle *l*) at the 4-digit HS level were 26 120. See Appendix Table 4A.2 for data we excluded and data we considered.
36. Appendix 4A.3 presents partial correlation coefficients among the dependent and independent variables.

REFERENCES

Amiti, M. and B.S. Javorcik (2008), 'Trade costs and location of foreign firms in China', *Journal of Development Economics*, **85**, 129–49.
Anderson, J.E. and E. van Wincoop (2002), 'Borders, trade and welfare', in S. Collins and D. Rodrik (eds), *Brookings Trade Forum 2001*, Washington, DC: Brookings Institution, pp. 207–44.
Anderson, J.E. and E. van Wincoop (2004), 'Trade costs', *Journal of Economic Literature*, **XLII**(3), 691–751.
Asia Pacific Economic Cooperation (APEC) (2002), *Measuring the Impact of APEC Trade Facilitation on APEC Economies: A CGE analysis*, Singapore: APEC.
Asian Development Bank (ADB) (2006), *Asian Development Outlook 2006: Routes for Asia's Trade*, Manila: ADB.
Balassa, B. (1961), *The Theory of Economic Integration*, Homewood, IL: Richard D. Irwin.
Bergstrand, J.H. (1985), 'The gravity equation in international trade: some microeconomic foundations and empirical evidence', *Review of Economics and Statistics*, **67**, 474–81.
Bergstrand, J.H. (1989), 'The generalized gravity equation, monopolistic competition, and the factor-proportions theory in international trade', *Review of Economics and Statistics*, **71**, 143–53.
Bernard, A.B., S. Redding and P.K. Scott (2004), 'Comparative advantage and heterogeneous firms', NBER Working Paper 10668.
Bougheas, S., P.O. Demetriades and E.L.W. Morgenroth (1999), 'Infrastructure, transport costs, and trade', *Journal of International Economics*, **47**, 169–89.
Brooks, D. and D. Hummels (2007), 'Infrastructure's role in Asia's trade and trade costs', paper Presented at the Finalization Conference on 'Infrastructure's Role in Reducing Trade Costs', organized by the Asian Development Bank Institute (ADBI), held in Tokyo, 25–26 June.

Cernat, L. (2001), *Assessing Regional Trading Arrangements: Are South–South RTAs More Trade Diverting?*, UNCTAD Policy Issues in International Trade and Commodities Study Series No. 16, Geneva: UNCTAD.

Clark, X., D. David and A. Micco (2004), 'Port efficiency, maritime transport costs and bilateral trade', NBER Working Paper 10353.

Davis, D. (1998), 'The home market effect, trade and industrial structure', *American Economic Review*, **88**(5), 1264–76.

De, P. (2005), 'Effect of transaction costs on international integration in the Asian Economic Community', in Asian Development Bank (ed.), *Asian Economic Cooperation and Integration: Progress, Prospects, Challenges*, Manila: ADB, pp. 365–88.

De, P. (2006a), 'Regional trade in Northeast Asia: why trade costs matter', CESifo Working Paper No. 1809, CESifo, Munich.

De, P. (2006b), 'Trade, infrastructure and transaction costs: the imperatives for Asian economic cooperation', *Journal of Economic Integration*, **21**(4), 708–35.

De, P. (2007), 'Impact of trade costs on trade: empirical evidence from Asian countries', ARTNeT Working Paper 27, Trade and Investment Division, UNESCAP, Bangkok.

De, P. (2008a), 'Trade costs and infrastructure: analysis of the effects of trade impediments in Asia', *Journal of Integration and Trade*, **12**(28), 241–66.

De, P. (2008b), 'Empirical estimates of trade costs for Asia', in D. Brooks and J. Menon (eds), *Infrastructure and Trade in Asia*, Cheltenham, UK and Northampton, MA: Edward Elgar, pp. 71–112.

Deardorff, A. (1998), 'Determinants of bilateral trade: does gravity work in a neoclassical world?', in J. Frankel (ed.), *Regionalization of the World Economy*, Chicago, IL: University of Chicago Press, pp. 7–32.

Dixit, A. and J. Stiglitz (1977), 'Monopolistic competition and optimal product diversity', *American Economic Review*, **67**, 297–308.

Djankov, S., C. Freund and C.S. Pham (2006), 'Trading on time', Working Paper, World Bank, Washington, DC.

Feenstra, R.C. (1998), 'Integration of trade and disintegration of production in the global economy', *Journal of Economic Perspectives*, **12**(4), 31–50.

Fink, C., A. Mattoo and I.C. Neagu (2002), 'Trade in international maritime services: how much does policy matter?', *The World Bank Economic Review*, **16**, 451–79.

Francois, J. and M. Manchin (2006), *Institutional Quality, Infrastructure, and the Propensity to Export*, London: CEPR.

Francois, J., H. van Meijl and F. van Tongeren (2005), 'Trade liberalization in the Doha Development Round', *Economic Policy*, **20**(42), 349–91.

Hummels, D. (1999), 'Toward a geography of trade costs', Working Paper, University of Chicago, Chicago.

Hummels, D. (2001). 'Time as a trade barrier', unpublished paper, Purdue University, West Lafayette.

Hummels, D. (2007), 'Transportation costs and international trade in the second era of globalization', *Journal of Economic Perspectives*, **21**(3), 131–54.

Hummels, D. and A. Skiba (2004), 'Shipping the good apples out? An empirical confirmation of the Alchian–Allen conjecture', *Journal of Political Economy*, **112**(6), 1384–402.

International Monetary Fund (2006), *Direction of Trade Statistics Year Book CD ROM 2005*, Washington, DC: IMF.

Krugman, P. (1980), 'Scale economies, product differentiation, and the pattern of trade', *American Economic Review*, **70**, 950–59.

Krugman, P. (1991), 'Increasing returns and economic geography', *Journal of Political Economy*, **99**, 483–99.

Krugman, P. and A.J. Venables (1990), 'Integration and the competitiveness of peripheral industry', in C. Bliss and J. Braga de Macedo (eds), *Unity with Diversity in the European Economy*, Cambridge: Cambridge University Press, pp. 56–75.

Kuroiwa, I. (2006), 'Production networks and spatial linkages in East Asia', in D. Hiratsuka (ed.), *East Asia's De Facto Economic-Integration*, IDE-JETRO, Basingstoke: Palgrave Macmillan, pp. 80–98.

Limao, N. and A.J. Venables (2001), 'Infrastructure, geographical disadvantage, transport costs, and trade', *The World Bank Economic Review*, **15**, 451–79.

Maersk Sealand (2007), *Historical Shipping Rates Database*, available at http://www.maerskline.com.

Nordås, H.K. and R. Piermartini (2004), 'Infrastructure and trade', Staff Working Paper ERSD-2004-04, Economic Research and Statistics Division, World Trade Organization, Geneva.

Obstfeld, M. and K. Rogoff (2000), 'The six major puzzles in international macro-economics: is there a common cause?', in B.S. Bernanke and K. Rogoff (eds), *NBER Macroeconomics Annual 2000*, Cambridge, MA: MIT Press, pp. 339–90.

Organization for Economic Co-operation and Development (OECD) (2003), *Quantitative Assessment of the Benefits of Trade Facilitation*, Paris: OECD.

Organization for Economic Co-operation and Development (OECD) (2005), *The Costs and Benefits of Trade Facilitation*, October, Paris: OECD.

Redding, S. and A.J. Venables (2004), 'Economic geography and international inequality', *Journal of International Economics*, **62**(1), 53–82.

Samuelson, P.A. (1954), 'The transfer problem and transport costs: the terms of trade when impediments are absent', *Economic Journal*, **62**, 278–304.

Steininger, K.W. (2001), *International Trade and Transport*, Cheltenham, UK and Northampton, MA: Edward Elgar.

United Nations (2007), *COMTRADE Database*, UN Statistical Division, New York.

United Nations Conference on Trade and Development (UNCTAD) (2006), *Review of Maritime Transport*, New York and Geneva: UNCTAD.

Venables, A. (2006), 'Shifts in economic geography and their causes', *Economic Review*, **91**(4), 61–85.

Wilson, J.S., C.L. Mann and T. Otsuki (2003), 'Trade facilitation and economic development: a new approach to quantifying the impact', *The World Bank Economic Review*, **17**(3), 367–89.

World Bank (2001), *Global Economic Prospects and the Developing Countries 2002: Making Trade Work for the Poor*, Washington, DC: World Bank.

World Bank (2002), *The Economic Impact of Trade Facilitation Measures: A Development Perspective in the Asia Pacific*, Washington, DC: World Bank.

World Trade Organization (WTO) (2006a), *Trade Profiles 2006*, Geneva, available at http://www.wto.org.

World Trade Organization (WTO) (2006b), *International Trade Statistics 2006*, Geneva, available at http://www.wto.org.

World Trade Organization (WTO) (2007), *World Tariff Profiles 2006*, Geneva, available at http://www.wto.org.

Yeaple, S. and S.S. Golub (2002), *International Productivity Differences, Infrastructure and Comparative Advantage*, mimeo.

APPENDIX

Table 4A.1   Classification of commodity groups

	Corresponding 2/4-digit HS (2002)	Remarks
Agriculture products	01–24, 50–53	Taken at 4-digit HS
Food	16–23	excluding HS 01 and HS 06
Fuels, mining and forest products	25–27, 44	Taken at 4-digit HS, excluding HS 45
Manufactures	28–43, 45–49, 54–70, 72–92, 94–96	Taken at 4-digit HS, excluding HS 44, 50–53, 71, 93
Chemicals	28–36, 38	Taken at 4-digit HS,
Pharmaceuticals	30	excluding HS 37
Rubber and plastics	39–40	
Leather	41–43, 64	
Paper and pulp	47–48	
Textiles and clothing	54–63	Taken at 4-digit HS,
Iron and steel	72–73	excluding HS 64–67, 71
Metal	68–70, 74–81	
Machinery and mechanical appliances	82–84	Taken at 4-digit HS, excluding HS 8415, 8418, 8471, 8473
Electrical and electronics	85, 90, 91, 92, 95	Taken at 4-digit HS,
Office and telecom equipment	8517–8548	including HS 8415, 8418, 8471, 8473
Electronic integrated circuits	8542	
Transport equipment	86–89	
Automobiles and components	87	

Table 4A.2   Excluded values by country and commodity groups

(a) By country

	Total excluded observations	Total no. of observations
China	263	8 594
India	1 029	7 558
Indonesia	311	8 699
Japan	505	7 852
Malaysia	2 052	8 881
Korea	354	7 682
Thailand	328	8 663
Total	4 842	57 929

(b) By commodity groups

Commodity group	Total excluded observations	Total no. of observations
Transport equipment	61	604
Automobiles and components	92	839
Chemicals	324	9 748
Electrical and electronics	1 007	5 775
Electronic integrated circuits	20	84
Food products	200	2 719
Fuels, mining and forest products	1 066	3 885
Iron and steel	165	3 741
Leather	26	1 001
Machinery and mechanical appliances	723	7 481
Metal	296	7 060
Office and telecom equipment	278	2 488
Paper and pulp	40	1 766
Pharmaceuticals	0	404
Rubber and plastics	88	3 334
Textiles and clothing	456	7 000
Total	4 842	57 929

Table 4A.3   Pair-wise correlation coefficients

	Import demand	Adv. tariff	Adv. total transport cost	Adv. inland transport cost	Adv. international transport cost
Import demand	1.0000				
Adv. tariff	−0.1241	1.0000			
Adv. total transport cost	−0.0856	0.0372	1.0000		
Adv. inland transport cost	−0.1088	0.0546	0.9942	1.0000	
Adv. international transport cost	−0.0696	0.0285	0.9955	0.9819	1.0000

5. Port competitiveness: a case study of Semarang and Surabaya, Indonesia[1]

Arianto A. Patunru, Nanda Nurridzki and Rivayani

1. INTRODUCTION

Ports have a significant role in economic development, especially in the trade and distribution of goods. Almost 85 per cent of the world's trade distribution relies on sea transportation. In the world's largest archipelago, Indonesia, ports are one of the idiosyncratic keys that can boost economic growth, along with the more common determinants. According to the Ministry of Transportation, approximately 90 per cent of Indonesia's external trade is transported via sea and only 10 per cent via land and air.

It is already known that distribution efficiency is one factor that determines producer competitiveness, which in this case is influenced by port performance. The decision to use one particular port instead of other ports is determined on the basis of cost calculation on the producer side. Producers would choose a port that is consistent with minimum distribution cost. There are several factors that can influence this cost. They include inland transportation cost, cost of using a forwarder, costs inside ports, time effectiveness in port (including for administrative procedures), bureaucracy and regulations applied in the port. Moreover, additional cost or illegal cost sometimes appears in the process, resulting in a lower competitiveness in the port sector.

In general, port-related competition can be defined on three different levels: inter-port competition, intra-port competition and intra-terminal competition. Inter-port competition arises when two or more ports or their terminals are competing for the same trade (World Bank, 2007). Some ports that experience this type of competition are Rotterdam, Hamburg, Bremerhaven and Antwerp in Europe; Hong Kong, Port Klang, Malaysia and Singapore. As an archipelagic country, Indonesia is subject to inter-port competition since it has hundreds of ports spread over the entire region. Some of them are located close to one another and thus are more likely to compete in luring customers from the same hinterlands.

The objective of this chapter is to explore the issues of ports in Indonesia, particularly to analyse inter-port competition and to identify the main factors that become the basis for users to determine which port they want to use.[2] Moreover, this study analyses the trade-off involved in using one particular port instead of other alternatives. Port users include cargo owners or exporting and importing firms that consistently use one port for their distribution activity, shipping companies etc. The information would be useful for the government in reviewing its current policy towards port development in Indonesia and for private agents to anticipate future trends in port business. The study employs two major approaches; it analyses secondary data; and it makes a qualitative analysis based on a series of in-depth interviews with port users as well as institutions that play important roles in Indonesia's port management.

The study focuses on the competitiveness of two key ports in Indonesia, namely Tanjung Perak Port in Surabaya, East Java Province, and Tanjung Emas Port in Semarang, Central Java Province. Tanjung Perak is the second-biggest port in Indonesia with high occupancy level, due to its role as an international port and as the gateway to eastern Indonesia. Tanjung Emas, on the other hand, is relatively less busy, notwithstanding similar characteristics as an international port.[3] These two ports are located in the same island, Java, and both are connected to large hinterland activities.

This chapter is organized as follows. The next section will discuss briefly the relevant issues of port competitiveness based on the literature reviewed. Section 3 gives a descriptive analysis of ports in Indonesia, covering the existing conditions, the role of the main institutions in Indonesian port management and other issues that relate to international trade activities in port, i.e. procedures and regulations. Furthermore, the section presents the profile of the two ports that are selected as the focus of this study, Tanjung Emas and Tanjung Perak. Section 4 analyses the findings in more detail, with regard to the port competitiveness aspects, from both supply and demand sides. The supply side is discussed by identifying the competitiveness of each port, while the demand side is captured by looking at the determinant factors of using each port and by analysing the trade-offs that might appear in using one particular port from a set of alternatives. Section 5 presents further points for discussion and Section 6 concludes.

2.   PREVIOUS STUDIES

The rationale for ports is to support trade activities, so demand for port facilities depends on the volume of trade flows. A port itself incurs high maintenance costs and it thus requires high investment. Once a port is built, the huge investment is largely sunk, and excess capacity might follow as a result. Huge investment in port infrastructure includes quay cranes, terminals, breakwaters, navigation and communication system facilities. Due to this high investment–slow return nature, ports are usually provided by the government. Evidence confirms that public sector monopolies in ports are often strong (Haralambides, 2002).

Hoyle and Charlier (1995) argue that port functions are related to hinterland growth, and that economic development requires port facilities, which leads to complex port–hinterland relationships. De Langen et al. (2005) divide the hinterlands into captive and contestable hinterlands. Captive hinterlands are all parts of a region over which a port has a competitive advantage, due to lower generalized transport costs that allow the port to handle the vast majority of cargoes. Contestable hinterlands, on the other hand, consist of all regions, with no single port having a clear cost advantage over competing ones.

Regions that are relatively more advanced (i.e. dominated by the services sector) are characterized by port development that applies the 'ships follow the trade' principle. In such regions, trade activities have usually been established both to meet the demand for end-users or for further production. As sea transportation dominates trade distribution, shipping lines find the regions with more potential in industrial and trade activities. Ships' routes are therefore adjusted to serve those regions.

In contrast, in regions with more conventional economies and where the trade mostly deals with raw material distribution, the 'trade follows the ship' principle is more common. This principle implies that the cargo owners will find the ports that have ship routes to deliver their cargoes. These ports might be located quite far from the cargo owners, or at least not in the same region as the cargo owners' location. Logically, a region with many industrial zones has more shipping routes and cargoes handled than other regions.

Another factor that also relates port performance and trade flows is port competitiveness. Port competitiveness becomes essential in the global network, in particular for a country that relies on seaborne trade. To increase its level of competitiveness, a port tends to capitalize on its strategic advantages and core competences in delivering efficient and affordable services to its users. Winkelmans (2003) mentions that ports can have a catalytic impact on the ongoing process of globalization only if they become cost-effective logistics centres in a world driven by a globalized economy.

Some indicators are commonly used to measure port competitiveness. Technical efficiency in handling ships and cargo are some of the indicators that have traditionally been used. In addition, other factors can measure competitiveness but are more difficult to quantify, such as geo-strategic location, history, trade and manufacturing patterns, government policies, logistics and supply chain management, niche advantages and ancillary activities. Fourgeaud (2000) suggests that in order to indicate port competitiveness, port performance could be expressed in traffic recording and parameters used in charging tariffs for port services. The basic means of assessment is to check whether organization and yard equipment can match the actual capacity of the main hoisting machines – generally quay cranes or gantries, which are the most expensive and high-performing pieces of equipment.

Port competition is indeed not just about getting more traffic, more tonnage, etc., but also about achieving a sustainable degree of generating added value in relation to the inputs and effort. As such, it becomes necessary to understand that the more effective a port is, the more efficient port management is needed and the more port management itself will become effective (Winkelmans, 2003).

The Indonesian Case

In Indonesia, inefficiency in ports could directly lead to higher transport costs, in particular for export-oriented and import-based industries. The inefficiency in logistics cost – i.e. transportation cost for cargoes – has forced firms to pass on the burden to consumers in the form of higher prices. LPEM-FEUI (2005) found that the share of Indonesia's total logistics cost was around 14 per cent of total production cost, while the best practice in Japan was only 4.88 per cent. The survey divided logistics costs into three types: input (from vendor to manufacturer), in-house (in the manufacturer), and output (from manufacturer to port). With such a framework, the study found that the highest cost is input logistics costs (Figure 5.1). Meanwhile, the average output logistics cost from manufacturers to port is about 4.04 per cent of total cost, higher than the ideal logistics cost perceived by the respondents (2.4 per cent) – Figure 5.2. Informal payments in road and port contributed about 22.12 per cent to the total inefficiency in output logistics cost (LPEM-FEUI, 2005).

3.   INDONESIAN PORT PROFILE

Indonesia is an archipelago that lies between two continents and two oceans. Its geographic position has given it a strategic comparative advantage in transportation routes. Driven by cost efficiency considerations and supply chain management principles, many of the world's shipping lines pass Indonesian maritime territory (Figure 5.3). Unfortunately, no

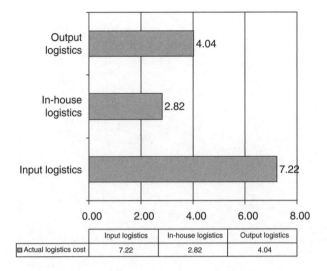

	Input logistics	In-house logistics	Output logistics
Actual logistics cost	7.22	2.82	4.04

Source: LPEM-FEUI (2005).

Figure 5.1 Comparison among input, in-house and output logistics costs (% of total production cost)

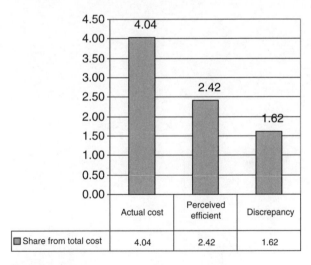

	Actual cost	Perceived efficient	Discrepancy
Share from total cost	4.04	2.42	1.62

Source: LPEM-FEUI (2005).

Figure 5.2 Output logistics costs (average) from manufacturers to port (% of total production cost)

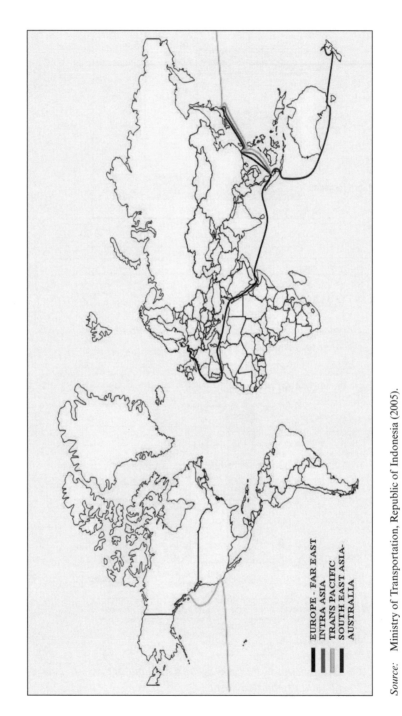

EUROPE - FAR EAST
INTRA ASIA
TRANS PACIFIC
SOUTH EAST ASIA-
AUSTRALIA

Source: Ministry of Transportation, Republic of Indonesia (2005).

Figure 5.3   International shipping lines route

Indonesian port is classified as a primary international port that serves international mother vessels (as opposed to, for example, the Port of Singapore in the region). Hypothetically, if Indonesia could exploit its potential to become a primary international hub port, the impact of such a port on the economy would be large.

Ports in Indonesia are classified into public ports and special ports. Public ports that consist of both commercial and non-commercial ports are designed to handle and give services to the public. Commercial ports operate under Pelindo or Indonesia Port Company (IPC), a state-owned company under the Ministry of State-owned Enterprises. The commercial public ports are identified by their ability to generate their own revenue. However, many commercial ports tend not to be profitable and only a few of them can accommodate many vessels as they are located in remote areas. The government via IPC then applies a cross-subsidy scheme between the commercial ports, in which more profitable ports subsidize others.

The non-commercial public ports are mostly developed to serve inter-island passengers and non-container cargoes. These ports operate under Ministry of Transportation. Currently they are also running at a loss. The government subsidizes these ports in order to keep them providing their public service role.

Currently in Indonesia there are 2047 ports: 112 commercial public ports, 523 non-commercial public ports and 1412 ports that are private (but usually classified as 'special ports', as they are typically owned and operated by private companies to handle specific cargoes, e.g. agriculture, forestry, etc.) (Table 5.1). Out of the 112 commercial-public ports in Indonesia, 85 are ports that serve international routes, and the rest are local ports. The international, commercial public ports include around 25 ports that are classified as 'strategic ports'. Such ports are equipped with modern facilities to handle most of the containerized cargoes, such as facilities for container shipping, loading/unloading, provision of supplies, maintenance–repair facilities, and also other services provided for ships. These ports not only serve international ports, but are also supported by high-potential hinterlands. However, some still suffer from insufficient infrastructure such as outdated handling equipment, inadequate berths and limited port back-up areas. Moreover, the existence of a strategic port is also affected by the demand for technology to handle the cargo. If the hinterland is relatively small, the requirement of high-technology port infrastructure to handle cargo is also limited.

Indonesian Shipping Law (UU.No.21/1992) requires that the management of a commercial public port operate under the IPC. The IPC itself consists of representatives from the Ministry of Communications, and the Ministry of State-owned Enterprises. Currently four IPCs serve four

Table 5.1   Indonesian port profile based on port management, 2005

Port type	Port management	Total	International (strategic ports)	Local ports
A. Public	**(1) Commercial ports**			
	IPC I (Belawan)	27		
	IPC II (Tanjung Priok)	29		
	IPC III (Tanjung Perak)	32		
	IPC IV (Makassar)	24		
	Subtotal	112	85	27
	(2) Non-commercial ports			
	Port office (under Ministry of Transportation)	523	10	513
B. Special	Mining, fishing, agriculture, forestry, etc.	1412	45	1367
	Total	2047	140	1907

Source: Ministry of Transportation, Republic of Indonesia (2005).

geographic areas and are headquartered in Belawan Port in North Sumatra, Tanjung Priok Port in Jakarta, Tanjung Perak Port in East Java, and Makassar Port in South Sulawesi. To date, IPC II and III seem to have more stable financial resources compared to the other two.[4]

In practice, IPC has a huge role in controlling the management of commercial ports in Indonesia. It is not only a regulator but it has also become a major player itself, resembling a monopolist. As the port authority, IPC dominates all services for freight and shipment in ports, starting when vessels entered the port, i.e. tugging services, berth services and so forth.

Like almost all state-owned companies in Indonesia, IPC consists of a mixture of public companies that are required to provide public services and to generate revenues for the government. Currently, only IPC II and IPC III record profits, while the other two have been incurring losses. By law, the IPCs have to subsidize each other to ensure financial sustainability of the entire organization and to comply with its public obligation. Because of this, IPCs seem to lack the incentive to improve their performance. This is evident even in infrastructure development. The monopolistic power adds to the slow improvement, particularly in low maintenance of port infrastructure. Ray and Blankfeld (2002) argue that different conditions of profit raised a need to merge and consolidate those IPCs into one or two management corporations, in order to increase management resource efficiencies, lower administration cost, and increase the potential to develop the less profitable ports by the more profitable ones. However, some parties are concerned that the idea of merging the IPCs could only create more monopolistic behaviour and not enhance an atmosphere of good competition. Whatever the case, the merger plan has not been applied until now.

In its operation, IPC applies tariffs to users. The rates plan is usually submitted by IPC to the Ministry of State-owned Enterprises. Subsequently, the tariffs are evaluated, involving the Ministry of Transportation and the Ministry of Finance, in addition to the Ministry of State-owned Enterprises. The rates are then discussed with the parliament to get approval. In order to get feedback from agents in the maritime industry, these tariffs are publicized in one of the regular meetings between IPC and associations inside ports, such as the shipping association, forwarding association, loading and unloading association, etc.

The final tariffs charged by each IPC are quite similar across its entire branch, especially for ports within the same IPC. For instance, tariffs applied in Tanjung Perak in Surabaya and those in Tanjung Emas in Semarang are relatively the same, as they both are under the coordination of IPC III.

Unfortunately, these tariffs may not reflect efficiency. As mentioned above, the lack of competition inside ports gives IPCs no incentive to improve their services. This is made worse by the cross-subsidy system set up by the government. Several complaints regarding IPC services have been raised by shipping companies, forwarders, or loading/unloading companies that have to waste a large amount of time not working due to lack of infrastructure and to inefficiency in port operation. Poor infrastructure is frequently characterized by insufficient pool or sailing channel depth, insufficient handling equipment, inadequate berths and limited port back-up areas; while port inefficiency usually takes the form of inadequate labour skills, under-utilization of port facilities, and cumbersome institutions and regulations in ports (we shall call the latter 'soft infrastructure' – see below).

The foregoing problems have led to general inefficiency in Indonesian ports, which is reflected by low performance in a number of key port indicators. The average berth occupancy ratio (BOR), which is the percentage of time vessels are berthed at port (i.e. the time berths are occupied relative to the total available time), is 60 per cent, relatively high compared, for example, to Westport in Port Klang, Malaysia, whose BOR is around 35 per cent.[5] Albeit approximate, this high BOR indicates a long waiting time. The average waiting time in Indonesian ports varies from three to five days, where loading and unloading activity takes up to 35 per cent of overall waiting time. This hampers the port users, as they have to spend more time inside the port, and experience a high-cost economy as several tariffs are calculated based on time.

One approach that has been proposed to solve the problem is to let private agents enter the port industry to foster more competition and to push towards higher efficiency. However, the current law states that any investor willing to build an international port in Indonesia must work together with the relevant IPC. This policy has been implemented in several strategic ports in Indonesia, where private sector firms are allowed to operate inside the ports such as in the privatization of terminal units, loading/unloading services, etc. Following such 'partial privatization' in some big ports in Indonesia (e.g. Jakarta's Tanjung Priok and Surabaya's Tanjung Perak), performance, especially in cargo handling, has increased. It is true that this does not necessarily imply a causal relation. But the interviews in the survey strongly supported the hypothesis that competition is needed to force the ports to improve, and one way to do this is through privatization.

Soft Infrastructure

In general, import clearance covers ship/port clearance, customs clearance and cargo clearance, i.e. all the procedures from vessel arrival to departure. Port clearance deals with procedures starting from vessel arrival, anchorage, berthing, followed by unloading cargoes and stacking in the container yard. Customs clearance includes all processes related to customs for import. Cargo clearance is a procedure started by taking out cargoes from the container yard to the gate. The activities are completed as the cargo reaches its importer. For cargoes packed in containers, activities are considered completed when the empty container is returned. This long procedure of import clearance involves many institutions. LPEM-FEUI (2006) identified at least 19. The Customs office asserted that export and import activities in the main port in Jakarta involve no fewer than 30 institutions (including port authorities, labour groups, shipping associations, transport officials, security officials – see also Ray and Blankfeld, 2002). The involvement of too many institutions has been a source of complaint by many cargo owners since it creates more transactions, which raises costs and leads to delays (Ray and Blankfeld, 2002). LPEM-FEUI's survey found that more than 60 per cent of respondents (shipping companies, shipping agencies and forwarding companies) considered the number of institutions involved as one of the key obstacles in both ship and cargo clearance (LPEM-FEUI, 2006) (Figures 5.4 and 5.5 respectively). It is concluded that problems related to 'soft infrastructure' in Indonesian ports play a more crucial role than those related to 'hard infrastructure'.

Other obstacles in ship and cargo clearance as identified in the LPEM-FEUI survey are additional payments, ship traffic, port infrastructure, congestion in the port area, quality of road infrastructure etc. Inadequate

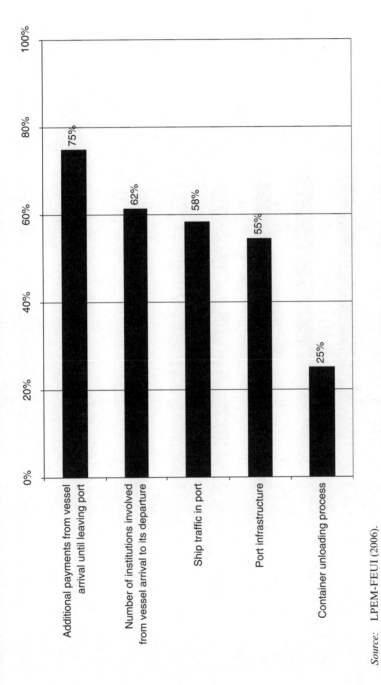

Source: LPEM-FEUI (2006).

Figure 5.4 Percentage of firms (as respondents) reporting obstacles in ship clearance to be moderate, severe, or very severe

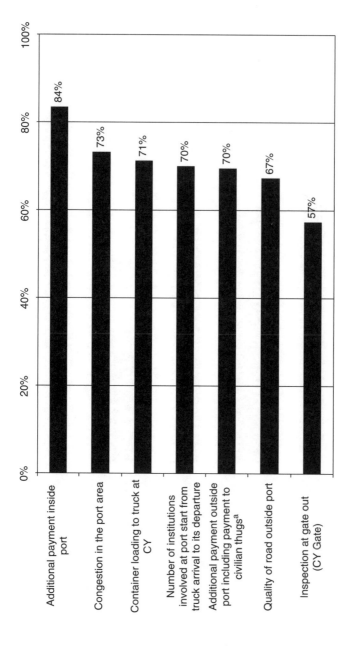

Note: [a] 'Civilian thugs' here refers to those civilians who collect money illegally (mostly with coercion) from business people. In some cases the money given is considered 'payment for security' as the paying businessman is guaranteed 'security' by the 'thugs' after the latter are paid.

Source: LPEM-FEUI (2006).

Figure 5.5 Percentage of firms (as respondents) reporting obstacles in cargo clearance to be moderate, severe, or very severe

port infrastructure creates problems for port users, such as limited number of gantry cranes, lack of breakwaters and insufficient water depth etc. These problems lead to longer delays, particularly at peak times. Anecdotal evidence has shown how such problems end up in informal payments to expedite the queuing.[6] This also shows that when infrastructure is inadequate, petty corruption is likely (LPEM-FEUI, 2006). That is, the problems in 'soft infrastructure' are not independent of those in 'hard infrastructure'. In fact, problems related to inadequate (hard) infrastructure in roads and ports are considered the highest source of inefficiency in output logistics (LPEM-FEUI, 2005). Furthermore, more than 60 per cent of respondents considered quality of roads outside the port as one of the obstacles in cargo clearance (Figure 5.5).

Other problems that hindered import procedures, and thus obliged the requirement of illegal additional payment, are problems in customs clearance. LPEM-FEUI (2006) identified some practices applied in import procedures, such as negotiation over tax of imported goods and over HS codes, late import notification, physical inspection bypass etc. These practices all contribute to the inefficient process, in the form of longer time and more costs required to clear an import. The extra payments and other inefficient practices in many institutions involved in ports imply weak law enforcement and lack of competition among service providers.

The additional payments in port have made Indonesia's terminal handling charge (THC)[7] the highest compared to those imposed in other Southeast Asian countries. In 2004, THC in Indonesia reached US$150 for a 20-foot container, while Thailand charged only US$60. However, there are many controversies on the issue of THC.[8] Some parties asserted that the official tariffs set by IPC and the shipping agency are about US$120, or US$30 lower than the total THC. The remaining is considered as document fees charged by shipping companies to cargo owners, including profit of those shipping companies. But this argument is denounced by shipping companies. Unclear, complicated handling processes and delays were the major problems that caused the high tariffs. Some trade-related factors also contributed to the higher THC, such as the imbalanced international trade volume that creates additional costs for empty containers, briberies at port, poor infrastructure in/outside the port, and other problems related to the clearance process, such as customs clearance.

As a response to this problem the government decided to cut the THC in November 2005. A 20-foot container now costs US$95, while a 40-foot container costs about US$150. Nevertheless, port users still complain about the additional rules applied after the reduction in THC, such as reposition fees for empty containers, trucking fees, lift on/off fees, value added tax and stacking fees.

The above discussion of 'soft infrastructure' applies in general to almost every key port in Indonesia. The remaining part of the chapter will explore in more detail the 'hard infrastructure' with specific reference to Tanjung Perak Port of Surabaya and Tanjung Emas Port of Semarang. Before the case studies are presented, we discuss the profile of Jakarta's Tanjung Priok Port to provide a background for comparison.

Tanjung Priok Port

Tanjung Priok Port is the largest port in Indonesia, with the most complete and modern facilities (Figure 5.6). The port is located in West Java and operates under the management of IPC II. In line with its development, it has played an important role as the main gateway of the Indonesian economy, especially Jakarta.

In order to improve its performance, mainly in efficiency and container service provision, as well as management and technology upgrade, Tanjung Priok Port underwent a privatization process by establishing Jakarta International Container Terminals (PT JICT) and Koja Container Terminal (Koja CT) in 1998. PT JICT is an affiliated company with a joint venture scheme between IPC II (48.9 per cent), Tanjung Priok Maritime Employees' Cooperative (0.1 per cent), and Grosbeak Pte, Ltd, a subsidiary of Hutchinson Port Holding (HPH) of Hongkong (51 per cent). Koja CT is an affiliated company of IPC II which established a joint venture scheme between IPC II (52.12 per cent) and PT Ocean Container Terminal (47.88 per cent).

Since privatization, the productivity performance of Tanjung Priok has increased, as reflected by an increase in the number of ships and goods in the last five years by more than 4 per cent per year. The flow of cargo at the container terminal reached more than 2.1 million TEUs, where the flow of ships passing through Tanjung Priok Port reached 17 000 ship units. This means that the port can serve 60 to 70 unit ships per day and has positioned itself as a hub port, of which 65 per cent of goods traffic is exported/imported goods, and the rest are inter-island.[9] However, we cannot conclude that this increase is the result of privatization alone, as other improvements have been conducted by the port's management.

Tanjung Perak Port

Tanjung Perak Port in Surabaya (Figure 5.7) is another one of the gateway ports in Indonesia. It has become a distribution centre from and to eastern Indonesia. This strategic position drives the port to become the second-biggest port in Indonesia after Tanjung Priok Port of Jakarta. Located in

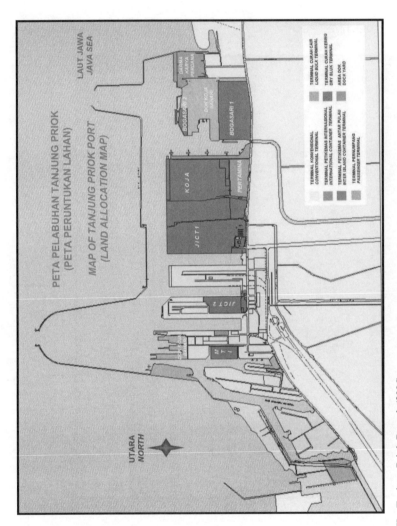

Source: IPC II – Tanjung Priok Branch (2006).

Figure 5.6 Tanjung Priok Port layout

127

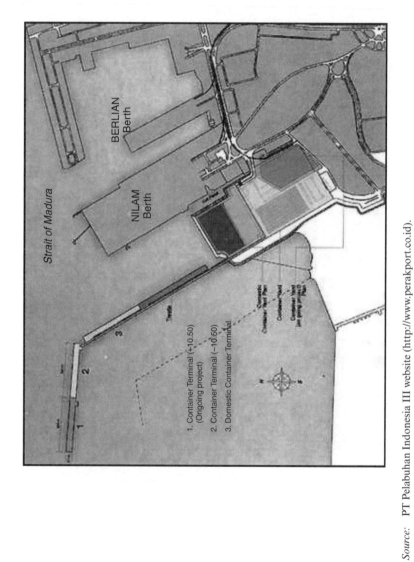

Source: PT Pelabuhan Indonesia III website (http://www.perakport.co.id).

Figure 5.7   Tanjung Perak Port layout

112° 43'22" east longitude and 07° 1'54" south latitude, the port has an advantage of being located in Madura Strait, for the Madura Island itself can be seen as a natural break water for the port.

In order to improve its overall performance and to solve its financial problems, IPC III privatized two of its terminal units: Terminal Petikemas Surabaya (TPS, Surabaya Cargo Terminal) in 1999 and Berlian Jasa Terminal Indonesia (BJTI) in 2002. Since BJTI is focused on cargo and container handling services at conventional terminals, it became a port terminal operator. TPS is now an affiliated company based on a joint venture scheme between IPC III and P&O Australia Ports Ltd, with IPC III holding 51 per cent and P&O Australia Ports Ltd 49 per cent shares. After the 1999 privatization, container throughput in TPS increased quite significantly. This is a result of several programmes conducted in order to increase the terminal's capacity, such as container yard expansion, and purchase of four units of new quay cranes from IMPSA Co. and 12 units of rubber-tyred gantry (RTG) from Konecranes Co. Both are large multinational companies specializing in manufacturing and service of cranes of various sizes and lifting capacities. Moreover, the terminal has applied a new computer system developed by Realtime Business Solutions, from Sydney, Australia, that displays the actual condition and activities of container handling in the terminal.

Profile of Tanjung Emas Port

Tanjung Emas Port (Figure 5.8) is located on the north coast of Central Java, with latitude coordinates of 06° 53'00"S to 06° 57'00"S and longitude of 110°24'00"E to 110° 26'02"E. In the past, this port, built in 1874, was known as the Semarang Port. During the period 1964–66, only vessels with less than 5 metres' draught (about 3500 DWT – dead weight tons) could anchor in Nusantara Pier of Tanjung Emas Port. Ships with more than 5 metres' draught should anchor outside the pier or even offshore, about three miles away. As the flow of ships and freight in the country started to increase, the government decided to develop the Semarang Port. Tanjung Emas Port was officially started in 1985, operating under IPC III. This port is classified as a first-class port, one level below the main ports.

As in Tanjung Perak Port, a container terminal was built in Tanjung Emas Port to meet the needs of domestic and international trade activities. In the past, the container terminal services division was integrated with Tanjung Emas Port Management (IPC Tanjung Emas). But since 2001, in order to improve its performance, the management separated this division into a new business unit called Terminal Peti Kemas Semarang

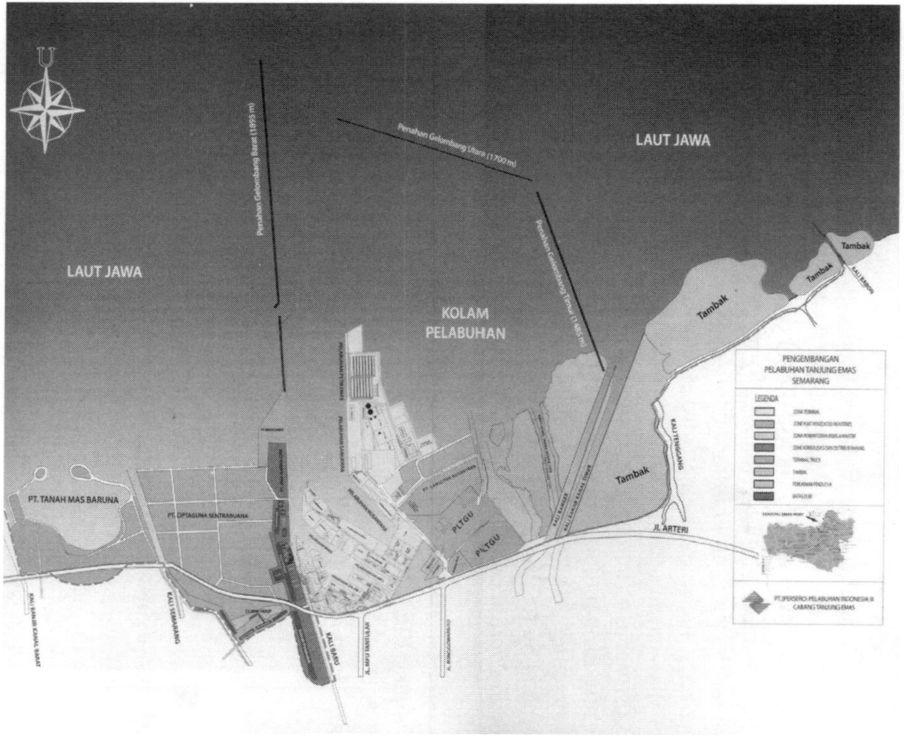

Source: IPC III – Tanjung Perak Branch (2005).

Figure 5.8   Tanjung Emas Port layout

(TPKS, Semarang Cargo Terminal). Since this expansion, TPKS has improved its facilities to support load–unload activities. Furthermore, TPKS has added one unit of container crane in 2005 and two more in 2007.

4. PORT COMPETITIVENESS ANALYSIS: SUPPLY AND DEMAND SIDE

Port competitiveness can be seen from both supply and demand sides. On the supply side, the analysis is focused on geographical aspects, port activities and infrastructure provided. Demand analysis, on the other hand, looks at the key factors that drive users to choose one port over another. This analysis can be expanded to identify the trade-off faced by users. For instance, high labour costs or less favourable maritime accessibility might be compensated with competitive port dues or high labour productivity.

Methodology

Qualitative analysis on the port competitiveness, from both demand and supply sides, employed information from in-depth interviews with cargo owners (importer and exporter) and shipping lines, in Surabaya and Semarang. Another group of respondents is formed by representatives of IPC (Tanjung Perak and Tanjung Emas Port), particularly selected to answer issues related to port management.[10]

The interviews used semi-structured, open-ended questions to get respondents' perceptions on port competitiveness. The questions looked at several aspects, such as port location and its hinterland, infrastructure at the port, existing regulations, institutions involved, tariff and other payments (including informal payments) at ports etc. For supply-side analysis, information was collected by combining in-depth interviews and secondary data of the two ports. The information from the survey was also used to analyse the demand side, from the view of both shipping lines and cargo owners. This could explain factors affecting the decision to choose a port.

A word of caution is in order here. It remains difficult to evaluate the operational efficiency of a particular port to measure port competitiveness, using this port indicator. Many physical and institutional factors influence productivity to an extent that makes these indicators incomparable. That is, there is no strict standard to compare any two or more ports, on a national or international basis, and the analysis must be made on a case-by-case basis.[11]

Supply Side: Competitiveness of Tanjung Perak Port and Tanjung Emas Port

As stated above, one type of port competition is inter-port competition. This occurs when two ports offer the same services and compete with each other to win market share. In Indonesia, this type of competition is evident in the case of Tanjung Perak Port in Surabaya and Tanjung Emas Port in Semarang. These two ports operate under IPC III, and offer similar services with relatively similar tariff rates. The following few factors are key determinants of competitiveness from the supply side.

Geographical aspects
Judging from its location, Tanjung Perak Port (Figure 5.9) has more advantage, as it is already widely known as the gateway to eastern Indonesia. Freight to eastern Indonesia is collected in this port and then redistributed to other ports such as Maluku, Kendari, etc. Its location in the Madura Strait has three characteristics that affect its performance, both directly and indirectly.

First, the sailing channel is longer. Second, Madura Island itself can be seen as an ideal natural breakwater for the port. Third, the sailing channel is not wide enough for mother vessels to enter the port. Widening of the channel is not possible due to geographical conditions. Based on this third characteristic, it seems unlikely that Tanjung Perak Port can expand its position to become an international hub port and to compete with other international hubs such as Singapore and the Port of Tanjung Lepas in Malaysia.

In 2005, the average turn-round time (TRT) for shipping in Tanjung Perak Port was 73 hours, while in Tanjung Emas Port it was only 41 hours (Table 5.2). This indicator might not be very relevant since TRT also depends on geographical characteristics. Tanjung Perak Port has a longer sailing channel compared to Tanjung Emas Port, as the former is located in Madura Strait. The western sailing channel is the main entry to Tanjung Perak Port; it is 25 miles long and 100 metres wide.

Meanwhile, Tanjung Emas Port lies on the north coast of Central Java facing the Java Sea. This condition makes the sailing channel much shorter, which might contribute to the lower TRT. However, this condition also creates negative impacts for the port. First, the sedimentation level of the coastal sea is quite high, as a result of deposits brought by two big rivers located on each side of the port. This causes delay to big vessels entering the port, and forces them to wait outside the port area. Second, the piers that are usually utilized to serve general cargoes are always flooded by seawater. This condition is caused by the higher sea

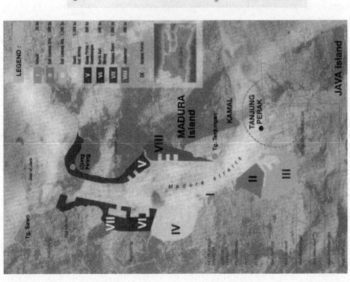

Source: IPC III – Tanjung Perak Branch (2005).

Figure 5.9 Tanjung Perak Port in East Java and Tanjung Emas Port in Central Java

Table 5.2   Port performance indicators: Tanjung Perak Port and Tanjung Emas Port, 2005

	Surabaya	Semarang
Ship services performance		
1. Turn-round time (hours)	73	41
Freight services performance		
1. General cargo (T/G/H)	51	55
2. Bag cargo (T/G/H)	23	38
3. Bulk cargo (T/G/H)	43	126
4. Liquid cargo (T/G/H)	132	171
5. Container cargo	7	n.a.
Facility utilization		
1. Berth occupancy ratio	53	50

Note: T/G/H is ton per gang (of labour) per hour.

Source: IPC and Ministry of Transportation, Republic of Indonesia (2005).

tide level, which makes the border between pier edge and seawater disappear. This has caused many difficulties. It especially hinders the freight load–unload activities and decelerates transportation inside and outside the port. The land transportation access to the port is really bad, slowing down container truck speed, and thus also contributes to road damage. Furthermore, the housing area around the port is very vulnerable, since houses are flooded when the port is. This problem, however, has been identified as a geological characteristic condition in Semarang, where the level of land is getting further below the sea level every year (known as 'rob condition'). Unfortunately neither the local government of Semarang nor the port authority has taken any significant action to solve this problem.

Despite the serious problem caused by the rob condition, freight services productivity in Tanjung Emas Port is still higher (for all types of cargo) compared to that in Tanjung Perak Port. The *Annual Report Evaluation of 24 Strategic Port Performances* published by the Ministry of Transportation stated that insufficient port equipment and facilities has lowered the operational performance of Tanjung Perak Port. On the other hand, berth occupancy rate (BER) in Surabaya is 53 per cent, slightly higher compared to Semarang at only 50 per cent. However, this rate is above the maximum acceptable international standard of 40 per cent.[12] In addition, the need to increase the depth of the channel is limited by the nature of the port's hinterland. Since the hinterland in Semarang is small, there is less incentive for

Table 5.3 *Operational activity in Tanjung Perak Port and Tanjung Emas Port, 2005–2006*

Activity	Unit	Tanjung Emas		Tanjung Perak	
		2005	2006	2005	2006
Vessels	Call	4 388	4 201	14 915	15 467
	GRT	17 253 982	17 213 029	60 590 286	60 005 935
Export	Ton	120 198	117 097	873 123	820 872
Import	Ton	454 248	462 306	3 560 909	3 547 427
	Total	574 446	579 403	4 434 032	4 386 299
Unload	Ton	1 448 140	2 201 414	4 050 943	4 345 773
Load	Ton	254 453	244 222	2 134 910	2 147 616
	Total	1 702 593	2 445 636	6 185 853	6 493 389

Note: GRT gross registered tons.

Source: IPC III (2007).

IPC Tanjung Emas to improve its infrastructure so as to allow bigger vessels to enter.

Port activity: cargo flows, hinterland and vessels frequency

Table 5.3 summarizes port activities in Tanjung Emas Port and Tanjung Perak Port. Tanjung Perak Port handles more international freight than Tanjung Emas Port. About 30 per cent of freight handled at Tanjung Perak Port is international and the rest is inter-island freight. In 2006, a total of 6.5 million tons of cargo were loaded and unloaded in Tanjung Perak Port, an increase of 4.1 per cent on the previous year. On the other hand, Tanjung Emas Port is dominated by domestic, rather than international, freight. In both ports, the shares of export to import freight volume are quite low, indicating that import activity is still dominant.

The value of imports into Tanjung Perak Port is higher than that of its exports. This is due to the nature of the industry that supports the Tanjung Perak Port hinterland. There are many manufacturing industries whose inputs consist of high-technology material that should be imported from other countries.

Being the gateway to eastern Indonesia, Tanjung Perak Port has been consistently expanding in freight flows. The port has become a transit port from and to the eastern islands of Indonesia, such as Sulawesi, Maluku, Nusa Tenggara and Irian Jaya. Moreover, the hinterland supporting Tanjung Perak Port is much greater than Tanjung Emas Port. The port is supported by small, medium and large industries in east Java, such as

Rambipuji Industrial Estate, which is located around 200 km from Tanjung Perak Port, and is planning to have its own main cargo facilities in Tanjung Perak Port. Surabaya Industrial Estate Rungkut (SIER), established in 1994, has around 290 large manufacturing firms built on 476 hectares of land and is located about 23 km from Tanjung Perak Port. Finally, Pasuruan Industrial Estate Rembang is located 60 km from the port, on 500 hectares of land. The types of commodity sent via the port vary, from raw materials to textiles to electronics goods.

Tanjung Emas Port itself is supported by a smaller hinterland, probably due to the fact that the port is located between two other main ports, Tanjung Priok Port in Jakarta and Tanjung Perak Port in Surabaya. As a consequence, the hinterlands of Tanjung Emas Port consist only of Semarang and other cities in Central Java Province, such as Jepara, Ungaran and Pekalongan. Commodities produced here are mainly furniture and textiles. Not surprisingly, those products are the main export commodities shipped via Semarang. The highest value of export commodity comes from Central Java Province and Yogyakarta in the form of furniture (52.74 per cent), polypropelene (45.02 per cent) and other commodities such as textiles, wood, garments, particle plywood, food/beverages and mushrooms. On the other hand, the largest import commodity is raw cotton (14.3 per cent), which is particularly used by textile companies, followed by machinery and spare parts (12.27 per cent).

The hinterland supporting a port determines not only the number and size of cargo flows, but also the frequency of vessel visits. This seems related to the 'ships follow the trade' principle, where Tanjung Perak Port is supported by a more developed hinterland; also its position as the gateway port of eastern Indonesia is an obvious advantage. Meanwhile, as a consequence of a smaller cargo volume in Tanjung Emas Port, the frequency of vessel visits to this port is also relatively low.

In 2006, the number of ship calls in Tanjung Perak was 15 500, three times higher than that in Tanjung Emas Port. In Tanjung Emas Port, the average ship visit rate is 65 ship calls per month, comprising about 70 per cent feeder ships from Singapore, Port Klang, Tanjung Pelepas Port etc., and about 30 per cent ships directly from Hong Kong, Taipei,China and Malaysia. The domestic routes are dominated by ships from Belawan, Medan (North Sumatera) and Tanjung Priok, Jakarta.

Infrastructure aspects
Tanjung Perak seems to be more competitive with respect to infrastructure (Table 5.4). The depth of the western sailing channel of Tanjung Perak Port varies between −9.7 to −12 mLWS (mean low water spring), while that of Tanjung Emas Semarang varies between −3.5 and −10 mLWS. A deeper

Table 5.4   *Infrastructure, facility and equipment: Tanjung Emas Port and Tanjung Perak Port*

	Tanjung Emas	Tanjung Perak
Sailing channel	−3.5 to −10 mLWS	−9.7 to −12 mLWS
Length of container terminal	495 m	1 870 m
Container freight station	9564 m^2	14 400 m^2
Pilot boat	1 unit	4 unit
Tug boat	3 unit	9 unit
Head truck	24 unit	59 unit
Chassis combo	28 unit	55 unit
Forklift	11 unit	20 unit
RTG (rubber-tyred gantry)	11 unit	23 unit

Note: mLWS is mean low water spring, a measure of channel depth.

Source: IPC III (2007).

sailing channel allows more large vessels to enter the port. The sedimentation problem that always appears in Tanjung Emas Port makes it difficult to maintain the sailing channel depth.

The length of container terminal indicates the capacity of berths to handle cargo. Tanjung Perak Port has a longer container terminal than Tanjung Emas. There are two container stations in Tanjung Perak, managed by Berlian Jasa Terminal International Company and Terminal Peti Kemas Surabaya, respectively. In Tanjung Emas Port, the container freight station is managed by Terminal Peti Kemas Semarang. Equipment provision in Tanjung Perak Port is also better than that at Tanjung Emas Port, as a consequence of more activities handled inside the port. The facilities and equipment currently available in TPKS are summarized in Table 5.4.

Studies have shown a negative correlation between port infrastructure and trade cost, where congestion due to poor infrastructure increases the time spent in the port, and therefore increases distribution cost. In addition, as the field observation of this study found, the availability of infrastructure in the ports also depends on the number of goods and vessels handled. So it is likely that infrastructure condition (e.g. congestion as a result) and trade cost affect each other both ways. Tanjung Emas Port, for example, has poorer infrastructure than Tanjung Perak Port. It also only handles a relatively small amount of freight compared to Tanjung Perak Port. Therefore congestion is unlikely, and the added cost to distribution is small.

Demand Side: Competitiveness of Tanjung Perak Port and Tanjung Emas Port

This section concentrates on the demand side of port usage that affects its competitiveness. The analysis refers to information from the survey to port users, in both Tanjung Perak Port and Tanjung Emas Port. Port users include cargo owners and shipping lines, each located in Surabaya and Semarang.

The view of shipping lines

The key strength of Tanjung Perak Port, according to the respondents, is its geographical aspect. The strategic location (as the gateway to eastern Indonesia and near Madura Strait) leads Tanjung Perak Port to act as a hub port to and from other ports in eastern Indonesia. Its hinterland is therefore quite extensive, both captive and contestable hinterland, not limited to East Java alone. In East Java itself, there are more industrial companies than in Central Java (Semarang). Respondents from shipping line associations reported that they prefer Tanjung Perak Port to Tanjung Emas Port, since there are more cargoes to be delivered via Tanjung Perak, dictated by its geographical advantage.

From the view of shipping lines as the port users, the major weakness of Tanjung Perak Port lies in its infrastructure, for example the limited space and amount of piers, the shallowness of the channel, the inadequate stacking area, and the insufficient tugboats and operators to serve the vessels. The limited depth of channel affects the inefficient vessels in delivering cargoes, in particular for big vessels, since they have to operate with idle cargo space, to keep the vessel safe when passing the channel area. These weaknesses could mean more time needed, and higher cost at the expense of shipping lines and end-users.

Tanjung Emas Port provides similar port services. However, the hinterland is relatively limited compared to that of Tanjung Perak Port. It covers only some cities in Central Java, with fewer industrial areas than East Java. The major weakness of Tanjung Emas Port is its geographical aspect. A constantly high sea tide creates critical problems for vessel activities or loading–unloading activity. It also affects the road transportation inside and outside the ports, since it frequently causes flooding. The high sea tide could also weaken the effectiveness of the breakwater in ensuring the safety of vessels when berthing. Such a problem was reported by shipping lines. A similar view was expressed by the Importers' Association, especially with respect to the flooding problem. According to the respondents, flooding hampers the distribution activity from port to final destination, in terms of delays and damage to trucks. The respondents suggested calling for the port authority to maintain the condition of the breakwater in the port, and to local government to improve the road condition. Another weakness related to port facilities is the condition of tugboats that are less powerful, as mentioned by the shipping line associations. This could contribute to the slowing down of vessel activities.

It is worth noting that trade activities are the major factor behind the development of the ports. Thus import/export imbalance is related more to hinterland characteristics. Even though port users, especially shipping lines, have in general clear ideas about the strengths and weaknesses of both Tanjung Emas Port and Tanjung Perak Port, their final decision in choosing one particular port is of course also affected by the volume of freight handled in the ports. That is, the greater the freight volume handled at a port, the more shipping lines would choose to use that particular port.

The view of cargo owners
The first factor that influences a cargo owner to choose a particular port is obviously the distance between its locations and the ports. An exporter will normally choose the closest port from where the good is produced. The Exporter Association in Semarang said that the exporters would use Tanjung Emas Port if vessels could deliver their cargoes directly from Tanjung Emas Port, albeit there are more ship routes to Tanjung Perak Port. Likewise, an importer will choose the closest port from where the good is needed by users such as manufacturing factories. It is possible (and is evident in the survey) that an importer is located in Semarang even though the factory is in Surabaya. In such a case, the importer would direct the imported cargoes to Tanjung Perak Port, as opposed to Tanjung Emas Port.

The second factor is the ship's fixed route. The exporter/importer might have to use a particular port based on a ship's fixed route even though the distance to reach the port is longer than that to alternative ports. Where there is no ship's route that matches the destination of exported cargoes, the cargo owners will find other ports, such as Tanjung Perak or even Tanjung Priok. Again, as dictated by the 'ships follow the trade' principle, shipping lines are more likely to choose a port based on the freight volume handled in the port, rather than on location alone.

The third factor is time. The exporter/importer will choose the port that can be reached immediately because, if the shipment does not meet the deadline as stated in the letter of credit (L/C), the L/C is rendered invalid. In interviews with importer/exporter associations, both in Semarang and Surabaya, respondents said that cargo owners would not process an overdue L/C. Hence, in general, cargo owners would not choose a port quite far from their location, especially if it requires longer road transportation time. This factor is of course very much related to the distance factor above.

The fourth factor is the destination port as determined by a foreign buyer/seller. This factor is subject to the trading system applied in a country. In Indonesia, virtually all import activities use the cost, insurance and freight (c.i.f.) system, while export activities use the free on board (f.o.b.) system. In import activities, this system lets the cargo owners (from other countries) pay the freight-related cost. As a consequence, the cargo owner determines which port to use. On the other hand, the f.o.b. system requires the exporters (from other countries) to pay the freight-related cost. Again, this means that the exporters decide which port the cargoes will depart from. This whole system limits the Indonesian importer/exporter in choosing a particular port. One respondent in Surabaya used Tanjung Priok Port in Jakarta to export its products, since the importer requested this, although the company is closer to Tanjung Perak Port. As it turned out, that importer prefers Tanjung Priok Port since it also imports other goods and loads them all into one container, i.e. an economies of scope consideration on the importer side.

The fifth factor is of course cost. An exporter/importer will surely aim for a lower distribution cost. In a country with a higher ratio of imports to exports (as is becoming more evident in Indonesia), using the direct call system could be more expensive. This is because the payment for an empty container after being used for import is borne by Indonesian importers. Meanwhile, if the feeder system is used instead, it takes more time since it has first to transit an international hub port. Consequently, the feeder system offers lower ocean freight cost than the direct call system. This has resulted in a smaller number of mother vessels (direct call) compared to feeder vessels. This phenomenon was especially evident in Tanjung Emas Port due to its relatively small freight volume handled. As a consequence, the number of direct call vessels in Tanjung Emas is lower than that in Tanjung Perak Port.

In addition to the five factors above, some more indirect trade-offs appear to occur in choosing between two ports. In the case of Surabaya's versus Semarang's port, the survey suggests the following additional observations.

First, the implementation of certain regulations might also cause a trade-off in selecting a port. There are cases regarding different interpretation of the Harmonized System (HS) codes for imported goods between importers and customs, followed by an extra charge in addition to the import tariff. However, the pattern varies, as reported by respondents. Tanjung Emas Customs, for example, is less strict than Tanjung Perak Customs. As a result, some importers in Surabaya prefer Tanjung Emas Port in Semarang to Surabaya's own Tanjung Perak Port, even though the former is more distant. The extra transportation cost that importers should pay given such a decision seems to be much lower than the extra charge for additional import tariffs they have to pay to custom officials. This practice usually occurs when the importer holds a General Importer Licence as opposed to Producer Importer Licence.[13] This in fact opens an opportunity for bad importers to take advantage by using the more lax officials in order to release their commodity through customs inspection. Moreover, the lack of a Hi-Co scan[14] system in Tanjung Emas Port customs also leads importers to use this port, as this lack of technology can reduce checking risks.

Second, there is also a trade-off between location and safety of delivering the cargoes. It is obvious that shippers should ensure that the cargoes they are handling can be delivered safely to their destination. One respondent suggested that a furniture exporter located in Boyolali (a small city in Central Java Province) prefers to use Tanjung Perak Port in Surabaya, although Boyolali is closer to Tanjung Emas Port. However, the lesser distance to Tanjung Emas Port is characterized by hilly roads. The road access to Surabaya, on the other hand, is flatter. The exporter chose Tanjung Perak Port because he did not want his furniture to get damaged in transportation to the port due to bad road conditions. As a consequence, the distance travelled is much greater, albeit with safer delivery.

5.   DISCUSSION

Inter-port competition betwen Semarang's Tanjung Emas Port and Surabaya's Tanjung Perak Port is not very evident. The respondents from IPC III in both Tanjung Perak Port branch and Tanjung Emas Port branch reported that any improvement of ports, in terms of performance and facilities, would be aimed directly at giving better services to the users, not to compete against each other or other ports. This state-owned corporation coordinates a total of 18 main ports, including Tanjung Perak and Tanjung Emas Ports. Most ports are not profitable. Tanjung Perak Port is in fact the most profitable port under IPC III coordination. As a consequence, however, IPC III should subsidize other groups of ports that report losses.

As for investment in an individual port, each port (or 'branch') might propose it to IPC III, as the coordinator. The IPC will then consider every proposal along with others in its priority list. The position in the list is subject to urgency, in addition to the break-even point period of the investment.[15] Not surprisingly, there are different levels of improvement efforts in ports with regard to facilities and equipment. The facilities in Tanjung Perak Port are more developed than those in other ports under IPC III, since it has the largest volume of freight handled. For example, Tanjung Perak Port has just launched a one-roof-service facility this year to improve its service.

Another interesting case is Bojonegoro Port, a port located nearby Tanjung Priok Port. This port was developed to become Indonesia's international hub container port. However, the financial crisis in 1997 badly affected the progress of its development.[16] In this case, the issue of a merger plan of IPCs has arisen, since the crisis left IPC with large debts.[17]

As a single authority, IPC is in a powerful position in organizing ports and in setting up tariffs. Therefore the difference in service rate – if any, considering that Tanjung Emas and Tanjung Perak are under one coordination (IPC III) – is not significant. As a consequence, service quality seems to be similarly stagnant, since there is no incentive for those ports to compete against each other.

This issue of the absence of competition between the two ports was also confirmed by shipping lines and importer/exporter associations. They also agreed that the tariffs and services are very similar. The absence of inter-port competition also confirmed that the port-choice decision completely depends on factors that promote efficiency, as explained in this chapter. In this regard, the decision to choose a particular port might be less relevant, since alternatives are lacking. However, both shipping lines and Indonesian cargo owners that were surveyed implied that the port performance and services should be improved. Promoting competition between ports is one way to do this.

Policy Implications

In general, port management is a role of government as public service provider in a country. However, the limited government financial capacity to develop ports hinders the provision of port services.

Ideas for increasing the role of private agents in ports have arisen since the 1980s (World Bank, 2007). In Indonesia, privatization has been applied gradually, particularly in ports with high domestic and international trade activities. However, privatization applied only to a few services, e.g. container terminal, as in Tanjung Priok, Tanjung Perak and Tanjung Emas Port. This framework of privatization could be expanded to cover other services provided at ports such as pilotage, tug assistance, vessel stevedoring, cargo handling, storage and yard services. Such privatization should not be limited to providers that are financially powerful but also to those who could improve the competitiveness of the port, employ modern management and technology, and guarantee the transfer of know-how to domestic providers. One type of privatization that may fit this is the one emanating from the public–private partnership framework, where, for example, local government has the authority to arrange its port service and management with the private sector directly.

One factor that is considered a binding constraint for privatization is the public service obligation (PSO) required by the government. As a state-owned enterprise that is subject to PSO, IPC cannot maximize its profits as a purely private company can. Privatization, albeit partial and gradual, should consider a proportional reduction of such obligation; i.e. it applies only to the remaining public share of the port services.

6. CONCLUSION

Maritime transport plays a significant role in trade distribution, which in turn supports the sustainable development of the economy. Almost all Indonesia's trade, both domestic and international, is transported via sea. Thus the development and the function of the Indonesian ports are essential in relation to some aspects of inland growth and economic development, in particular trade activities.

Port competitiveness is a function of whether port users (cargo owners and shipping lines) would choose one particular port among a set of alternatives. Infrastructure and port facilities are dominant factors in port competition but there are also other factors that affect port users in their choice of port. However, the final decisions on port choice were not necessarily dictated by the user's opinion with regard to infrastructure and port facilities.

The study finds that there are some important trade-offs in choosing ports. Based on the survey, the implementation of certain regulations might influence port users to choose another port. Importers located in the hinterland of Tanjung Perak Port may prefer Tanjung Emas Port since customs in the latter is less strict than in the former. This could imply extra transportation cost since Tanjung Perak Port is relatively more distant. Another trade-off is between location and safety in delivering the cargoes. Geographical condition could prompt the exporter to choose the more distant port to ensure that the cargoes are delivered safely.

Currently competition is not evident among ports in Indonesia. This is due to the fact that all ports are controlled by one authority, the IPC. However, users demand that ports operate more efficiently. A certain degree of competition in port handling services might be needed to drive service providers to improve their performance. Higher competition could lead to more options for port users and in turn might alter their decisions in favour of more efficient ports. In addition, competition among ports is likely to be contagious to the hinterlands, as they would themselves compete over the ports.

If the control of two ports falls under two different private bodies, competition between the two ports is more likely. However, given the public nature of port services, privatization might have to be done gradually. A few key ports in Indonesia have taken this course, and it is expected that the improvement will spread to other ports as well. Obviously port competition is relevant only within a certain limit of geographical areas, as distance is a key factor in choosing a particular port. This implies that complete privatization of *all* ports is not necessary. Priority should be given to the most important ports.

However, the drive to competition should also be seen as an opportunity to improve 'soft infrastructure', with a focus on increasing efficiency. For example, privatization as a means to foster competition will force the port management to cut unnecessary clearance processes and to eliminate any illegal collections.

The study recommends the authority to encourage competition among key ports in Indonesia. This might be achieved by gradually minimizing the authority of the IPC to manage them. One suggestion is to give the opportunity for private operators to provide services to shipping lines and cargo owners. As of the time of writing, the government is preparing a draft of a new shipping law (UU Pelayaran). One of the issues that is being considered is the movement towards more competition and away from monopoly.

Finally, the findings from this study should, however, be accepted with caution. The limited number of observations limits the generalization to every port in Indonesia.[18]

NOTES

1. We thank Toshihiro Nishizawa and Mario Lamberte for helpful comments and suggestions.
2. We do not analyse the other two types of port competition; i.e. intra-port competition and intra-terminal competition.
3. The biggest port of the country is Tanjung Priok in Jakarta. The study chooses Surabaya and Semarang since both are geographically closer compared to Surabaya–Jakarta or Semarang–Jakarta. The close geographical proximity and relatively similar characteristics are needed to assess the competition issue. Many other studies have looked at the Tanjung Priok case.
4. This was confirmed by an IPC official during the field interview.
5. Westports Malaysia, http://www.westportsmalaysia.com/.
6. This is also confirmed by field interviews.
7. THC involves a cost recovery mechanism whereby shipping lines claim charges to offset port costs that are not covered in freight handling fees.
8. THC is set by agreement at international trade conferences – associations of ship owners

operating in the same trade routes. In Indonesia, the membership of the conference is dominated by global shipping companies, i.e. foreign fleets.

9. Indonesia Port Corporation II – Tanjung Priok Branch (2006).
10. See Appendix Table 5A.1 for respondents' description.
11. United Nations Conference on Trade and Development (1997).
12. BOR is defined as the percentage of time vessels are berthed at port.
13. General Importer Licence (API) is a basic licence to import goods. It is usually held by traders that import final goods to be sold to end-consumers, without further production process. Producer Importer Licence (API-P) is a licence to import goods that are used for particular production processes. This licence is usually held by producers who use imported goods as raw materials, intermediate inputs, or machines for their production.
14. Hi-Co scan is an X-ray scanner used by Customs for cargo inspection.
15. It is not however clear what constitutes 'urgency'.
16. However, the chairman of the Investment Coordinating Board (BKPM) asserted that central government was fully committed to support the development of this port, in cooperation with Banten Province government (www.gatra.com, 31 January 2006).
17. However, this has been denied by the IPC II (Ray and Blankfeld, 2002).
18. For more references, see for example Blankfeld and Fritz (2002) and Ray and Blankfeld (2002).

REFERENCES

Blankfeld, Richard and Don Fritz (2002), 'Indonesia shipping and port sector policy review', Technical Report published by Partnership for Economic Growth, a Project under USAID.

De Langen, Peter W. and Athanasios A. Pallis (2005), 'Analysis of the benefits of intra-port competition', Working Paper, Erasmus University Rotterdam, http://ideas.repec.org/p/wpa/wuwpio/0510003.html.

Fourgeaud, Patrick (2000), *Measuring Port Performance*, Washington, DC: The World Bank.

Haralambides, H.E. (2002), 'Competition, excess capacity, and the pricing of port infrastructure', *International Journal of Maritime Economics*, **4**, 323–47.

Hoyle, Brian and Jacques Charlier (1995), 'Inter-port competition in developing countries: an East African case study', *Journal of Transport Geography*, **3** (2), 87–103.

Indonesia Port Corporation (IPC) II – Tanjung Priok Branch (2005), *Annual Report 2005*, Jakarta: Pelindo II.

Indonesia Port Corporation (IPC) II – Tanjung Priok Branch (2006), *Tanjung Priok Port Directory 2006*, Jakarta: Pelindo II.

Indonesia Port Corporation (IPC) III – Tanjung Emas Branch (2005), *Tanjung Emas Port Directory 2005*, Semarang: Pelindo III.

Indonesia Port Corporation (IPC) III – Tanjung Perak Branch (2005), *Port of Tanjung Perak Profile*, Surubaya: Pelindo III.

LPEM-FEUI (2005), *Competitiveness of Indonesian Industries from Logistics Perspective: Inefficiency in the Logistics of Export Industries*, Final Report, in collaboration with Japan Bank for International Cooperation (JBIC).

LPEM-FEUI (2006), *Customs Study: A Report from the 2006 Survey*, Final Report, in collaboration with the World Bank.

Ministry of Transportation, Republic of Indonesia (2005), *Annual Report Evaluation of 24 Strategic Port Performances 2004*, Jakarta: Ministry of Transportation RI.

Overseas Shipowners' Representatives Association (2005), 'Setting the record straight: THC and the future of shipping in Indonesia', mimeo.

Ray, David and Richard Blankfeld (2002), 'Reforming Indonesia's port', Technical Report published by Partnership for Economic Growth, a Project under USAID.

United Nations Conference on Trade and Development (1997), *Review of Maritime Transport 1997*, Geneva: UNCTAD.

Winkelmans, Willy (2003), 'Port competitiveness and port competition, two of a kind?', paper presented at the 23rd IAPH World Port Conference, 24–30 May, Durban, South Africa.

World Bank (2007), *Port Reform Toolkit*, 2nd edn, Washington, DC: World Bank.

APPENDIX

Table 5A.1   Respondents for in-depth interviews

Company/Institution	Position
Surabaya	
Indonesia Port Corporation III Tanjung Perak Branch	One Stop Service Manager (PPSA)
Indonesia Port Corporation III Tanjung Perak Branch	Public Relations
Indonesia Port Corporation III Tanjung Perak Branch	Operational Dept
Indonesian National Shipowners' Association (Surabaya Branch)	Chairman
Indonesian National Shipowners' Association (Surabaya Branch)	Head, Division of Foreign Affairs
Indonesian National Shipowners' Association (Surabaya Branch)	Head, Division of Domestic Affairs
Indonesian National Shipowners' Association (Surabaya Branch)	Secretary
Indonesian Exporters' Association of East Java	Deputy Chairman
Indonesian Exporters' Association of East Java	Trade and Craft Industry Sector Adviser
Importers' Association of Indonesia (East Java)	Chairman
Importers' Association of Indonesia (East Java)	Assistant Secretary
PT Atriamoda Transportindo (International Freight Forwarding and Agencies)	Surabaya Branch Manager
PT Hagajaya Kemasindo Sarana (International Freight Forwarding)	Branch Manager
PT United Waru Biscuit Manufactory	Human Resource Dept
PT Panggung Electric Citrabuana	Risk Management Dept
Semarang	
Indonesia Port Corporation III Tanjung Emas Branch	Operational Manager
Indonesian National Shipowners' Association (Semarang Branch)	Chairman
Indonesian National Shipowners' Association (Semarang Branch)	Secretary I
Importers' Association of Indonesia (Central Java) and Indonesian Exporters' Association of Central Java	Chairman
PT Atriamoda Transportindo (International Freight Forwarding and Agencies)	Semarang Branch Manager
PT Forindo Mitra Buana	Operational Dept
PT Dasa Karindo Utama (Shipping Company)	Manager
PT Bahari Haluan Samudera Semarang (Shipping Company)	Branch Manager
PT Bahari Haluan Samudera Semarang (Shipping Company)	Operational Dept
PT Djakarta Lloyd (Shipping Company)	Branch Manager
PT Apac Inti Corpora	Div. Man. Logistics
PT Apac Inti Corpora	Despatch Import Manager

6. Infrastructure and trade costs in Malaysia: the importance of FDI and exports*

Tham Siew Yean, Evelyn Devadason and Loke Wai Heng

1. INTRODUCTION

Among developing countries, Malaysia is one of the most highly integrated into the world economy, as reflected by A.T. Kearney's Globalization Index for 2006, in which Malaysia ranked nineteenth. International trade and foreign direct investment (FDI) play an important role in Malaysia's integration with the world economy, as seen in A.T. Kearney's indices on trade and FDI integration, where Malaysia ranked second and eleventh, respectively. The entry of transnational corporations (TNCs) through FDI has not only contributed towards Malaysia's exports, but imports have also increased due to the fragmentation of production across various countries in East Asia. In turn, Malaysia's progressive integration into the regional production networks that are forged by the TNCs operating in East Asia can be attributed to its relatively strong locational advantages.

Excellent infrastructure is one of the locational advantages valued by foreign investors. In fact, the reliability and quality of infrastructure, roads, and air service are three out of the 20 critical location factors that have been found to be very influential in determining the FDI competitiveness of a country (World Bank, 2003, p. 51). In the case of Malaysia, the TNCs operating in the country are producing mainly for export, due to the relatively small domestic economy. Good and reliable transport infrastructure is therefore critical as it affects the relative cost of moving goods across international borders. In particular, with progressive tariff liberalization, this cost is perhaps even more important than tariffs in determining the cost of landed goods. Export competitiveness is therefore no longer confined to the cost of producing a good within the country alone, but also encompasses the ability to deliver goods and services in time and at a low cost. In view of this, the objective of this chapter is to examine the development of

148

transport infrastructure in Malaysia and its contribution towards reducing trade costs through its impact on FDI and trade in the country. The chapter is organized as follows: an overview of the development of transport infrastructure in Malaysia from 1991 until 2006 is presented in Section 2. This is followed by an analysis of the inflow of FDI and its impact on the trade in Malaysia in Section 3. Section 4 analyses the impact of transport infrastructure development on trade costs. The last section summarizes the main findings, and offers some policy suggestions for future development of transport infrastructure in the country.

2. OVERVIEW OF TRANSPORT INFRASTRUCTURE DEVELOPMENT IN MALAYSIA, 1991–2006

Infrastructure Development

Malaysia has invested and continues to invest heavily in transport infrastructure since achieving Independence in 1957.[1] The main objectives for the government's sustained investment in infrastructure development are to ensure the timely and adequate supply of facilities that can meet the development requirements of the country (Malaysia, 1991, p. 145; 2001a, p. 177). In turn, this sustained investment in infrastructure development has enabled Malaysia to be ranked above most of her ASEAN (Association of Southeast Asian Nations) neighbours and China, with the exception of Singapore, in terms of the overall quality of infrastructure in the country by the World Economic Forum (as cited in ADB et al., 2005).

From 1991 until 2005, Malaysia spent a total of RM (Malaysian ringgit) 63 billion for the development of transport infrastructure in the country (Table 6.1). A further RM 30.3 billion was allocated for the period of the Ninth Malaysia Plan (9MP: 2006–10).[2] The amount spent constituted an average of 21 per cent of the total development expenditure of the country from 1991 until 2000. In the last five-year plan, the total expenditure on transport infrastructure amounted to 28 per cent of total development expenditure, while in the current plan, the amount allocated is 15 per cent of total development expenditure.

Based on the same table, it can be seen that road development has consistently taken the largest share (60–65 per cent) of the amount spent or allocated for developing the transport infrastructure in the country. Besides government expenditure, the private sector also expended RM 15.2, RM 7.9 and RM 4 billion respectively during the Sixth, Seventh and Eighth Malaysia Plans under the country's privatization programme.

Table 6.1   Government expenditure on infrastructure development in
*   Malaysia, 1991–2010 (RM million)*

Transport type	1991–1995 6MP, expenditure	1996–2000 7MP, expenditure	2001–2005 8MP, expenditure	2001–2010 9MP, allocation
Total transport (RM million)	11 594.7	20 484.2	30 936.5	30 304.4
% of total development expenditure of the government	21.2	20.7	28.1	15.2
Roads	7 572.6	12 269.5	18 451.4	17 303.1
	(65.3)	(59.9)	(59.6)	(57.1)
Urban transport	95.2	404	706.6	1 565.5
	(0.8)	(2.0)	(2.3)	(5.2)
Rail	1 735.4	5 450.3	5 270.1	3 634.9
	(15.0)	(26.6)	(17.0)	(12.0)
Ports	410.9	1 089.2	2 443	1 290
	(3.5)	(5.3)	(7.9)	(4.3)
Airports	1 780.6	1 271.2	1 779.3	2 868.5
	(15.4)	(6.2)	(5.8)	(9.5)
Rural roads	n.a.	n.a.	2 286.1	3 642.4
	n.a.	n.a.	(7.4)	(12.0)

Notes:
MP – Malaysia Plans.
Numbers in parentheses show percentage of total transport expenditure.
n.a. – not available.

Source: Seventh, Eighth and Ninth Malaysian Plans.

The second-largest share of the amount expended for the development of transport infrastructure accrued to rail development, with the exception of the Sixth Malaysia Plan (6MP: 1991–95), when the amount spent on airport infrastructure took a slightly bigger share at 15.4 per cent due to the development of the Kuala Lumpur International Airport (KLIA). Port development took the second-smallest share of the amount spent on transport infrastructure during the Sixth and Seventh Malaysia Plans (7MP: 1996–2000), while urban transport development had the smallest share. However, during the Eighth Malaysia Plan (8MP: 2001–05), the amount spent on port development more than doubled from RM 1.1 billion to RM 2.4 billion due to expansion in capacity and upgrading of port and port-related facilities (Malaysia, 2001b, p. 275). The development of rural roads has been increasingly emphasized since the 8MP, with the amount allocated increasing to RM 3.6 billion in the 9MP or a share

Table 6.2   Road development indicators, 1990–2005

Indicator	Level of development			
	1990	1995	2000	2005
Road density[1]	0.16	0.19	0.20	0.24
Road development index[2]	0.7	0.74	0.75	0.85
Road service level[3]	n.a.	2.96	2.98	3.02

Notes:
[1] Road density measures road length over the total area.
[2] Road development index measures the level of road development taking into account both area and population size of the country.
[3] Road service level measures total road length per 1000 population.

Source: Seventh (p. 348); Eighth (p. 270) and Ninth Malaysian Plans (p. 377).

of 12 per cent of the total amount allocated for transport infrastructure development.

Road Development

The total road network, comprising federal and state roads, increased from a total of 53 984 km in 1990 to 77 673 km in 2005. The total amount spent for road development from 1991 to 2005 amounted to RM 38.4 billion from the government and another RM 27.1 billion from the private sector.

Road density has increased from 0.16 in 1990 to 0.24 km of road per km^2 in 2005, representing a 50 per cent increase in road coverage and accessibility in any given area (Table 6.2). The road development index also showed improvement from 0.7 in 1990 to 0.85 in 2005, while the road service level improved from 2.96 km per 1000 population to 3.02 km from 1995 to 2005.

Generally, the road infrastructure is better on the west coast of Peninsular Malaysia compared with the east coast and East Malaysia, as the major cities and industries are located on the west coast. A major development during the period under study is the construction of highways and expressways to connect all major cities and towns on the west coast. The development of these highways and expressways was guided by the Highway Network Development Plan (1993–2004). Major road networks were privatized since the passing of the Federal Roads (Private Management) Act in 1984, in order to accelerate the construction of major expressways or highways and to reduce the fiscal burden. During the 8MP, (2001–05), 16 privatized highway projects were undertaken to construct an additional 604.5 km of the national road network, involving a capital expenditure of RM 18.0 billion (Malaysia, 2006a, p. 224). Most of these projects were implemented through the Build–Operate–Transfer (BOT) System, which requires the private sector to construct, operate and maintain the facility using its own funds and, in return, to collect tolls from the road users during the concession period. At the end of the concession period, the facilities will be transferred at no cost to the government. PLUS Expressways Bhd is the biggest of the highway concessionaires, operating approximately 85 per cent of the country's highways. As of 2006, the total length of these toll highways was 1238 km. While some privatized highways are interstate in nature, quite a few are localized to Kuala Lumpur to ease traffic congestion in the capital city.

The North–South expressway, linking the northern tip of Peninsular Malaysia (Kayu Hitam in Kedah state[3]) to the southern tip (Johor Baru), was constructed progressively by sections from 1981 to 1994. It spans 847 km and has reportedly lowered perceived vehicle operating and time saving cost by 25 per cent per trip, after taking into account toll charges (Malaysia, 1996, p. 344). This expressway is also linked to the Kuala Lumpur International Airport (KLIA) via the North–South Central Link expressway. It is part of the Asian Highway Network, which also connects into Thailand and Singapore.

In the case of Penang, since the state is geographically and administratively divided between the island of Penang and Seberang Perai on the peninsular side, the Penang Bridge was constructed in 1982 and completed in 1985 to link the island with the hinterland. Due to the heavy volume of traffic, the bridge is set to be broadened from the current two lanes to three lanes. Penang is linked to the North–South expressway on its Seberang Perai side. In 2006, the government announced that a second bridge will be built under the Ninth Malaysia Plan.

Johor, the southernmost state in Malaysia, is linked to Singapore via the Johor Causeway and the Malaysia–Singapore Second Crossing. This second link cost RM 1.6 billion and was ready in 1997 (Malaysia, 1996, p. 346).

Apart from the expressways, various roads were constructed or upgraded to alleviate traffic congestion as well as to provide connections with ports and industrial estates in the country. For example, access roads were constructed to the Port of Tanjung Pelepas in the southern part, as well as to the Kulim Hi-Tech Industrial Park in the north.

Railway Development

The existing rail infrastructure links Malaysia to Singapore in the South and up to Kunming in China under the Trans Asia Link project, endorsed by ASEAN. The total track length is 2262 km in Peninsular Malaysia. The main infrastructure programmes undertaken during the period include the strengthening and rehabilitation of railway tracks, computerization, double tracking, purchase of additional locomotives, and construction of additional stations and facilities such as inland container depots. Special links were constructed to the Port of Tanjung Pelepas (1999), the West Port of Port Klang (1998) and also to the North Butterworth Container Terminal (NBCT) (2000).

The sole provider of rail carrier services is the Malaysian Railway Limited (or Kereta Tanah Melayu Bhd (KTMB)), a fully owned government entity. In 1997, the government entered into a management agreement with a private consortium for the management takeover of the company. Subsequently, the company was restructured into three major strategic business units (SBUs), namely freight, inter-city and commuter. These three units operate as autonomous business entities, while the corporate headquarters provided support in terms of policy formulation and strategic directions (Malaysia, 2006a, p. 378). KTMB provides containerized freight services, conventional freight services (for bulk carriers, cement, etc.) and international freight service to Thailand and Singapore.

In terms of speed, moving cargo from Port Klang to Bangkok takes only 60 hours by rail as compared to five to seven days by ship (Nesathurai, 2003, p. 7). More importantly, containers transshipped by rail do not have terminal handling charges and hence confer a significant savings on shippers. Consequently, quite a number of the major shipping lines are using the container services of KTMB to save the time and cost of moving goods internationally.

Airport Development

Malaysia has 45 airports, including six international airports, 19 domestic airports and 20 STOLports (Malaysia, undated, p. 12).[4] The six international airports are the Kuala Lumpur International Airport (KLIA), Penang International Airport, Langkawi International Airport, Senai International Airport (in Johor state) in Peninsular Malaysia, Kota Kinabalu International Airport in Sabah and Kuching International Airport in Sarawak in East Malaysia.

Various airport capacity expansion projects were implemented during the period, including the building of a new cargo complex at Penang International Airport. During the period, the capacity at the old international airport (Subang International Airport) was expanded while the new international airport (KLIA) was being built. KLIA is designed to be a regional hub and its development has three phases. Its first phase was completed on 30 June 1998, after seven years of conceptualization with a capacity of 25 million passengers per annum and one million tonnes of cargo (Malaysia, 2001b, p. 278). Phase 2 (2003–08) will expand the facility to handle up to 35 million passengers per year by 2008, while Phase 3 will expand this further to 45 million passengers per year by 2012. There is sufficient land and capacity to develop facilities to handle up to 100 million passengers and 5 million tonnes of cargo per annum, including four runways by 2020 and two mega-terminals, each with two linked satellite buildings. A free commercial zone is established there to support storage, value-added and distribution activities.

Malaysia Airports Holdings Berhad (MAHB), a privatized entity, manages and operates all the airports in the country, with the exception of the Senai Airport in Johor and the Kertah Airport in Terengganu. MAHB was formed in 1992 and listed on the Kuala Lumpur Stock Exchange in November 1999. The major shareholder is Khazanah National Bhd, a government investment holding company (73 per cent), while the foreign share amounted to 2.6 per cent in 2005 (MAHB, 2005, p. 239).

A low-cost carrier terminal (LCCT) was constructed on a fast-track basis at the beginning of June 2005 and was fully operational by March 2006, at an approximate cost of RM 108 million (www.lcct.com.my 7 May 2007). The LCCT is located about 20 km from KLIA Main Terminal Building and has the capacity to handle 10 million passengers per year with the scope of expanding to 15 million passengers per year. There are plans to expand the LCCT as well as to construct a rail link between the Main Terminal Building and the LCCT.

Port Development

Due to the geographical make-up of the country, there are 100 ports and cargo handling facilities spread throughout the country, including Sabah and Sarawak in East Malaysia. There are 13 major ports, with North Port and Westport in Port Klang and the Port of Tanjung Pelepas in Johor ranked within Asia's top ten in the best seaport category (Table 6.3).

Based on the government's supply-driven policy, numerous port development projects have been implemented over time, including: (i) privatization of ports; (ii) development of Port of Tanjung Pelepas (PTP); (iii) appointment of Port Klang as the National Load Centre; (iv) expansion of the capacities of different ports; and (v) entry of foreign partners in the two leading ports in the country.

As part of the government's privatization programme, the container terminal at Port Klang was privatized in 1986. Subsequently, other ports were

Table 6.3   Structure of the port industry in Malaysia, 2006

Federal ports	
Bintulu Port Authority	Bintulu Port Sdn Bhd
Johor Port Authority	Port of Tanjung Pelepas
	Johore Port Berhad
	Tanjung Langsat Port Sdn Bhd
Kemaman Port Authority	Petronas
	Kuantan Port Consortium Sdn Bhd
Kemaman Port Authority	Kuantan Port Consortium Sdn Bhd
Penang Port Commission	Penang Port Sdn Bhd
	Langkawi Port Sdn Bhd
	Kedah Cement Jetty Sdn Bhd
Port Klang Authority	Northport (Malaysia) Bhd
	Kelang Multi Terminal Sdn Bhd
	Syarikat Pekhidmatan Pelaburan Gabungan Sdn Bhd (Malacca Port)
State ports	
Marine Department	Lumut Maritime Terminal Sdn Bhd
	Kertih Port Sdn Bhd
	Labuan Port (not privatized)
	Sg. Udang Port Sdn Bhd
Miri Port Authority	(Not privatized)
Kuching Port Authority	(Not privatized)
Rajang Port Authority	(Not privatized)
Sabah Ports Authority	Sabah Port Sdn Bhd

Source: Malaysian Maritime Yearbook, 2005/2006.

also privatized to improve operational and managerial efficiency of port services. Privatized ports are listed in Table 6.3.

Malaysia's newest port, the Port of Tanjung Pelepas (PTP), is located at the southwestern tip of Peninsula Malaysia, at the mouth of Pulai River. PTP's location is in one of the few areas in the region that has a natural deep draught for international shipping. The port is linked by highway or rail to Peninsular Malaysia and Thailand. It is also adjacent to the Second Link, connecting Malaysia and Singapore across the Johor Straits. This makes it adjacent to the same confluence of major shipping routes as Singapore's port. PTP's development entails five phases, extending to the year 2020. The total development will embrace a full range of facilities from container to liquid, dry, bulk and conventional cargo. Phase 1 began in 1995 and was completed in 1999. Operations began in October 1999 with the official opening on 13 March 2000.

Table 6.4   Selected port developments projects

Northport, Port Klang

Phase 2 of Container Terminal 3 is being implemented and berth 14 of the project was ready for commercial operation in 2005. The new terminal with 15 m natural depth will complement 2.73 km container berths in operation and will raise total handling capacity to 4 million TEUs.

Westport, Port Klang

An additional 600 m container terminal is being developed, it increased the total berth length of the terminal at Westport to 2.6 km in 2005.

Penang Port

Under the NBCT Phase IIB Expansion Project, NBCT will be extended a further 200 m to a 900-metre berth. NBCT will be able to handle 1 million TEUs per annum.

Port of Tanjung Pelepas

An additional 2.16 km container berth is being developed under Phase 2 development project.

Sabah Ports

A dedicated container terminal is being developed at Sepangar Bay. The terminal with 400 000 TEUs capacity will be ready for operation in 2006 and will eventually handle Kota Kinabalu Container Terminal traffic and will be developed as the hub for the BIMP EAGA region.

Bintulu Port

A new 1000 m general cargo berth is being developed at the second inner harbour basin. This will allow the current container terminal to be extended to close to 1 km when the general cargo operation is shifted from its present location to the new terminal.

Kuantan Port

A dedicated 400 m container terminal has been developed and plans are on the drawing board to expand container, cruise and liquid chemical berths.

Source: Malaysian Maritime Yearbook, 2005/06.

In 1992, the government designated Port Klang as the National Load Centre to which cargoes from other ports in the national port system would be directed. Various measures were undertaken to improve the capacities of Port Klang, including the introduction of an electronic data interchange (EDI) system to facilitate automated processing of trade documents and to link the port with the other relevant government agencies.

Table 6.4 highlights some of the development projects undertaken for some of the Malaysian ports. Consequently, the capacity in Malaysian ports has expanded rapidly from 174 to 443 million tonnes from 1995 until

Table 6.5   Port capacity, number of berths, cranes, ship calls and volume of cargo handled at ports, 1995–2010

Indicator	1995	2000	2005	2010
Port capacity (million tonnes)	174.1	324.9	443.3	570.0
Number of berths	173.0	221.0	233.0	242.0
Number of cranes[1]	51.0	131.0	217.0	265.0
Number of ship calls	70 098.0	81 313.0	98 345.0	130 000.0
Volume of cargo handled (million tonnes)	152.3	223.9	369.4	539.0
General	30.1	23.3	44.7	47.0
Liquid bulk	60.7	87.5	103.8	202.0
Dry bulk	23.7	28.6	38.2	44.0
Containerized cargo	37.8	84.5	182.7	246.0
Container (million TEUs)	n.a.	4.9	12.1	18.0

Note: [1] Includes gantry and multipurpose cranes.

Source: Eighth (p. 277) and Ninth Malaysian Plans (p. 379).

2005, while the volume of cargo handled has increased from 152 to 369 million tonnes (Table 6.5).

Foreign participation in the privatized ports started in 2000 when AP Moller-Maersk bought a 30 per cent stake in PTP. Hutchinson Port Holdings, a subsidiary of Hutchinson Whampoa Limited (HWL), also took a 30 per cent share of Kelang Multi Terminal Sdn Bhd, the owner and terminal operator for Westport in 2000.

3.   FOREIGN DIRECT INVESTMENT AND INTERNATIONAL TRADE, 1991–2006

Foreign Direct Investment Inflows

Malaysia has sought foreign direct investment (FDI) since opening its first free trade zone (FTZ) in 1972.[5] FDI policies were further liberalized for the manufacturing sector after the economic crisis in 1985 as 100 per cent foreign equity was allowed for firms that exported more than 50 per cent of their output.[6] Generous incentives were also provided to attract investment into the manufacturing sector with the enactment of the Promotion of Investment Act (PIA), 1986. This was accompanied by tariff reforms, especially for light industries. Tariffs continued to fall under Malaysia's current commitments in the World Trade Organization (WTO) and the ASEAN Free Trade Area (AFTA).

The shift towards an FDI-led, export-oriented industrialization from 1985 onwards was greatly assisted by fortuitous external circumstances as the Plaza Accord of 1985 exerted foreign exchange pressures for the industries in newly industrialized economies (NIEs) to relocate to lower-cost producing countries in Southeast Asia. Capital outflows from the NIEs were also further encouraged with the withdrawal of the Generalized System of Preferences (GSP) from these economies. Malaysia was well placed to receive these investments due to its relatively stable political, economic and social environment coupled with good infrastructure, generous incentives, relatively low wages and a relatively well-educated labour force. Consequently, the country rapidly became part of the regional production networks that were being created by the TNCs operating in East Asia. By 1993, Malaysia had become one of the ten largest developing host countries for FDI inflows. In that year, FDI accounted for as much as 8.6 per cent of GDP (gross domestic product) and 23.4 per cent of gross fixed capital formation (GFCF) (Table 6.6).

Inflows dropped sharply to 3.8 per cent of GDP and 14 per cent of GFCF in 1998 due to the emergence of the Asian financial crisis and its negative impact on corporate profits, retained earnings and investor confidence in the region. In response to the crisis, the government further liberalized its FDI policy by allowing 100 per cent foreign ownership in the manufacturing sector, regardless of its export orientation. The recovery of the economy in 1999 helped to restore inflows to 4.9 per cent of GDP and 22.5 per cent of GFCF. However, the global slowdown and decline in global FDI flows resulted in an all-time low in the inflows of foreign capital in 2001 when FDI accounted for 0.6 per cent of GDP and 2.5 per cent of GFCF. Although inflows recovered in 2002, they fell again in 2003 due largely to the acquisition of foreign interests in the oil and gas sector by a Malaysian company on the expiry of joint-venture contracts, as well as large loan repayments to parent companies abroad (Central Bank, 2003, p. 46). They fluctuated from 2004 until 2005, with FDI averaging 3.5 per cent of GDP and 17 per cent of GFCF. In 2006, net inflows increased to RM 26 billion or 4.7 per cent of GDP due to higher investments in petroleum refining and the petroleum-related products industry, and the liberalization of the financial sector, especially in Islamic financing (Central Bank, 2006, p. 48).

Although theoretically infrastructure is one of the locational advantages of host economies, there is very little empirical evidence supporting its relative importance in the case of Malaysia. Two recent studies that have attempted to quantify its relative importance in attracting FDI into

Table 6.6   Trends in FDI in Malaysia, 1991–2006

	Net* FDI in Malaysia, RM billion	Nominal GDP, RM billion	FDI as % of GDP	GFCF in current prices, RM billion	FDI as % of GFCF
1991	11.1	135.1	8.2	30.6	36.3
1992	13.1	150.7	8.7	53.5	24.5
1993	14.8	172.2	8.6	63.4	23.4
1994	12.0	195.5	6.1	76.4	15.7
1995	14.6	222.5	6.6	107.8	13.5
1996	18.4	253.7	7.2	121.4	15.1
1997	17.8	281.8	6.3	121.5	14.6
1998	10.6	283.2	3.8	76.0	14.0
1999	14.8	300.8	4.9	65.8	22.5
2000	14.4	343.2	4.2	87.7	16.4
2001	2.1	334.4	0.6	83.3	2.5
2002	12.2	362.0	3.4	83.8	14.2
2003	9.4	395.2	2.4	87.1	10.8
2004	17.6	450.2	3.9	91.8	19.1
2005	15.0	495.2	3.0	98.9	15.2
2006[e]	25.9	548.4	4.7	112.3	23.0

Notes:
* Net FDI is defined as inflows of FDI after taking account of outflows arising from the liquidation of FDI in Malaysia and loan repayments to related companies.
[e] Estimated figure for 2006.

Sources: 1991–2002 from Tham (2004, p. 191), 2003–06 updated from Central Bank of Malaysia for net FDI and GDP, and the Ministry of Finance, Malaysia for GFCF, *Economic Report*, Kuala Lumpur, various years.

Malaysia are Hasan (2004) and Sharma et al. (2004). In the case of the former, the three main determinants of FDI inflows into Malaysia from 1970 to 2000 were found to be the exchange rate, exports and infrastructure development (Hasan, 2004, p. 167). However, the proxy used to capture infrastructure development in Malaysia is the annual net developmental expenditure that covers the government's spending on infrastructure development as well as other aspects of social development such as education. It is therefore significantly overstated as the expenditure on infrastructure constituted approximately an average of 20 per cent of total development expenditure from 1991 to 2000 (Table 6.1). On the other hand, Sharma et al. (2004, p. 13) found a negative and significant relationship between FDI inflows and physical infrastructure for Malaysia from 1971 to 2004. This unexpected relationship is probably due to the use

Table 6.7   FDI inflows into Malaysia by sectors, 1999–2004 (US$ million)

Sector	1999	2002	2004	1999 – 2004
Total	**3 895.1**	**3 203.4**	**4 624.2**	**18 537.5**
Manufacturing	1 946.3	897.0	3 508.0	9 592.9
Services	115.0	n.a.	1 678.5	2 752.0
Trade and commerce	n.a.	n.a.	450.4	605.4
Financial intermediation and services	n.a.	n.a.	1 118.7	1 880.7
Real estate	115.0	n.a.	23.0	159.5
Other services	n.a.	n.a.	86.4	106.4
Agriculture, fishery and forestry	n.a.	n.a.	13.8	− 53.5
Construction	n.a.	n.a.	− 23.0	− 29.0
Mining and quarrying	722.4	1 089.0	− 596.6	3 056.3
Others	1 111.4	1 217.4	43.4	3 218.8

Note: n.a. – not available.

Source: Malaysia (2006c).

of per capita electricity consumption as a proxy for infrastructure development. In contrast, openness was found to have a positive and significant impact on the inflows of FDI into Malaysia. It is possible that the difficulties in constructing a good proxy for infrastructure development may have contributed to the shortage of empirical evidence on its role in attracting FDI into Malaysia.

Due to the lack of empirical evidence, the role of infrastructure development in attracting FDI into Malaysia will be inferred from the sectoral pattern of FDI and its location in the country. Overall, the share of the manufacturing sector in the total inflows of FDI into Malaysia was about 65 per cent of total FDI for the period 1990 until 1997 (Tham, 2004, p. 192). However, this fell to about 52 per cent for the period 1999–2004 due to the loss of comparative advantage in labour-intensive manufacturing while the shortage of skilled workers in the country also hindered the government's drive to attract technology-oriented FDI into the manufacturing sector (Table 6.7).

Within manufacturing, approved investment in the electrical and electronics (E&E) subsector has fluctuated over time, from RM 3.7 billion in 1990 to RM 10.9 billion in 2005, although its share in total approved investment in manufacturing increased progressively for the period 1990–2000 (Table 6.8). Despite the drop in its share in 2005, it still constitutes half of the total approved investment in manufacturing.

Table 6.8 FDI shares* in manufacturing, by industry (%)

Industry	1990	1995	2000	2005
Food	1.85	1.31	2.93	3.22
Beverages & Tobacco	0.05	0.02	0.59	0.37
Textiles & Textile Products	4.96	5.18	3.98	0.86
Leather & Leather Products	0.17	0.24	0.02	0.02
Wood & Wood Products	3.08	8.12	0.85	0.46
Furniture & Fixtures	0.72	1.21	0.58	0.37
Paper, Printing & Publishing	2.12	1.07	1.15	0.73
Chemicals & Chemical Products	9.80	9.87	3.19	5.13
Petroleum Products	15.33	14.40	9.58	0.78
Rubber Products	0.31	0.84	3.63	1.27
Plastic Products	2.42	1.94	1.58	3.51
Non-Metallic Mineral Products	1.02	13.72	8.30	0.37
Basic Metal Products	25.75	5.19	2.33	2.54
Fabricated Metal Products	1.73	3.12	0.89	1.51
Machinery Manufacturing	6.62	2.53	2.28	18.00
Electrical & Electronic Products	**21.40**	**25.96**	**55.48**	**49.76**
Transport Equipment	1.59	5.05	1.48	2.97
Scientific & Measuring Equipment	0.45	0.03	0.90	8.05
Miscellaneous	0.63	0.20	0.28	0.07

Note: * FDI shares refer to FDI in each industry as a share of total FDI (in %). FDI refers to the approvals given (not the applications filed).

Source: Unpublished data obtained from Malaysian Industrial Development Authority (MIDA).

The regional distribution of FDI within Malaysia shows a consistent bias towards the three relatively rich states on the west coast of Peninsular Malaysia: Selangor, Penang and Johor due to their relatively good infrastructure and amenities (Tham, 2004, p. 196). The two major electronics hubs are located in Penang and the Klang Valley in Selangor. The first FTZ was established at the Bayan Lepas FTZ in Penang in 1972 and attracted eight multinationals in the electronics industry to set up their offshore bases in Penang (*Penang Development News*, January 2003, p. 1).[7] Subsequently, another FTZ was developed on the Seberang Perai side of Penang, or the Prai FTZ to further increase FDI in the state. Similarly, Selangor also utilized FTZs to attract FDI with Sungai-Way FTZs as one of the pioneer FTZs in the state.[8] Out of the 12 FTZs in the country, four are devoted to electronics: Batu Berendam (Malacca), Hulu Kelang (Kuala Lumpur), Bayan Lepas (Penang) and Prai (Penang). In addition, there are industrial parks specifically for electronics, such as the Technology Park (Kuala Lumpur), Kulim Hi-Tech Park (Kedah), Shah Alam (Selangor) and Subang Hi-Tech Park (Selangor).[9]

Since both the input and output of the E&E sector are trade dependent, it is not surprising that most of the FDI in this sector is located in Penang and the Klang Valley in the state of Selangor. These two states are well served by roads, ports and airports. Thus, although the government's planning and investment in infrastructure development was not targeted at attracting FDI *per se*, nevertheless the overall development of roads, ports and airports has enhanced the locational advantages of the country. However, there are clearly other factors that can influence the inflow of FDI into the country besides infrastructure development. For example, the amount of investment approved for this sector fell from RM 9.2 billion in 1996 to RM 2.9 and RM 1.9 billion respectively in 1997 and 1998 due to the negative impact of the financial crisis. Post-crisis, approved investment in this sector increased steadily to a peak of RM 10.2 billion in 2001 before falling to RM 4 and RM 3.6 billion in 2002 and 2003 respectively despite the continued development of roads, ports and airports. It subsequently increased to RM 6.9 and RM 10.9 billion in 2004 and 2005 respectively. Therefore, while infrastructure development may have contributed towards the inflow of FDI in the E&E subsector, other factors also affected the foreign investors' interest in this sector.

Trade Patterns in Manufactured Goods

International trade is critical for Malaysia's economy due to its relatively small domestic market. Malaysia was the nineteenth-largest exporting country and the twenty-third-largest importer in 2006, according to the WTO's *International Trade Report* for 2006.

Malaysia's push to industrialize since the early 1970s through the liberalization of investment and trade has led to a dramatic shift in its exports. Although Malaysia was predominantly a primary commodity producer at the time of Independence in 1957, manufactured goods have grown progressively to be more important in its trade structure. By 1990, manufactured goods accounted for 84 per cent of total exports and their share grew to 94 per cent in 2005 (Table 6.9). Similarly, manufactured imports also commanded a high share of total imports, increasing from 90 per cent of total imports to 99 per cent for the same duration (Table 6.9).

Figure 6.1 presents the trade flows in manufactures between Malaysia and the world. Malaysia was generally a net exporter of manufactures throughout the period 1990 to 2006. The 1990s witnessed a continued expansion of exports and imports. Figure 6.1 shows that the gap between

Table 6.9   International trade in manufactures (%)

Year	Share of manufactures in total exports	Share of manufactures in total imports
1990	84.09	90.26
1991	83.63	88.81
1992	73.00	88.29
1993	87.99	81.96
1994	84.28	81.87
1995	84.32	81.80
1996	80.53	79.50
1997	79.30	79.17
1998	83.50	82.26
1999	84.19	81.20
2000	82.74	85.93
2001	95.29	96.29
2002	96.25	97.13
2003	95.51	99.83
2004	95.18	99.31
2005	93.74	99.48

Note: Refer to Appendix 6A.2 for trade classification.

Source: Calculated from Bank Negara Malaysia, *Quarterly Economic Bulletin*, various years.

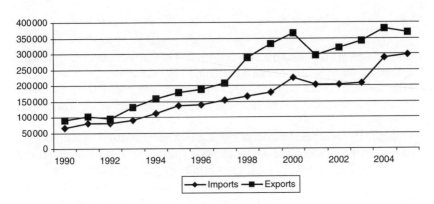

Note: The values of imports (M) and exports (X) are deflated by the import price and export price indices based on constant 1980 prices.

Sources: Bank Negara Malaysia, *Quarterly Economic Bulletin*, various years; Department of Statistics, *Malaysia: External Trade Statistics*, various years.

Figure 6.1   Total imports and exports in manufacturing (RM million)

Table 6.10   Manufacturing export structure (%)

Industry	1990	1995	2000	2005
Food	9.93	7.94	4.65	6.99
Beverages & Tobacco	0.11	0.19	0.28	0.68
Textiles & Textile Products	5.46	4.07	3.81	2.99
Leather & Leather Products	0.02	0.06	0.03	0.03
Wood & Wood Products	10.15	5.65	3.14	1.93
Furniture & Fixtures	0.52	1.09	1.42	1.53
Paper, Printing & Publishing	0.46	0.37	0.31	0.39
Chemicals & Chemical Products	1.27	2.00	2.23	5.77
Petroleum Products	13.38	4.40	5.18	9.16
Rubber Products	3.98	2.41	0.93	1.65
Plastic Products	0.19	0.69	0.99	2.10
Non-Metallic Mineral Products	0.60	0.52	0.29	0.30
Basic Metal Products	2.05	1.51	1.35	2.45
Fabricated Metal Products	0.63	0.90	0.72	1.15
Machinery Manufacturing	3.51	11.98	20.92	20.96
Electrical & Electronic Products	**25.76**	**34.24**	**32.98**	**35.56**
Transport Equipment	2.17	2.51	0.69	1.40
Scientific & Measuring Equipment	1.20	1.38	1.59	2.46
Miscellaneous	2.84	2.24	1.82	2.83

Note: Refer to Appendix 6A.2 for trade classification.

Source: Calculated from the *Malaysia: External Trade Statistics*, various years.

the two has grown considerably since 1997. The pattern of trade in manufactured goods in Malaysia can be explained by several key factors, namely, (i) the composition of manufactured goods exported, (ii) FDI in the manufacturing sector, and (iii) exchange rate movements before the imposition of the ringgit peg in 1998.

Table 6.10 presents the composition of exports in total manufactured exports. In 1990, the largest groups contributing to total manufactured exports are E&E (26 per cent), petroleum products (13 per cent), wood products (10 per cent) and food (10 per cent) in 1990. Only E&E has remained a key contributor to exports over the period of study. Traditional sectors (mainly resource based) such as food, petroleum and wood products have declining shares of total manufactured exports over time, while modern sectors such as E&E and machinery command increasing shares of total exports. By 2005, the shares of E&E and machinery manufacturing had increased to 36 per cent and 21 per cent, respectively.

Table 6.11 Destinations of Malaysia's E&E exports, 2004

Destination	Value (US$)	Share (%)
China	2 421 005 571	5.58
China, Hong Kong SAR	5 212 470 273	12.01
Japan	3 660 090 162	8.44
Singapore	8 397 231 370	19.35
Thailand	1 658 097 243	3.82
USA	9 046 400 714	20.85
Sub-total		70.05
World	43 391 188 591	100.00

Source: UN COMTRADE database.

Generally, the shift toward a larger share of E&E as well as machinery-manufactured goods does not imply that Malaysia has moved into industries requiring skill- and capital-intensive production processes and thus no longer specializes in exporting unsophisticated, labour-intensive manufactures. Within the skill- and capital-intensive industries, Malaysia is still involved in relatively labour-intensive segments of component production and assembly activities (Devadason, 2006).

Despite efforts made to diversify the export base of the manufacturing sector, there is still a high concentration in the exports of E&E. Malaysia is the world's largest exporter of semiconductor devices and audio-visual equipment (Wong and Tuck, 2007). Principal markets for Malaysia's exports of electronics are the USA, Singapore, Hong Kong, China and Japan (Table 6.11).

Malaysia's manufactured exports in general are tied to the FDI in that sector. FDI and exports were found to be positively correlated during the period 1985–2002 (Malaysia, 2006c, p. 131). In fact, the share of foreign establishments (comprising foreign-controlled companies and the Malaysian branches of limited companies) in total manufactured exports increased from 64 per cent in 1990 to 73 per cent in 1995 (Tham, 2004, p. 220). This share subsequently fell marginally to 70 per cent during the period 2000 until 2002 (Malaysia, 2006c, p. 131). There are currently more than 900 E&E companies operating in Malaysia with total exports amounting to US$76.6 billion. In 2006, the 17 US-based member companies of the Malaysian-American Electronics Industry Association exported about US$19.2 billion worth of electronics components and parts, representing 63 per cent of Malaysia's total exports to the USA (MIDA, 2007). Since these exports from the TNCs operating in Malaysia are part of the regional production networks, they also have high import content. E&E imports,

Table 6.12   Manufacturing import structure (%)

Industry	1990	1995	2000	2005
Food	5.92	3.92	3.49	4.75
Beverages & Tobacco	0.34	0.26	0.20	0.67
Textiles & Textile Products	3.67	2.31	1.38	1.34
Leather & Leather Products	0.07	0.17	0.08	0.12
Wood & Wood Products	0.13	0.22	0.29	0.32
Furniture & Fixtures	0.13	0.10	0.11	0.30
Paper, Printing & Publishing	1.79	1.60	1.08	1.21
Chemicals & Chemical Products	5.21	4.30	4.25	7.87
Petroleum Products	4.50	1.87	4.01	7.30
Rubber Products	0.62	0.58	0.69	0.85
Plastic Products	2.52	2.01	1.97	2.53
Non-Metallic Mineral Products	0.67	0.86	0.31	0.28
Basic Metal Products	5.53	5.68	4.19	6.30
Fabricated Metal Products	2.04	1.61	1.43	1.61
Machinery Manufacturing	15.65	15.94	13.57	16.80
Electrical & Electronic Products	**21.67**	**29.55**	**38.38**	**36.03**
Transport Equipment	8.80	7.22	5.52	4.45
Scientific & Measuring Equipment	2.78	2.38	2.70	2.87
Miscellaneous	1.82	1.49	1.77	1.61

Note: Refer to Appendix 6A.2 for trade classification.

Source: Calculated from the *Malaysia: External Trade Statistics*, various years.

which accounted for 36 per cent of total manufactured imports in 2005, remains as the dominant subsector within manufactured imports since 1990 (Table 6.12).

Given the dependence of Malaysian exports on electronics exports, the country's trade volume is inevitably vulnerable to the global electronics cycle. For example, the global downturn in 1995/96 due to excess capacity contributed towards the deterioration in export growth in 1995/96 just before the onset of the financial crisis (Figure 6.1; Doraisami, 2004, p. 717). The subsequent upturn in the global electronics cycle between 1999 and 2000 enabled the recovery of electronics exports, thereby contributing towards the V-shaped recovery of the economy in 1999 after the economic recession in 1998 as a result of the crisis. Another downturn in the global electronics cycle in 2001/2002 (Matthews, 2005, p. 25) again negatively affected the exports and imports of the country, as shown in Figure 6.1.

Before the ringgit was pegged to the US dollar on 1 September 1998, Malaysia adopted a basket peg system with the US dollar, yen and other currencies. However, in reality the US dollar had an overwhelming weight (Doraisami, 2004, p. 716) and its sharp appreciation between June 1995 and April 1997 led to an appreciation of the currencies that were pegged to it, including the ringgit, thereby leading to an erosion of the export competitiveness of Malaysia. This, together with the downturn of the global electronics cycle, was found to be responsible for the deterioration in export growth before the onset of the Asian financial crisis. The peg was maintained right up to July 2005 before it was dismantled and replaced by a managed float system based on a basket of currencies.

4.   INFRASTRUCTURE AND TRADE COSTS

Malaysia's investment in infrastructure has enabled the country to develop an extensive network of roads and railways as well as to upgrade and improve its port and airport facilities. This in turn has contributed towards the set of locational advantages that attracted FDI into the country. Although deterioration in some locational advantages such as labour cost and the shortage of skilled labour has reduced the relative attractiveness of Malaysia as a host economy after the financial crisis, there appears to be some recovery since 2005 with the liberalization of financial services for Islamic banking.

FDI in manufacturing has contributed positively towards exports. Apart from the evidence shown in Section 3, the Pearson correlation between FDI in the E&E subsector and the export volume of this subsector was also found to be positive and significant at the 10 per cent level.[10]

Before moving on to examine the impact of infrastructure development on trade costs, it is important to first highlight some salient features of trade costs in Malaysia. Given the significance of the E&E sector in Malaysia's exports, we focus our analysis on trade costs (here freight, insurance and tariff costs over time) only in this sector. Our analysis in the next few paragraphs shows two key features of trade costs in the country: (i) the bulk of trade costs in Malaysia comes from freight and insurance costs as tariff costs have considerably declined over the years; (ii) the E&E goods are exported by both sea and air and the choice of export mode (i.e. either by air or by sea freight), is product specific and hence price (freight charge) insensitive.

We employ the data of US imports of E&E goods from Malaysia.[11] This data set is used as the USA is a significant importer of Malaysia's E&E products. It is also the only set of data on trade costs that is available. The original data record the US imports from Malaysia using the HS code at

Table 6.13   *Average freight & insurance and tariff rates for Malaysia's*
             E&E exports to the USA, 1991 and 2004 (%)

SITC	Average freight and insurance rates						Average tariff rate	
	By sea		By air		By all modes			
	1991	2004	1991	2004	1991	2004	1991	2004
761	3.509	5.851	7.073	1.820	3.457	5.295	5.000	2.324
762	2.923	3.485	12.827	5.878	3.078	3.929	2.105	1.257
763	1.491	1.614	13.881	3.076	1.797	2.265	1.384	0.450
764	1.770	2.144	4.389	1.535	3.382	1.561	0.940	0.124
771	1.804	1.785	8.166	3.047	5.542	2.868	0.604	1.359
772	1.915	1.905	6.901	4.343	3.783	3.590	2.405	1.450
773	4.171	5.992	11.928	6.341	4.685	6.305	0.412	2.275
774	–	2.293	2.064	2.202	2.064	2.251	3.908	0.460
775	3.344	5.903	15.266	45.305	3.453	6.958	0.487	1.189
776	1.208	2.376	1.336	0.813	1.332	0.722	0.158	0.001
778	2.725	3.658	2.616	3.423	2.645	3.448	1.271	1.423

Note: Exports of SITC 774 by sea in 1991 were zero.

Source: Calculated from data provided by David Hummels.

the 10-digit level. It is converted into the SITC at the 3-digit level to make them comparable with the trade data used in Section 3 (Appendix Table 6A.3).

Bulk of Trade Costs from Freight and Insurance Costs

Table 6.13 shows that the average freight and insurance rates by all modes[12] is higher than the average tariff rates for almost all product categories within E&E in 1991, with the exception of SITC 761 and 774. By 2004, all the product categories under study record higher average freight and insurance rates than average tariff rates. The average tariff rate has fallen from 1991 to 2004 for most of the products shown in the table due to progressive tariff liberalization under Malaysia's current commitments in the WTO. There are some products where the average tariff rate was zero or close to zero in 2004 (SITC 763, 764, 774 and 776). However, the average freight and insurance rates show distinct differences by modes; i.e., while the average sea rates have tended to increase from 1991 to 2004, a converse pattern can be observed for the case of the average air rates, with the exception of SITC 774, 775 and 778.

Table 6.14   Mode of transport for Malaysia's E&E exports to the USA

SITC	1991			2004		
	% of exports moved by sea	% of exports moved by air	Average freight and insurance costs by all modes (%)	% of exports moved by sea	% of exports moved by air	Average freight and insurance costs by all modes (%)
761	98.8	1.2	3.457	86.7	13.3	2.324
762	98.0	2.0	3.078	82.3	17.7	1.257
763	97.3	2.7	1.797	54.1	45.9	0.450
764	64.2	35.8	3.382	14.5	85.5	0.124
771	40.8	59.2	5.542	20.2	79.8	1.359
772	62.2	37.8	3.783	27.6	72.4	1.450
773	93.2	6.8	4.685	24.2	75.8	2.275
774	–	100.0	2.064	53.5	46.5	0.460
775	99.8	0.2	3.453	97.4	2.6	1.189
776	0.5	99.5	1.332	0.1	99.9	0.001
778	35.7	64.3	2.645	44.6	55.4	1.423

Note: Exports of SITC 774 by sea in 1991 were zero.

Source: Calculated from data provided by David Hummels.

E&E Goods Exported by both Sea and Air, and Transport Mode is Product Specific

Malaysia's exports of E&E goods to the USA are delivered either by sea or by air. Table 6.14 shows the mode of transport of Malaysia's exports to the USA for the years 1991 and 2004. On the whole, electrical goods are shipped mainly by sea (e.g. SITC 761, 762 and 775) since these goods are generally bulky and durable, Electronic goods are mainly delivered by air (e.g. SITC 764, 776) because these goods are less bulky (and hence take relatively less space compared with electrical goods) and at the same time require greater storage care (for example, low temperature to be maintained during the shipment), which is easier when they are shipped by air. In addition, comparing exports for the two years, there is an overall increase in the use of air freight with the exception of SITC groups 774 and 778.

To investigate further whether the choice of transport mode is price sensitive or product specific and hence price insensitive, we conduct a simple regression analysis on the following equation using the same data set. This regression will test on the responsiveness of the choice of export mode on freight charges.

$$\ln(X_{it}^{air}/X_{it}^{ocean}) = a + b\ln(f_{it}^{air}/f_{it}^{ocean}) \qquad (6.1)$$

where

> i = product
> t = year
> a = constant
> (X^{air}/X^{ocean}) = relative exports of E&E by air to exports of E&E by ocean to the USA (in volume)
> (f^{air}/f^{ocean}) = relative average freight and insurance costs by air to average freight and insurance costs by ocean (in *ad valorem* terms)

The pooled results indicate that relative shipping costs significantly influence the relative quantity of exports moved by air. The relationship is negative, which signifies that the higher the relative average costs of air to ocean shipping, the lower the shipment of exports of E&E by air. The significant relationship between relative shipping costs and relative exports does not hold, however, when fixed effects are imposed (see Appendix Table 6A.4 for detailed regression results). The results support our earlier suggestion that while the E&E sector as a whole may respond to relative changes in freight charges (the pooled results), some E&E goods are not sensitive to freight charges on the transport mode choice (the fixed effects results) but instead the export mode may be determined by other factors, such as the importance of cargo timeliness or the weight-to-value ratio (see Hummels, 2007).

The divergent results between the pooled and the fixed effect analysis may also be due to the shift in product composition within E&E exports of Malaysia to the USA over time. Appendix Table 6A.4 shows that while SITC 776 has generally constituted the largest export share within E&E, distinct shifts in product composition are observed for categories SITC 762, 763 and 764. Both the share of exports of SITC 762 and 763[13] have reduced with time, while the share of SITC 764 has grown in importance, with its share more than doubling between 1991 and 2004. SITC 764 has emerged as the leading export category in the recent past. Despite the shift in product composition, as mentioned above, the exports of E&E remain highly concentrated on a few products throughout the period of study. Export shares for SITC 771, 772, 773, 774, 775 and 778 remain hardly changed for the entire period (see Appendix Table 6A.5).

In 2004, the leading exports, based on their export share in total E&E exports, are SITC 764 followed by SITC 776. These two products contributed nearly 70 per cent of total E&E exports to the USA and they are exported mainly by air (see Table 6.14). The Third Industrial Master Plan has noted that electronics and information, communications and technology (ICT) products, being high-value and time-sensitive cargo, are mainly exported by air through Penang International Airport (60 per cent) and KLIA (40 per cent) as these two airports are located in the electronics hub in Penang and the Klang Valley in Selangor (Malaysia, 2006c, p. 710).

Development of Infrastructure and the Movement of E&E Goods across Borders

This section will examine how the development of roads and airports has expedited the export of E&E goods produced by the TNCs. Notably, the development of highways and expressways has facilitated the movement of electronics goods that are produced outside the FTZ in Bayan Lepas as well as the goods produced from the mainland to Penang International Airport. For example, Intel has five factories in Malaysia, three on Penang island and two at the Kulim Hi-Tech Park. There is a new factory being built in Kulim Hi-Tech Park that is scheduled for production in 2008/09. Semiconductor chips from Intel are exported through both Penang Airport (70 per cent) and KLIA (30 per cent) (interview, Intel).[14] With the North–South Expressway, Intel factories at the Kulim Hi-Tech Park in the north can reach Penang Airport faster. The estimated time saved is 45 minutes. The highway also provides an alternative route to KLIA for the export of goods in the event of any problem on the Penang bridge or for flexibility of flight connectivity and timing purposes. A recent bomb hoax caused the Penang bridge to be closed for more than two hours as well as a massive jam (*The Star*, 5 April 2007, p. 1). Goods rerouted to KLIA as a result of any jam on the Penang bridge would need five hours by the North–South expressway from Kulim Hi-Tech to KLIA instead of eight hours by the old trunk road.

Total cargo handled by Penang Airport increased steadily from 30.3 to 184.9 thousand tonnes from 1990 to 2004, and from 159.6 to 651.7 thousand tonnes from 1998 to 2004 for KLIA (Ministry of Transport, 2005). The total number of passengers increased from 1.9 million to 2.9 million from 1990 to 2006 in the case of Penang Airport, while in the case of KLIA it increased from 6.4 million in 1998 to 23.2 million in 2005. MASkargo, a wholly owned subsidiary of the national carrier, Malaysia Airlines (MAS), has doubled its cargo volume compared with the time when it operated out of the old international airport (or the Subang International Airport) (MASkargo, interview). Transshipment cargo was only 30 per cent of total cargo at the old airport while it is 55 per cent of total cargo at the new one. The setting up of KLIA has provided facilities and sufficient capacity to increase business.

However, several factors may lessen the positive impact of the infra-structure's development on trade costs. First and foremost is the traffic congestion on the island as land transport is a slow and burdensome process due largely to the congestion on the Penang bridge (SERI, 2004, p. 4). The Penang bridge is overloaded with vehicles and any accident or security scare can paralyse the traffic and have a strong adverse impact on the cycle time of air and sea freight delivery for the manufacturers located on the mainland such as at Kulim and Sungai Petani. The proposed second Penang bridge that is estimated to cost RM 3 billion is a 24 km bridge linking Batu Kawan, Seberang Prai to Batu Maung on Penang Island. It will ease the traffic congestion at the current bridge as well as shorten the distance that is taken to the airport since its link on the island is located nearer to Penang Airport than the existing bridge.

Second, the security of freight trucks is a problem as trucks carrying valuable cargo such as semiconductor chips are susceptible to hijacking. Incidences of cargo theft in warehouses even within the vicinity of the airport have also increased security risks in the country itself. From 1999 until 2001, it was reported that there were 49 cases of hijacking of trucks and 69 incidences of warehouse break-ins that were worth RM 8.6 billion and RM 6.8 billion, respectively (*New Sunday Times*, 2 December 2001, F2). While these incidences have reportedly reduced over time, security and hijacking continues to be a problem and increases the costs of trucking relative to neighbouring competitors who do not have such a problem (interview, AFAM, DHL). Intel also emphasized the need to increase the security level in order to reduce road hijacking and warehouse robbery (interview, Intel).

Third is the connectivity of airports in Malaysia. This is important as it affects the port-to-port charges, which are the largest component of the trade costs in door-to-door services provided by the global integrators. Penang International Airport is a medium-sized airport with 15 passenger airlines flying through the airport as opposed to 83 passenger airlines flying through Changi Airport. Further, there are only ten scheduled cargo operators at Penang Airport compared to the 21 airlines with all-cargo or with passenger-cum-all-cargo operations that operate scheduled services into Singapore. KLIA has 46 passenger airlines and six cargo airlines operating through this airport, with four more passenger airlines scheduled to operate there in 2007. Due to the better connectivity at Changi Airport, port-to-port charges for flying through Changi can be lower than flying through KLIA or even Penang (interview, DHL). This is despite the cost of trucking the goods down to Singapore (including the security costs), and the lower labour cost in Malaysia compared to Singapore. It is reported that as much as 25–30 per cent of air-freight throughput is channelled through neighbouring airports (Malaysia, 2006c, p. 727). Intel also reported that some of their chips from Malaysia are exported through Singapore due to the flexibility of flight connectivity and timing of flights in Changi that suit their needs (interview, Intel).

The national carrier, Malaysia Airlines (MAS), is currently using code-share agreements instead of being a member of global alliances to forge international air links. It has been reported that MAS is switching from its current point-to-point expansion plan to a hub-and-spoke model, with the assistance from its code-share partners to enable it to reach further, faster and cheaper (*New Straits Times*, 7 April 2007).

Fourth is the speed of processing of documents at the airports. Computerized customs clearance is provided at Port Klang and at KLIA. Firms in the FTZs in Penang can have the goods processed for export within 3–6 hours since they do not have to pay any duties.[15] However, firms outside the FTZs do not have 100 per cent paperless processing and customs clearance takes much longer than in the FTZs. Moreover, the current electronic data interchange (EDI) system that is in use is not inter-active, and is not seamlessly integrated into the computer system of various government departments and cargo terminal operators. Given that IT applications are one of the key components in maintaining competitive-ness, the current system is at a disadvantage compared to the advanced interactive EDI systems that are being used by other international airports in Singapore and Hong Kong.

5.   CONCLUSION

Malaysia's investment in infrastructure has developed an extensive road system complemented by railways, ports and airport development. This development has served to attract FDI into the country and to increase exports as well as imports. Consequently, the export of manufactured goods has become progressively important in terms of its contribution to total exports. In particular, the share of E&E goods in total manufactures has increased over time.

Given that the two electronic hubs are Penang in the north and the Klang Valley in the centre of the peninsular, and the importance of time in the delivery cycle of these goods, E&E goods are exported mainly through Penang Airport and KLIA. Although Penang Airport is the nearest airport for the E&E manufacturers from the northern part of Malaysia, the goods are often trucked down to KLIA and even to Singapore for export. Given that Penang Airport handled 222 000 tonnes of cargo and 2.8 million passengers in 2005, rather than its capacity of

360 000 tonnes and 5 million passengers, improving the connectivity of the airport is of paramount importance. It will require the national carrier, MAS, as well as other airlines, to expand their networks by increasing flights to business hubs in India and China as well as other countries. Reducing the landing and parking charges will also provide incentives for new carriers to use the two major international airports in the country. It will also require the airport to create security measures and more secure facilities as well as improved usage of e-logistics and an ICT-based process for customs to encourage more freighters and wide-body aircrafts to fly into Penang.

In the medium- and longer-term interest of the country, Penang Airport can be further developed to serve industries in the northern part of the country while KLIA can be used to serve the southern part of the country, especially with the development of the Iskandar Development Region in the south. KLIA's capacity is unlikely to be exhausted in the short or medium term, given its expansion plans up to 2020.

However, in the case of Penang, the building of the second bridge that will link Batu Kawan at Seberang Perai to Batu Maung near Penang Airport is the first major infrastructure activity in Penang since the first bridge was constructed in 1985 and the last stretch of the North–South expressway was completed in the early 1990s. Hence it is expected to stimulate industrial development at Seberang Prai. This, coupled with appropriate FDI policies to improve the FDI climate of Penang, will increase the demand for airport facilities at Penang Airport. Thus the twin strategies of expanding the number of cargo freighters and commercial planes flying into Penang Airport as well as expanding the physical capacity of Penang Airport will contribute towards lowering the trade costs of exporting and importing E&E goods in Malaysia.

NOTES

*   This report forms part of the Asian Development Bank Institute (ADBI)'s project on 'Infrastructure's Role in Reducing Trade Costs'. The authors have benefited greatly from the feedback of colleagues and participants at the Finalization Conference that was held on 25–26 June in Tokyo.
1.   Malaysia inherited a relatively good system of rail and road infrastructure at the time of Independence.
2.   This refers to the latest of the five-year plans in the country that are used to guide the medium-term development of Malaysia.
3.   Malaysia is a federation of 13 states and three federal territories.
4.   STOLports are Short Take–Off Landing airports, which serve communities in the less accessible areas.
5.   FTZs were initially areas specifically established for manufacturing companies that produce or assemble products mainly for export. FTZs enable these export-oriented

companies to enjoy minimal customs formalities and duty-free import of raw materials, component parts, machinery and equipment required directly in the manufacturing process as well as minimal formalities in exporting their finished products. Subsequently, FTZs were divided into free industrial zones (FIZs), where manufacturing and assembly takes place, and free commercial zones (FCZs) for warehousing and commercial purposes. There are 14 FCZs in the country.

6. Before 1986, foreign equity was limited to 30 per cent under the New Economic Policy (NEP) that was promulgated in 1970 to promote growth and redistribution.
7. They are Advanced Micro Devices Export Sdn Bhd, Agilent Technologies Sdn Bhd, Clarion (M) Sdn Bhd, Fairchild Semiconductor Sdn Bhd, Hitachi Semiconductor Sdn Bhd, Intel Malaysia Sdn Bhd, Osram Opto Semiconductors Sdn Bhd and Robert Bosch (M) Sdn Bhd.
8. See Appendix Table 6A.1 for a list of the FIZs in Malaysia.
9. The Technology Park (established in 1998) occupies 120 acres and caters for R&D, while the Kulim Hi-Tech Park (established in 1993) occupies 1486 hectares and caters specifically for high-tech manufacturing (Lai and Yap, 2004).
10. The correlation coefficient for the 13 observations spanning the period 1991 to 2003 was 0.487.
11. We thank David Hummels for providing us with the data.
12. The average freight and insurance costs are expressed in *ad valorem* terms, namely the cost of shipping relative to the value of the good (see Hummels, 2007).
13. Note that both products of SITC 762 and 763 are mainly shipped by sea while SITC 764 has shifted its mode from ocean to air (see Table 6.14). Thus the shifts in product composition over time are reflected in larger exports of E&E products using air shipment relative to ocean.
14. Another firm that is also producing on the mainland side of Penang also stated that they exported their goods through Penang Airport (60 per cent), KLIA (30 per cent) and Singapore (10 per cent).
15. Apparently having to pay duties slows down customs clearance considerably.

REFERENCES

Asian Development Bank, Japan Bank for International Cooperation and World Bank (2005), *Connecting East Asia: A New Framework for Infrastructure*, Manila, Tokyo and Washington, DC: Asian Development Bank, Japan Bank for International Cooperation and World Bank.

Central Bank (2003), *Annual Report 2003*, Kuala Lumpur: Central Bank.

Central Bank (2006), *Annual Report 2006*, Kuala Lumpur: Central Bank.

Devadason, E. (2006), 'Aspects of labour demand and international trade: evidence from Malaysian manufacturing', unpublished thesis, Kuala Lumpur: University of Malaya.

Doraisami, A. (2004), 'Trade causes of the Asian crisis: the Malaysian experience', *World Economy*, **27**(5), 715–26.

Hasan Zubair (2004), 'Determinants of FDI flows to developing economies: evidence from Malaysia', In H.S. Kehal (ed.), *Foreign Direct Investment in Developing Countries*, Basingstoke: Palgrave Macmillan, ch. 8.

Hummels, D. (2007), 'Transportation costs and international trade in the second era of globalization', *Journal of Economic Perspectives*, **21**(3), 131–54.

Lai, M.-C. and S.-F. Yap (2004), 'Technology development in Malaysia and the newly industrializing economies: a comparative analysis', *Asia-Pacific Development Journal*, **11**(2), 53–80.

Malaysia (undated), *Transport Statistics Malaysia: 2003–2004*, Putrajaya: Ministry of Transport.

Malaysia (1991), *The Second Outline Perspective Plan: 1991–2000*, Kuala Lumpur: National Printing Department.

Malaysia (1996), *Seventh Malaysia Plan 1996–2000*, Kuala Lumpur: National Printing Company of Malaysia.

Malaysia (2001a), *The Third Outline Perspective Plan: 2001–2010*. Kuala Lumpur: National Printing Company of Malaysia.

Malaysia (2001b), *Eighth Malaysia Plan 2001–2005*, Kuala Lumpur: National Printing Company of Malaysia.

Malaysia (2006a), *Ninth Malaysia Plan 2006–2010*, Kuala Lumpur: National Printing Company of Malaysia.

Malaysia (2006b), *Malaysian Maritime Yearbook, 2005/2006*, Klang: Malaysian Shipowners' Association (MASA).

Malaysia (2006c), *The Third Industrial Master Plan: 2006–2020*, Kuala Lumpur: National Printing Company of Malaysia.

Malaysia Airports Holdings Berhad (MAHB) (2005), *Annual Report 2005*, available at http://www.malaysiaairports.com.my, accessed 25 September 2008.

Matthews, John A. (2005), 'Strategy and the crystal cycle', *California Management Review*, **47**(2), 6–32.

MIDA (2007), Information obtained from the website, www.mida.gov.my.

Ministry of Transport (2005), *Transport Statistics Malaysia 2003–2004*, Putrajaya: Ministry of Transport.

Nesathurai, A. (2003), 'Key players in the logistics chain', available at http://www.mima.gov.my/mima/htmls/papers/pdf/nesa/logchain.pdf, accessed 11 July 2008.

Sharma, K., J. Nayagam and H.H. Chung (2004), 'Foreign direct investment in Malaysia: trends, patterns and determinants', Working Paper Series No. 14/06, Charles Sturt University, Faculty of Commerce, Australia.

Socio Economic & Environmental Research Institute (SERI) (2004), 'Logistics in the Penang industrial zones', *Economic Briefing to the Penang State Government*, **6**(7), 1–6.

Tham Siew Yean (2004), 'Malaysia', in D.H. Brooks and H. Hill (eds), *Managing FDI in a Globalizing Economy: Asian experiences*, Basingstoke: Palgrave Macmillan, ch. 6, pp. 189–238.

Wong Koi Nyen and Tuck Cheong Tang (2007), 'Foreign direct investment and electronics exports: exploratory evidence from Malaysia's top five electronics exports', *Economics Bulletin*, **6**(14), 1–8.

World Bank (2003), *Benchmarking FDI Competitiveness in Asia*, Washington, DC: World Bank.

Newspapers

New Sunday Times, 2 December 2001, 'Insider tip-offs aid hijackings', Focus, p. 2.
The Star, 5 April 2007, 'Traffic snarl', p. 1.
New Straits Times, 7 April 2007, 'The right connection', Biznews, p. 45.

Interviews Conducted

DHL, Air-freight Forwarders' Association of Malaysia (AFAM), Intel, MASKargo, and an anonymous logistics manager of a TNC in Malaysia.

APPENDIX

Table 6A.1   Free industrial zones (FIZs)

No.	FIZ	State
1	Sungai Way	Selangor
2	Teluk Panglima Garang	
3	Port Klang	
4	Hulu Kelang	Wilayah Persekutuan
5	Bayan Lepas	Penang
6	Prai	
7	Peringgit I, II, III	Melaka
8	Tanjung Keling	
9	Batu Berendam	
10	Johor Port	Johor
11	Port of Tanjung Pelepas	
12	Sama Jaya	Sarawak

Source: Malaysian Industrial Development Authority (MIDA).

Table 6A.2   Trade classification

Industry group	SITC (Rev. 3)
Food	011, 012, 016, 017, 022, 023, 024, 025, 034, 035, 036, 037, 041, 042, 043, 045, 046, 047, 048, 054, 056, 057, 058, 059, 061, 062 071, 072, 073, 074, 075, 081, 091, 098, 222, 223, 411, 421, 422, 431
Beverages & Tobacco	111, 112, 121, 122
Textiles & Textile Products	261, 263, 264, 265, 266, 267, 268, 269, 651, 652, 653, 654, 655, 656, 657, 658, 659, 841, 842, 843, 844, 845, 846, 848
Leather & Leather Products	611, 612, 613, 211, 212
Wood & Wood Products	633, 634, 635, 244, 245, 246, 247, 248
Furniture & Fixtures	821
Paper, Printing & Publishing	641, 642, 251
Chemicals & Chemical Products	511, 512, 513, 514, 515, 516, 522, 523, 524, 525, 531, 532, 533, 541, 542, 551, 553, 554, 562, 591, 592, 593, 597, 598
Petroleum Products	333, 334, 335
Rubber Products	621, 625, 629, 231, 232
Plastic Products	571, 572, 573, 574, 575, 579, 581, 582, 583
Non-Metallic Mineral Products	661, 662, 663
Basic Metal Products	671, 672, 673, 674, 675, 676, 677, 678, 679, 681, 682, 683, 684, 685, 686, 687, 689
Fabricated Metal Products	691, 692, 693, 694, 695, 696, 697, 699 711, 712, 713, 714, 716, 718, 721, 722, 723, 724, 725, 731, 733, 735, 737, 741, 742, 743, 744, 745, 746, 747, 748, 749, 751,
Machinery Manufacturing	752, 759
Electrical & Electronic Products	**761, 762, 763, 764, 771, 772, 773, 774, 775, 776, 778**
Transport Equipment	781, 782, 783, 784, 785, 786, 791, 792, 793
Scientific & Measuring Equipment	871, 872, 873, 874, 881, 882, 883, 884, 885
Miscellaneous	892, 893, 894, 895, 896, 897, 898, 899

Note: The Standard International Trade Classification (SITC) Revision 2 was revised to Revision 3 in 1988.

Source: Based on the classification adopted by the Malaysia Industrial Development Authority (MIDA).

Table 6A.3   Description of electrical and electronics products

No.	Rev. 3	Product description
		(76) Telecommunications and Sound-Recording or Reproducing Apparatus and Equipment
1	761	Television receivers with radio-broadcast receivers, sound recorders or reproducers
2	762	Radio-broadcast receivers with sound recorders or reproducers
3	763	Sound recorders or reproducers; television image and sound recorders or reproducers; prepared unrecorded media
4	764	Telecommunications equipment, n.e.s; their parts, and accessories used in Division 76
		(77) Electrical Machinery, Apparatus and Appliances, n.e.s. and Electrical Parts Thereof (Including Non-Electrical Counterparts, n.e.s., of Electrical Household-Type Equipment)
5	771	Electric power machinery (other than rotating electric plant), and parts thereof
6	772	Electrical apparatus, resistors, other than heating resistors; printed circuits; switchboard and control panels, n.e.s., and parts n.e.s.
7	773	Equipment for distributing electricity, n.e.s.
8	774	Electro-diagnostic apparatus for medical, surgical, dental or veterinary sciences and radiological apparatus
9	775	Household type, electrical and non-electrical equipment, n.e.s.
10	776	Thermionic valves and tubes; photocells; etc., and parts thereof, n.e.s.
11	778	Electrical machinery and apparatus, n.e.s.

Note: As for Appendix 6A.2.

Table 6A.4   Results for regression estimations

	Equation (6.1)	
	Pooled	Fixed effects
constant	−1.511***	−2.174***
	(0.255)	(0.116)
f^{air}/f^{ocean}	−1.239***	−0.026
	(0.231)	(0.153)
R^2	0.177	0.177
No. of observations	143	143

Notes:
The dependent variable is the export quantities shipped by air relative to ocean for equation (6.1) and total exports in quantities for equation (6.2).
Figures in parentheses represent standard errors.
***: significant at 1 per cent.

Table 6A.5   Percentage share of each product in E&E exports, 1991–2004

SITC	1991	1992	1993	1994	1995	1996	1997	1998	1999	2000	2001	2002	2003	2004
761	3.73	4.17	4.76	4.88	4.00	4.51	4.74	5.73	6.98	6.20	7.59	12.10	9.48	7.59
762	17.27	18.32	16.61	16.65	15.10	13.03	10.64	11.26	9.77	7.71	8.19	7.52	7.54	7.34
763	13.60	14.20	13.91	15.32	12.88	11.50	10.36	10.08	9.81	10.14	11.59	8.10	8.09	8.12
764	**14.81**	**14.89**	**12.58**	**12.23**	**10.95**	**11.83**	**10.22**	**11.62**	**12.75**	**18.36**	**22.60**	**25.50**	**35.96**	**36.66**
771	1.77	1.62	1.19	0.94	1.04	1.37	1.72	1.56	1.28	1.21	1.10	0.82	0.97	1.11
772	1.13	1.25	1.55	1.52	1.23	1.52	2.24	2.82	2.26	2.24	1.57	1.56	1.52	1.82
773	0.27	0.28	0.27	0.30	0.34	0.34	0.33	0.60	0.47	0.30	0.30	0.32	0.24	0.15
774	0.02	0.02	0.02	0.01	0.01	0.01	0.05	0.04	0.02	0.01	0.01	0.16	0.13	0.15
775	0.58	0.94	0.97	0.97	0.85	1.08	1.02	1.16	0.75	0.76	0.96	1.04	1.44	2.77
776	**45.16**	**42.41**	**46.31**	**45.39**	**51.55**	**53.13**	**56.48**	**52.39**	**54.10**	**51.72**	**44.47**	**41.31**	**33.20**	**32.58**
778	1.66	1.89	1.84	1.77	2.04	1.69	2.20	2.73	1.82	1.35	1.63	1.57	1.41	1.71

Source: Calculated from data provided by David Hummels.

7. Infrastructure development in a fast-growing economy: the People's Republic of China

Liqiang Ma and Jinkang Zhang

1. INTRODUCTION

The People's Republic of China (PRC) has experienced high economic growth driven by exports and investment since its reform and opening-up policy implemented in 1978. The fast-growing economy calls for rapid infrastructure development. In order to facilitate trade and investment, a large amount of investment has been allocated to transport infrastructure construction since 1978, which has achieved unprecedented development. In particular, investment in coastal ports construction has been enlarged in order to enhance the role of ports as gateways to international markets. Furthermore, local governments have made big efforts to improve physical infrastructure in order to attract foreign direct investment (FDI), which is mostly involved in exporting activities. The majority of export-oriented FDI flowed to coastal regions which have geographical advantages for exporting activities; these coastal regions subsequently became important manufacturing and exporting bases of China. Due to this uneven regional development, infrastructure and logistics services in coastal regions are much more advanced than in inland regions. However, as labour costs and land costs are becoming more expensive in costal areas, foreign investors are looking for new manufacturing locations in inland China, which is endowed with cheaper labour, cheaper land and abundant natural resources. Thus transport costs from inland areas to costal ports is an important part in total trade costs when enterprises are doing international business in inland areas. However, transport costs for goods originating from inland provinces are very high due to poor logistics infrastructure[1] and logistics services.[2] Congestion occurs due to the shortfall of transport capacity, which is caused by overwhelming traffic growth driven by trade and the relatively lagged expansion of capacities in various transport infrastructure. High transport costs constitute an impediment to trade and investment in the country.

Meanwhile, other trade costs in addition to transport costs (freight, insurance and time costs) occur when doing business internationally, such as policy barriers (tariffs and non-tariff barriers), information costs, contract enforcement costs, legal and regulatory costs, local distribution costs (wholesale and retail), and costs associated with using different currencies (Anderson and van Wincoop, 2004). As trade liberalization globally continues to reduce policy trade barriers, the effective rate of protection provided by transport costs is higher than that provided by tariffs (Hummels, 1999a and b). In particular, tariff costs of international trade have reduced largely for China after its accession to the World Trade Organization (WTO). Transport costs are therefore a more important component in total trade costs.

This chapter tackles the issues of infrastructure and trade costs in the context of China. It focuses on China's rapid growth and regional disparity, the major industrial and export clusters, rapid congestion in seaports and inland provinces, and subsequent infrastructure needs. The case study of China's exports to the USA in this chapter tests how far the tariff costs have been reduced compared with transport costs in the last two decades. Another case study on China's seaports provides evidence that infrastructure development has a significant role in facilitating trade and lowering trade costs. The study on the Port of Shanghai focuses on the role of the port as an export and logistics centre for its hinterland, and how high the transport cost is from the inland province to the port. The study on the Port of Shenzhen depicts a case where that port forms crucial infrastructure for special economic zones, which conduct export-oriented activities. A special focus will be on how congestion at seaports and on inland railways, highways or waterways impedes trade growth and increases trade costs.

The rest of the chapter is organized as follows. Section 2 overviews infrastructure development in the fast-growing economy; Section 3 studies the issue of trade costs using US imports from China as a case study; Section 4 focuses on China's coastal ports study: Shanghai and Shenzhen; Section 5 offers concluding remarks, which provide policy recommendations based on the findings from the study.

2. INFRASTRUCTURE DEVELOPMENT IN THE FAST-GROWING ECONOMY

China covers roughly 9.6 million km^2 with a population of 1314.5 million in 2006. The geographical features range from the west, filled with mountains, plateaux and deserts, the centre, full of valleys, rivers and meadows, to the east, endowed with relatively flat areas (see Appendix Figure 7A.1).

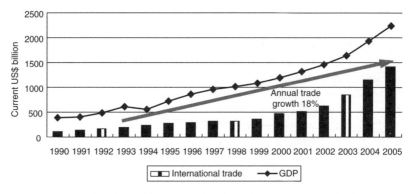

Source: Based on data from China Economic Information Network: http://cei.gov.cn.

Figure 7.1   *GDP and trade growth of China, 1990–2005*

In 2006, the GDP of China reached 20 940 trillion renminbi (RMB), with 10.7 per cent real growth.[3] China was the world's third-largest trader after the USA and Germany, registering US$1.76 trillion in foreign trade, up 24 per cent year on year, and an aggregate trade surplus of US$177 billion. On 11 December 2001, China entered the WTO. On 21 July 2005, the renminbi exchange rate regime was reformed by moving into a managed floating exchange rate system with reference to a basket of currencies (see Appendix Table 7A.1).

As Figure 7.1 shows, from 1990 to 2005, China experienced a high annual GDP growth rate of about 10 per cent, and an even higher growth rate of trade at 18.2 per cent. The ratio of the value of exports to GDP was 16 per cent in 1990, and increased to 21 per cent in 2000 and 34 per cent in 2004.[4]

During the period of fast growth in trade after 1978, transport infrastructure of China developed rapidly. However, for most of the period between 1949 and 1978, transportation was a relatively low priority in the nation's development. Inadequate transportation systems hindered domestic trade. Meanwhile, the country had a very small amount of international trade before it started its open-door policy and economic reform. Therefore seaport development was also very slow. As a result, the underdeveloped transportation system constrained the pace of economic development throughout the country.

Since 1978, China has opened the door to the outside world, and invigorated the national economy through reform. Special economic zones have been set up, with Shenzhen, Zhuhai, Shantou and Xiamen as the four initial ones, followed by the Yangtze River Delta and the Pearl River Delta. Last, but not least, Pudong, the eastern part of Shanghai, has been newly designated as a special economic zone. All these zones are located in the coastal area. In order to attract more FDI, the Chinese government has put a higher priority on updating infrastructure conditions. Improvements were also made throughout the transportation sector, especially in coastal areas. Historic changes have taken place in the transportation sector during the 30 years from 1978.

By the end of 2005, the total length of transportation lines in China had reached 4.17 million km, 22 times and 3.3 times the lengths in 1949 and 1978 respectively. Developing from nothing, the length of expressways reached 41 000 km in 2005. There are 3641 newly built berths at major harbours, of which 769 are 10 000-ton-class berths, and there are 135 civil airports. In 2005, the various transport means carried 8025.8 billion tons-km of freight, which increases 8.2 times over 1978.

Railways

China's first railway was built in 1876. In the 73 years that followed, 22 000 km of track were laid, but only half were operable when China was founded in 1949. Between 1949 and 1978, more than 29 700 km of lines were added to the existing network, mostly in the southwest or coastal areas where previous rail development had been concentrated.

Between 1978 and 2005, newly constructed lines opened to traffic reached 27 300 km, of which electrified lines totalled 18 400 km. In 2005, the length of railway lines opened to traffic reached 75 400 km, 19 400 km of which had been electrified, and 24 497 km of which is the double-track line. Total railway length by 2005 is a 45.9 per cent increase over that of 1978.

However, over the past decades, the main focus of railway development has been on electrifying the existing network, rather than on increasing capacity. Furthermore, most of the trunk lines are ageing; and there is also a general shortage of double-track lines, resulting in over-use of the railway. Consequently, current railway transport is becoming very congested. Even so, with just 6 per cent of the railway lines in the world, China has achieved one-quarter of turnover of freight transport in the world. Additionally, railway transport is also number one in the world in terms of rail passenger transport, freight transport, turnover of freight transport and freight traffic density.

Although more and more new lines and double-track lines have been constructed, the railway freight transport system is unable to meet the transportation needs incurred by rapid economic expansion. For example, in 2006, more than 280 000 freight cars were needed every day, and railway capacity in that year could satisfy only 35 per cent of the needs. Thus, even today, many freight goods have to be transported by truck.[5]

Highways and Roads

In 1949, the length of highways in China was just over 80 000 km, and more than one-third of the counties nationwide were not accessible by road. However, by 2005, the total length of highways opened to traffic had reached 1.93 million km (see Figure 7.2). Now all counties, towns and townships are accessible by road. From 1950 to 1978, highway construction increased ten times in terms of length. In this period, the central government's main target was to have all counties nationwide connected by road.

Due to the fast-growing economy, high-speed truck freight transport was urgently required. After 1987, China began to build a large number of expressways to connect all province capitals and other important cities. By 2005, there were 4100 km of newly built expressways. In terms of total length of expressway, China ranks as second just after the USA. During this period, road construction investment focused mainly on the expressway. Therefore it can be seen that the length of highway did not increase significantly after 1978, as shown in Figure 7.3. By contrast, the length of expressway increased dramatically, especially from 1997. However, expressway construction still cannot keep pace with demand brought about by rapid economic expansion, as the total length of expressway is just 2 per cent of the total highway in China.

Water Transport

China's mainland coast is over 18 000 km long, and its rivers total 220 000 km in length. Such excellent natural conditions lend themselves to developing inland river transport and ocean shipping. The major inland navigable rivers in China are the Yangtze and the Pearl. Before 1978, water transport was mainly inland, since there was little international trade. After 1978, the open-door policy was implemented and greatly stimulated international trade. Most goods have to be exported or imported through the ports. Meanwhile, due to increasing congestion of the railways, the government also came to see water transportation as a much less expensive alternative to new road and railway construction. Therefore it launched a large number of port construction and improvement projects, and also gave high priority for the port infrastructure construction and water transport industry, which had often been mismanaged or neglected in the past.

In 1978, navigable inland waterways in China totalled 136 000 km. However, they declined to 123 300 km in 2005, because of the construction of dams and irrigation works, and increasing sedimentation. Meanwhile, the volume of waterway cargo transportation increased to 4967.2 billion tons-km in 2005, compared with 377.9 billion tons-km in 1978. More than

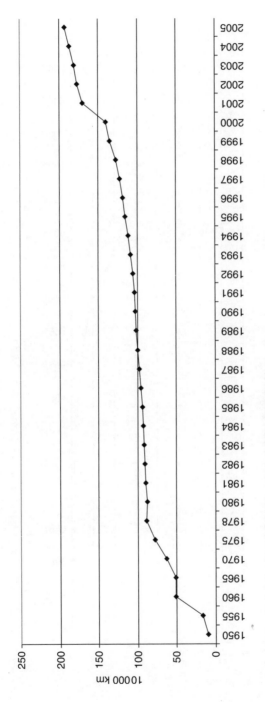

Figure 7.2   Length of highway route in China, 1950–2005

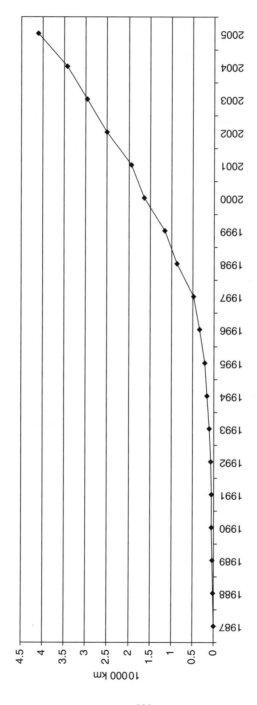

Figure 7.3   Length of expressway route in China, 1987–2005

188

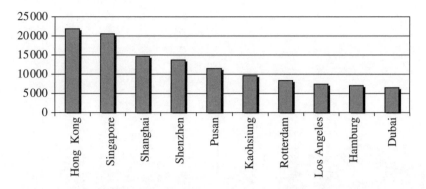

Source: *Containerization International Yearbook*, 2005.

Figure 7.4   World port rank in 2004 (in 1000 TEU)

72 per cent of inland water transport cargo was transported on the Yangtze River from Chongqing to Shanghai. This route also connects the inland provinces' foreign trade with overseas markets through Shanghai Port.

The major coastal ports of China are connected to more than 1100 ports in more than 100 countries. These ports handled around 14 per cent of the world's total container cargoes in 2003. Shanghai Port and Shenzhen Port rank as the third- and fourth-largest ports in the world in terms of container throughput as of 2003 (see Figure 7.4). Other Chinese ports have also developed very fast, which affects the international shipping transport industry (see Figure 7.5). As a result, Chinese ports are becoming the busiest in the world.

On the other hand, Chinese ports are also becoming the most congested ports in the world. The inadequacy of port and harbour facilities has been a longstanding problem for China but has become an even more serious obstacle due to increased foreign trade. This situation is mainly caused by the long-term neglect of port construction and access transport by means of highway, railway and inland waterway. Beginning in the 1980s, the government gave priority to port construction. In 1980, there was a total of 686 berths at major coastal ports, 197 of which were 10 000-ton-class berths. In 2005, there were 3641 berths, 769 of which were 10 000-ton-class berths. But even such construction cannot keep pace with fast-growing foreign trade.

Civil Aviation

Civil aviation underwent tremendous development during the 1980s. The domestic and international air service was greatly increased. By 2005

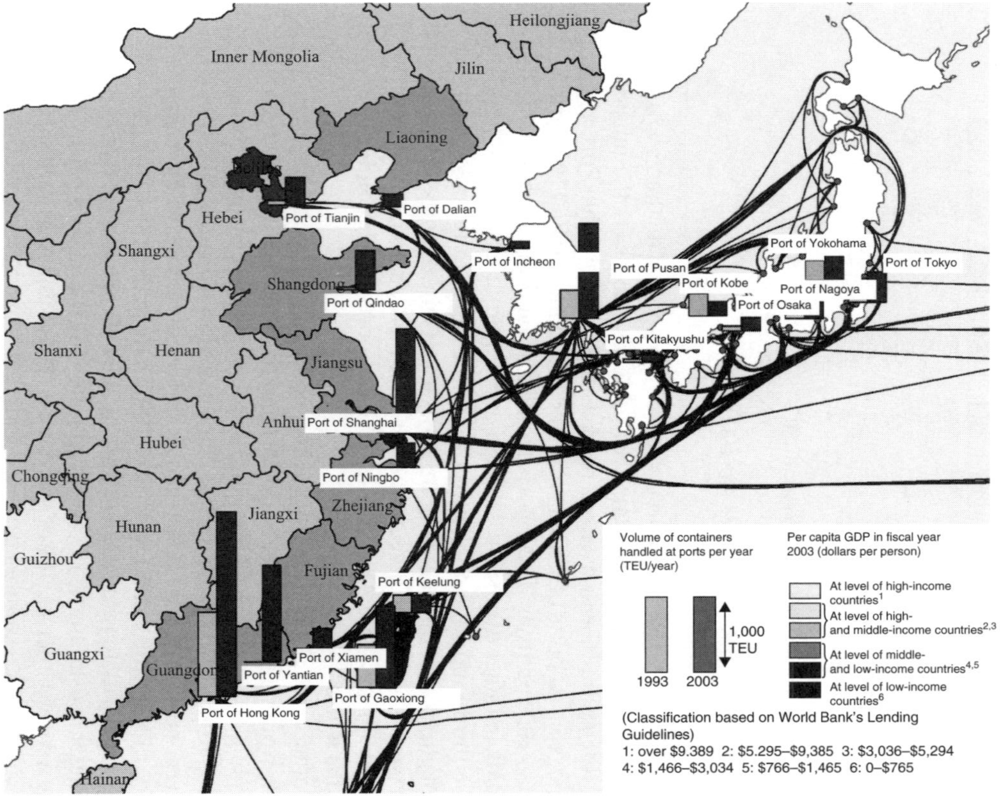

Source: Adapted from Ieda and Liqiang Ma (2005).

Figure 7.5 Fast-growing Chinese ports

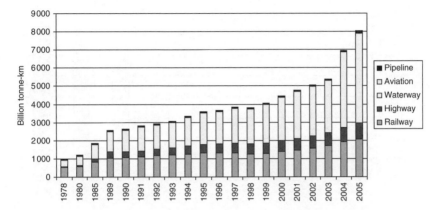

Figure 7.6   China freight transport turnover, 1978–2005

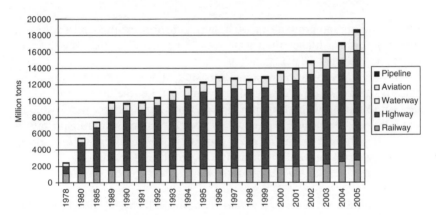

Figure 7.7   China freight transport, 1978–2005

China had more than 1 995 500 km of air routes and more than 855 000 km of these were international. In 2005 civil airlines handled 3 million tons, which was 48 times the freight goods carried by air transport in 1978. However, compared with other transport modes, air freight transport still accounts for a very small share due to its high transport cost (see Figures 7.6 and 7.7).

In the 1980s the central government increased its investment in airport construction, and some local governments also granted special funds for such projects. Almost all airports located at each provincial capital were expanded. Some new airports were also constructed in those cities. In 2005, China had more than 135 civilian airports. Between 1990 and 2001, the

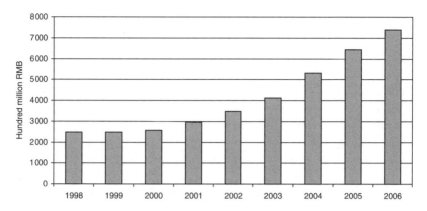

*Figure 7.8   Fixed assets investment on transport industry in China,
1998–2006*

compound annual growth rate of freight transport by air was 16 per cent,
which was much higher than waterway (5 per cent), expressway (3.7 per
cent) and railway (1.6 per cent).[6]

China's transportation system consisted of long-distance hauling by
railways and inland waterways due to low cost. On the other hand, roads
are a popular mode of transport for short-distance cargo mainly due to
the relatively developed expressway network. Waterborne transportation
dominated freight traffic in east, central, and southwest China, along
the Yangtze River and its tributaries, and in Guangdong Province
and Guangxi-Zhuang Autonomous Region, served by the Pearl River
system.

Due to the open-door policy and economic reform, international trade
has increased significantly during the past decades. This has made a huge
demand on the infrastructure, especially transportation industry. The
Chinese government has also invested a huge amount of money in transport infrastructure, especially in the past eight years (see Figure 7.8).

Finally, infrastructure development is also very unbalanced across
the regions. Most major port facilities were developed along China's
coast. The railway and highway infrastructure condition of the eastern
region of China is much better than that of the western region. This
makes it difficult for the western region to be integrated into the world
economy.

Figure 7.9 compares the growth rate of some indicators from 1991 to
2005. Although China experienced high growth in transport infrastructure
investment in most years, the growth cannot keep pace with the even higher
trade growth after 2002.

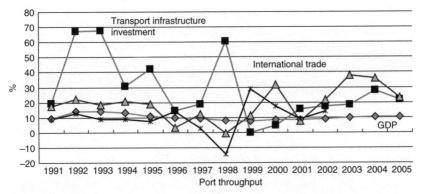

Notes:
The GDP growth rates from 1993 to 2004 are the revised figures by China's National
Bureau of Statistics (NBS), in accordance with the first national economic survey.
Data for port throughput growth from 2003 to 2005 are not available.

Source: Based on data from Ju Tian Zheng Quan Institute.

Figure 7.9   Growth rate of major indicators in China, 1991–2005

3. TRADE AND TRADE COSTS: US IMPORTS FROM CHINA

Definition

> Trade costs, broadly defined, include all costs incurred in getting a good to a final
> user other than the marginal cost of producing the good itself: transportation
> costs (both freight costs and time costs), policy barriers (tariffs and non-tariff
> barriers), information costs, contract enforcement costs, costs associated with
> the use of different currencies, legal and regulatory costs, and local distribution
> costs (wholesale and retail). (Anderson and van Wincoop, 2004, p. 691).

China has been gradually integrating into the world economy since 1978.
Trade volume has increased significantly in the last two decades. Moreover,
the progress of trade liberalization has been speeding up since China's entry
into the WTO in 2001. Trade costs, therefore, have decreased as a result of
scale economies and tariff reduction. In view of this, doing business with
other economies has become less costly.

It is too complex to explain the determinants of China's broadly defined
trade costs as a whole, as the country has different geographical characteristics, regional disparities in terms of economic and trade development,
different levels of infrastructure development in different regions, and
different policies were implemented for different regions at the beginning of

Table 7.1   Sino-US ocean and air trade in 2005

Transport modes	US imports from China				US exports to China			
	Volume		Value		Volume		Value	
	Billion pounds	Growth rate (%)	Billion US$	Growth rate (%)	Billion pounds	Growth rate (%)	Billion US$	Growth rate (%)
By all modes	129.6	19.2	235.2	24.0	74.2	2.0	34.4	13.0
Ocean trade	127.8	19.0	180.4	21.0	73.9	2.0	23.4	16.0
Air trade	1.8	21.0	54.8	37.0	0.3	3.0	11.0	8.0

Source: Based on information from http://www.tdctrade.com.

reform and the opening-up policy. However, we can gain useful insights by studying trade costs in the context of China.

Based on the available data, trade costs in this section are confined to freight, insurance and duty when the USA ships goods from China.[7] We investigate these trade costs, and their trends from 1991 to 2004.[8]

In addition, trade costs incurred when moving goods from door to port[9] and at the port[10] will be presented in Section 4, which focuses on how port development facilitates trade and reduces trade costs, and how less developed infrastructure and poor logistics management in inland provinces remain quite high costs for exporting activities, as evidenced below.

Data and Methodology

The USA is China's top trading partner: its share in China's exports increased from 8.5 per cent in 1990 to 21.5 per cent in 2005, as shown in Table 7.1. Moreover, shipping between the USA and China in 2005 grew at a faster pace than that between the USA and the world market. According to The Colography Group's Annual IS International Cargo by Commodity and Country database, China was the largest market in terms of vessel value, for US imports and exports. US ocean imports from China grew by 21 per cent and air imports grew by 37 per cent in terms of trade value, and by 19 per cent and 21 per cent in terms of cargo volume.

Studies of trade costs of Sino–US trade are valuable in investigating the issues arising from trading with other countries. Moreover, US import data at the HS 10-digit[11] level as the primary data source provide import value and imports quantities from China by modes of transportation. Furthermore, this source provides detailed data on freight and insurance,

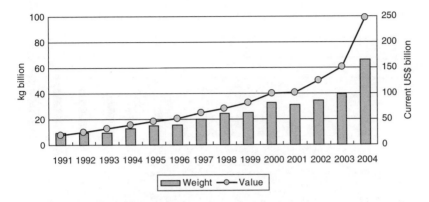

Figure 7.10   US imports from China in weight and value terms, 1991–2004

and the duty paid for each commodity. The aggregate values of imports, freight and insurance (transport costs), and import duties between 1991 and 2004 are computed by modes of transportation for this study.

Findings

Share change by mode of transportation

As shown in Figure 7.10, the value (in nominal terms) of US imports from China in 2004 was over 13 times that in 1991. Accordingly, the freight transported from China to the USA increased significantly during the same period. In 2004, 66.33 billion kg of goods were transported from China to the USA, of which 65.46 billion kg were transported by ocean vessel and 870 million kg by air, which doubled the figures for 2000.

Most cargo transported from China to the USA in both value and weight terms was by ocean vessel, but there was an increase in the share of air cargo in both terms. Around 99 per cent of the cargo from China to the USA is transported by ocean vessel. Goods transported by air are usually higher value–weight ratio commodities, or those with special requirements for timing or storage, such as fish, fresh vegetables, cut flowers, machinery and mechanical appliances, parts and accessories. Most goods under product code 84 ('machinery and mechanical appliances, including parts' by the HS 2-digit classification) were transported by air in 2004, which accounted for a large share of the air cargo from China to the USA.

The value share of cargo transported by air increased from 9.5 per cent in 1991 to 27.6 per cent in 2004, which has tripled in the last two decades. The relatively high value–weight ratio exports are becoming a larger share of China's exports to the USA (see Figures 7.11 and 7.12).

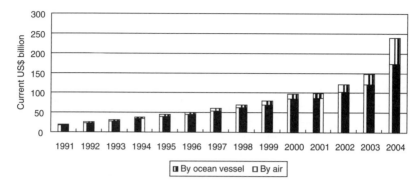

*Figure 7.11   Value share by transport modes: US imports from China,
            1991–2004*

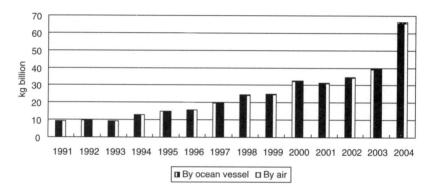

*Figure 7.12   Weight share by transport modes: US imports from China,
            1991–2004*

To sum up, from 1991 to 2004: (a) US imports from China have increased significantly; (b) most cargo transported from China to the USA is by ocean vessel; (c) the share of air cargo has been increasing; (d) the share of air cargo has kept relatively constant in terms of weight but tripled from 9.5 per cent to 27.6 per cent in terms of value, which reflects the change in pattern[12] of China's exports to the USA on the one hand and the robustness of the air cargo industry on the other.[13]

Measuring freight costs: aggregate *ad valorem* freight costs

The recent *Review of Maritime Transport 2006* (UNCTAD, 2006) estimated freight costs as a percentage of import (c.i.f.) value for selected countries and regions in 1990, 2000, 2003 and 2004. It shows that the share of global freight payments in import value (3.6 per cent) was slightly lower in 2004 than in 1990 (3.7 per cent). The estimation also indicates that freight costs incurred in developed market-economy countries continue to be lower than those incurred in developing countries. The share for developed countries has been fluctuating around 3 per cent and for developing countries around 6 per cent in recent years. This difference is mainly attributable to global trade structures, regional infrastructure facilities, logistics systems, and the distribution strategies of shippers in developed and developing countries.[14]

However, the estimates may be misleading due to their data sources and the methodology used. Some factors could lower aggregate expenditures on transport. Concerning the data, estimates of freight costs derived from balance-of-payments data are generally considered somewhat lower than actual freight costs. World total and regional total imports and their freight costs could also be distorted because of slow reporting by some countries.

Despite the shortcomings of data sources, the methodology is also questionable. First of all, the estimates are weighted averages, derived by computing aggregate freight payments relative to aggregate import value. This yields 'aggregate *ad valorem* freight costs', in other words, a percentage of aggregate freight costs in aggregate import value, which is a weighted average of *ad valorem* freight costs for individual products, weighted by the share of each product in trade.

These factors mean that aggregate *ad valorem* freight costs reflect two dimensions of information: the actual freight costs for an individual product; and the share of each product in trade – the product composition of trade.

Are trade costs going up or down?
Despite the flaws of using aggregate *ad valorem* freight costs, they can still give rise to some useful observations on trade costs. Based on the estimates for this case, we can see if transport costs are a larger or smaller impediment to Chinese trade today than in the past, compared with duty costs. We use a similar methodology to estimate *ad valorem* trade costs composed of freight costs and duty costs, and to investigate if the expenditures on freight are going up or down.

Ad valorem trade costs in this case are measured as a percentage of import value (f.o.b.) of product i, that is, the extra costs incurred when the USA imports US$100 (f.o.b.) worth of product i from China. Expressing trade costs on product i at time t as C_{it}, and imports as M_{it}, aggregate trade costs relative to aggregate imports (f.o.b.) are then

$$\frac{C_t}{M_t} = \frac{\sum_i C_{it}}{\sum_i M_{it}} = c_{it}s_{it}$$

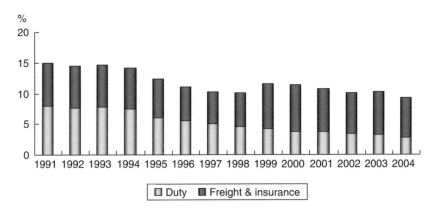

Figure 7.13   Aggregate ad valorem *trade costs of US imports from China
by all modes of transportation, 1991–2004*

where

$$c_{it} = C_{it}/M_{it}$$
$$s_{it} = M_{it}/\sum_i M_{it}$$

In other words, aggregate *ad valorem* trade costs are a weighted average of *ad valorem* trade costs on individual products, weighted by the share of that product in the trade. The data set (US Imports of Merchandise database, HS 10-digit) provides 'import value (f.o.b)', 'freight and insurance charges' and 'tariff duties paid' for each product,[15] which makes it possible to separate 'transport costs (freight and insurance)' from 'duty costs'. Then we can see if trade costs have been going up or down over years. Moreover, this data set records the mode of transportation for each product, which provides information to track the changes of trade costs by different modes: ocean vessel and air.

- *Declining trade costs are mainly due to tariff reduction rather than transport costs reduction. Transport costs show an increasing share in total trade costs compared with duty costs.*

Figure 7.13 shows the trends of trade costs incurred when the USA imports US$100 worth of goods from China. The trade costs were steadily decreasing from US$15 in 1991 to US$9.3 in 2004. The costs of freight and insurance were decreasing relatively slowly and fluctuated over several years. In contrast, duty costs were continuously decreasing from US$8 in 1991 to US$2.8

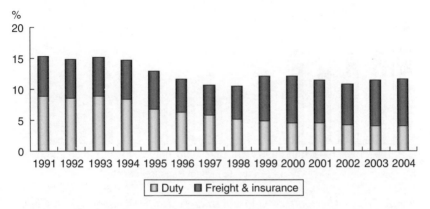

Figure 7.14   Aggregate ad valorem *trade costs of US imports from China
by ocean vessel, 1991–2004*

in 2004. Before 1995, the costs of duty accounted for over half of the trade costs, while it is becoming a smaller share in the trade costs after 1995. In 2004, the share of duty costs in the total trade costs was only 30.1 per cent.[16]

- *Trade costs by air declined dramatically, benefiting from a rapid decrease in duty costs for high-value goods and development of the aviation industry. Lower air transport costs played an important role in the growing fragmentation of trade.*

Furthermore, the trends are very different when comparing trade costs by different modes of transportation: ocean vessel and air. Figures 7.14 and 7.15 show that trade costs decreased mainly because of the declining duty for goods transported by both ocean vessel and by air. The figures show the fluctuating trends of freight and insurance cost for ocean trade and the steady decrease of that for air trade. The *ad valorem* costs of freight and insurance by air were higher than those by ocean before 2002 but afterwards they were lower. This indicates that air trade has developed rapidly in the past two decades: we can see the steadily increasing share of cargo transported by air but a decreasing share of cargo transported by ocean vessel in terms of trade value and weight.[17]

Explanations: A View from Compositional Change of Trade

The most important feature related to transport costs and infrastructure is the weight–value ratio of the traded goods. Hummels and Skiba (2004) estimate that a 10 per cent increase in product weight–value leads to a 4 per

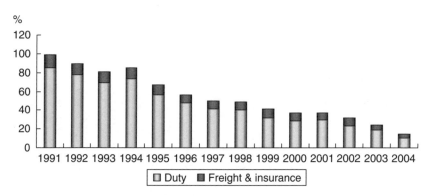

Figure 7.15   Aggregate ad valorem *trade costs of US imports from China by air, 1991–2004*

cent increase in *ad valorem* shipping costs. We calculate the weight–value ratio for China's trade over time in order to determine if it has decreased in the past decade.

Weight–value ratios

The COMTRADE data using the HS at the 6-digit level provide trade value and quantity for about 5000 commodities. Brooks and Hummels (2007) calculated the weight of the trade bundle for US imports from other countries based on HS 6-digit data. We use a similar method to calculate weight–value ratios for China's trade.

We use world export data between 1988 to 2006 to calculate the median weight–value ratio for each HS 6-digit product i, w_i, measured in kg per US$2000. Thus each product (4933 products in total) has a unique weight–value ratio. It is reasonable to assume that a dollar of some particular product weighs the same when shipped from one country to another. There are also other reasons to use world export data to get the unique weight–value ratio for each product. Moreover, export data are recorded as f.o.b., which excludes freight and insurance. Thus the ratios only reflect weights and f.o.b. value. If using import data recorded as c.i.f., the ratios will vary because freight and insurance may reflect different origins and destinations. Therefore the unique ratio computed based on world export data can be applied to any country pairs no matter what the differences of origins and destinations.

We then multiply the weight–value ratio by the share of product i in the trade bundle of country c at time t, s_{cit}. Summing over products yields the aggregate weight–value ratio for each country's imports and exports at a point in time:

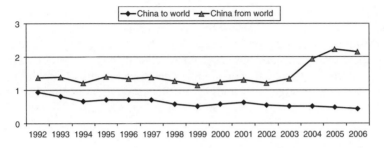

*Figure 7.16   Weight–value ratio of China's trade with the world,
1992–2006*

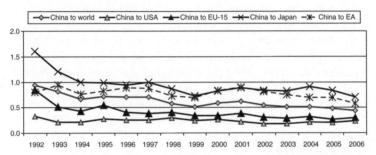

*Figure 7.17   Weight–value ratio of China's exports to major trading
partners, 1992–2006*

$$W_{ct} = \sum_i s_{cit} w_i$$

Weight–value ratio is declining for China's exports

First of all, we calculate W_{ct} for China's trade (imports and exports) with the rest of the world (see Figure 7.16). The ratios for China's exports are lower than 1 and were decreasing continuously from 1991 to 2006. The ratios for China's imports are above 1, with prominent increases since 2002. The trends show that China's exports are getting 'lighter' and imports are getting 'heavier'. This trend also reflects the significant increase of imports of materials since 2000.

Furthermore, we calculate the ratios of China's exports to the USA and major partners. Figure 7.17 shows that China's exports to Japan and East Asian developing countries (EA) are much higher than its exports to the USA and the European Union (EU). All experienced declining trends, which reflects the change in composition of China's exports from high weight–value goods to low weight–value goods.

The lower weight–value ratio of trading goods can lower the aggregate *ad valorem* transport costs. This means that even if *ad valorem* freight costs on individual products f_{it} were the same over time, the aggregate *ad valorem* transport costs would still be expected to decline if the composition of trade changed from high weight–value to low weight–value ratios. Combining the compositional change with findings in this section shows that transport costs have not declined as much as shown in Figures 7.13, 7.14 and 7.15.

4.   CASE STUDY OF CHINA'S SEAPORTS: SHANGHAI AND SHENZHEN

Seaports comprise significant infrastructure for the development of the national economy in general and foreign trade in particular. Around 90 per cent of China's foreign trade goods are transported through seaports.[18] There are around 150 coastal ports in China. By the end of 2005, there were 4933 productive berths,[19] and the comprehensive cargo throughput capacity reached 2.89 billion tons. The cargo throughput handled reached 3.38 billion tons in 2005, with a shortfall of about 0.47 tons. There were 208 container berths, throughput capacity reached 58.78 million TEU and actually handled container throughput reached 71.9 million TEU, with a shortfall of 13.12 million TEU.

Shanghai Port, as a gateway to China's trade, has a long history. Since 1978, trade volume has increased greatly, which has caused serious port congestion. Meanwhile, infrastructure improvement in Shanghai Port and nearby regions was conducted to solve this bottleneck. The study on Shanghai Port has implications for several ports in developing Asian countries, which are suffering from similar serious congestion. Furthermore, the study shows how economic and trade growth calls for port development in capacity on the one hand and in efficiency on the other. It also shows how both factors affect trade costs.

Shenzhen Port was a brand new port which played a prominent role in the development of Shenzhen City. Shenzhen City was established based on a small fishery village at the beginning of China's reform and opening-up policy. Shenzhen Port serves as a gateway for the economic development zones, and the industry parks located in and around Shenzhen City. The study of Shenzhen Port has implications for developing countries that expect to benefit from exported-oriented economic zones located close to ports. Moreover, the study also shows how port development facilitates trade, especially in reducing trade costs.

Meanwhile, an investigation of the infrastructure changes outside the port is useful in assessing how they can facilitate the goods movements from seaports to Shanghai and Shenzhen, then to the vast economic hinterland of China. Special focus is given to the high transport costs from the inland area to coastal ports, such as Shanghai and Shenzhen.

Port of Shanghai: Trade Growth Needs for Port Development

Shanghai Port is located at the convergence point between the eastern coast of China and the Yangtze River. Its direct economic hinterlands include the Yangtze River Delta area of Jiangsu–Zhejiang–Shanghai. It also provides transshipment services for the middle and upper banks of the Yangtze River including Sichuan, Chongqing, Hunan, Hubei, Jiangxi and Anhui.

Shanghai has a highly developed economy. In 2005, its per capita GDP was US$6283.7, ranking the highest among 31 regions of China (see Appendix Table 7A.3). In the same year, goods throughput at Shanghai Port accounted for around 10 per cent of that for China's coastal ports. As estimated by Shanghai Statistics, in a single day commodities valued at US$961 million cross the Customs, and 1 214 200 tons of cargo are handled at local ports.

Economic and trade development: Shanghai and the Yangtze River Delta

Shanghai borders on Jiangsu and Zhejiang Provinces on the west, the East China Sea on the east and Hangzhou Bay on the south. North of the city, the Yangtze River flows into the East China Sea. It is the central location along China's coast. In 2005 Shanghai had 18 districts and one county, as shown in Appendix Figure 7A.2. Shanghai plays a significant role in the nation's economic and trade development. As an international metropolis-oriented city, it strives to serve the nation and leads the growth of the Yangtze River Delta region, even the larger areas of the upper and middle Yangtze River. With only 1 per cent of the population and 0.06 per cent of the land area in the nation's total, Shanghai contributes 4.6 per cent of the nation's total GDP (see Appendix Figure 7A.3).

Yangtze River Delta port cluster   The Yangtze River Delta (YRD) is composed of 16 cities in Shanghai, southern Jiangsu, and eastern and northern Zhejiang.[20] The YRD is an important economic area of China, with Shanghai as China's financial and logistics centre, and Zhejiang and Jiangsu forming an increasingly important manufacturing base.

The YRD's manufacturing industries are developing rapidly, partly as a result of the influx of foreign investment. Cities that have the largest industrial production include Shanghai, Suzhou, Wuxi, Hangzhou, Ningbo and

Table 7.2   Major industries in the YRD and their shares (%) in PRC industrial output

Industries	Shanghai	Jiangsu	Zhejiang
Textile industry	2.80	23.90	23.20
Garments & other fibre products	7.10	21.10	19.20
Raw chemical materials and chemical products	6.40	19.20	7.60
Chemical fibre	1.90	30.20	37.00
Smelting and pressing of ferrous metals	6.20	14.10	2.90
General purpose machinery	11.60	18.20	15.30
Special purpose equipment	6.50	14.20	8.30
Transport equipment	8.90	8.90	7.90
Electrical machinery & equipment	7.20	15.10	12.90
Telecommunication equipment, computers and other electronic equipment	12.70	19.60	3.90

Sources: Statistical Yearbooks of PRC, Shanghai, Jiangsu and Zhejiang, 2006; http://www.tdctrade.com.

Nanjing. The YRD's total industrial output reached US$781.4 billion in 2005, which accounted for about 25.4 per cent of China's total (see Appendix Table 7A.4).

While the Pearl River Delta excels in the assembly of light consumer goods, the YRD is more focused on heavy industries such as machinery, chemicals and other upstream industries, i.e. the production of raw materials, intermediate goods and capital goods including electronic parts, textile and chemical fibre etc. (see Table 7.2). For example, in terms of volume, Shanghai and Jiangsu together accounted for more than 57 per cent of the national total output of integrated circuits; Jiangsu and Zhejiang together accounted for 70 per cent of the country's total output of chemical fibres in 2005. Within the YRD region, while Jiangsu and Zhejiang are the major production sites of garments, textiles, chemical fibre and machinery, Shanghai also produces a relatively large share of chemicals, machinery and motor vehicles. Shanghai alone produced 17 per cent of the country's total output of sedans in 2005.

The YRD is one of the leading industrial bases as well as an important export base. From 2001 to 2005, its exports rose by an average of 44 per cent per annum to US$276 billion in 2005, 36 per cent of national total exports. Major export items include machinery, transportation equipment, electrical equipment and parts, garments, textiles and raw material products. Major export markets include the USA, the EU, Japan, Hong Kong and Korea.

From 2001 to 2005, the YRD's imports grew by an average of 32 per cent per annum to US$227 billion in 2005. As a manufacturing base, major imports of the YRD include raw materials, chemical products, electrical equipment, parts and components. Major import sources include the EU, Japan, the USA, Taipei,China, Korea and Hong Kong.

The YRD is one of the largest transportation hubs in China, and its transport infrastructure is highly developed. As at the end of 2005, the total length of expressways in Shanghai, Jiangsu and Zhejiang was 5312 km, 13 per cent of the national total. In 2005, total passenger and freight traffic of Shanghai, Jiangsu and Zhejiang accounted for 17 per cent and 16 per cent respectively of the national total.

Airport density in the YRD is among the highest in the world. As one of the largest airports in China, Shanghai's Pudong International Airport, with the second runway opened in 2005, can handle about 36.5 million travellers per year. It is estimated that visitor arrival will amount to 70 million person-times in Shanghai during the World Expo period from May to October 2010. To deal with the influx of visitors, the Pudong International Airport will be expanded, with the third runway scheduled for completion by 2008.

The YRD is also an important gateway for waterway transportation. In 2005, out of the top ten ports in China in terms of container throughput, two are located in the YRD, namely Shanghai Port and Ningbo Port. In particular, the port at Shanghai is the largest container port in China, handling over 18 million TEUs in 2005, an increase of 24.3 per cent on 2004. Ningbo Port, ranked as the fourth largest in China, handled 5.2 million TEUs in 2005, an increase of over 30 per cent on 2004.

Highways are the main transportation mode within the YRD region. For example, in 2005, highways accounted for 95 per cent of Jiangsu's total passenger traffic and 68 per cent of total freight traffic. A network of highways linking all cities in the YRD is being constructed to shorten travelling times among different cities within the delta, giving rise to a 'metropolitan region within a three-hour drive'.[21]

Increasing the cargo throughput of Shanghai Port
There was a very small amount of cargo throughput of the Port of Shanghai before the mid-1980s. It was 1.91 million tons in 1949, 10.11 million tons in 1954, 50.39 million tons in 1973, and 100.65 million tons in 1984. As Figure 7.18 shows, the cargo throughput handled in Shanghai Port has increased since the mid-1980s. The annual growth from 1985 to 2000 was 4.04 per cent, while the annual growth from 2000 to 2005 was 16.74 per cent. The cargo throughput of Shanghai has surged between 2000 and 2005. In 2005, the Port of Shanghai ranked first in the world in terms

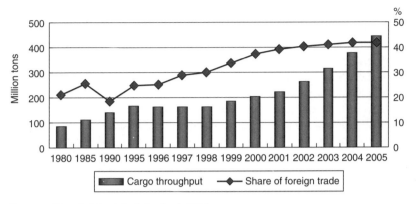

Source: Shanghai Statistical Yearbook, 2006.

*Figure 7.18   Cargo throughput of Shanghai Port and share of trade,
1980–2005*

of cargo throughput, at 443.17[22] million tons, and third in terms of container throughput, at 18.08 million TEUs.

Because of the tremendous economic growth of Shanghai and its vast hinterland, the port is facing opportunities and challenges from keen competition from ports of neighbouring economies such as Pusan, Kaohsiung and Kobe.[23] The main reason for this is that the shipping centre is limited by the shallow draught of the Yangtze River. Without planned projects, there will be very serious congestion at the Port of Shanghai. More seriously, the majority of the containers from the Yangtze River would be transshipped elsewhere, which in turn would depress the status of Shanghai as an international trade hub.

In recent years, the number of transshipped containers from Shanghai via Hong Kong accounted for 20 per cent of the total container throughput of Shanghai. For example, based on 1999 Shanghai throughput figures, of Shanghai's turnover of 4.21 million TEUs, about 1 million TEUs were transshipped via Hong Kong and comprised about one-sixteenth of the 16.2 million TEUs handled by Hong Kong in 1999. The container throughput reached 8 million TEUs in 2005.

Figure 7.18 shows that the share of cargo throughput of foreign trade in total cargo throughput of Shanghai was increasing. It was around 20 per cent from 1980 to mid-1990, around 30 per cent from mid-1990 to 2000, and has reached over 40 per cent since 2000. The Port of Shanghai has been enhancing its role of facilitating international trade. Figure 7.19 shows a strong growth of international container throughput.

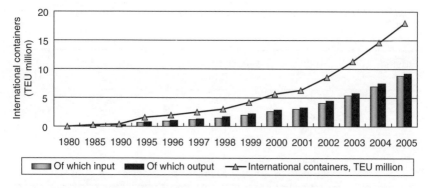

Source: Shanghai Statistical Yearbook 2006.

Figure 7.19   *International container throughput in Shanghai, 1980–2005*

Table 7.3   *Transport to the US west coast of a container from an inland province of China*

	US$ per TEU	Percentage of total
Land access to port	2300	63
Port handling	200	5
Maritime transport	750	21
Port handling	150	4
Port to final destination	250	7
Total	3650	100

Source: Carruthers (2003).

High transport cost from inland province to coastal port

Table 7.3 provides a breakdown of the costs for goods transported from the inland province of China to final destination of a foreign market (US west coast). It shows that a very high proportion of costs are incurred in movement from inland province to coastal port.

Table 7.4 shows the distance, time and cost by different modes of transportation from ports (Wuhan and Chongqing) of the upstream Yangtze River to Shanghai.[24] This indicates that the trade costs for inland regions are quite high, and weaken the competitiveness of exports from the inland provinces. Cheaper rates by inland waterway or railway are usually not available due to limited capacity. On the other hand, truck transportation is more attractive because it takes much less time than by rail or by barge.

Table 7.4   Cost of multimodal transport in the Yangtze River for one TEU, 2006[25]

Origin	Mode	Distance to Shanghai (km)	Transit time (days)	Cost (US$)
Wuhan	Rail	1063	5	365
	Truck	1100	2	1280
	Barge	1043	4	183
Chongqing	Rail	2425	8	525
	Truck	2756	3	2560
	Barge	2335	8	390

Source: Comtois (2006).

As a result, a large amount of goods is transported by truck at a much higher cost, about four to six times the cost by rail or barge.

Even road transport is usually congested due to poor infrastructure conditions and connectivity.

Inland transportation in China becomes a bottleneck because a lack of inland infrastructure and inefficient logistics processes increase transportation costs. The labour costs and land rent are increasing in coastal areas, and firms are seeking new locations in inland provinces. Besides the poor inland infrastructure, many inland provinces are without waterway gates or have a poor rail infrastructure network. Transport costs are quite high via road.

In addition to these costs, limited capacity and low efficiency[26] of seaports cause bottlenecks. At port side, mega-vessels demand greater port efficiency, but port operators are facing inflexible regulatory environments and higher operating costs. As suggested by an international expert,[27] China's ports need to increase productivity by almost 50 per cent, but maintain or reduce service cost. There is also a lack of collaboration among different stakeholders of the industry to achieve higher levels of supply chain efficiency at both port of origin and port of destination.

Shenzhen Port: Port Development Promotes Trade

Economic and trade development: Shenzhen
Shenzhen is located at the Pearl River Delta (PRD), which has been the most economically dynamic region of China since the launch of China's reform programme in 1978. The PRD covers nine prefectures of Guangdong Province and Hong Kong and Macau (see Appendix Figure 7A.4 and Appendix Table 7A.5).

Although the PRD economic zone encompasses only 0.4 per cent of the land area and only 3.2 per cent of the 2000 Census population of mainland China, it accounted for 8.7 per cent of GDP, 35.8 per cent of total trade, and 29.2 per cent of utilized foreign capital in 2001. These figures show the remarkable level of economic development that the PRD economic zone has achieved and the international orientation of the region's economy. This orientation has attracted numerous investors from all over the world who use the Greater PRD region as a platform for serving global and Chinese markets. Since the onset of China's reform programme, the PRD economic zone has been the fastest-growing portion of the fastest-growing province in the fastest-growing large economy in the world.[28]

The PRD started producing labour-intensive consumer goods such as food and beverages, toys and clothes in the early 1980s. After 1985, industrial relocation, mainly from Hong Kong, accelerated the growth of light industry in the PRD until the early 1990s, followed by heavy industry featuring high-tech electronic equipment and machinery, chemical products and autos playing a leading role in industrial output and export.

The PRD is a major manufacturing base for electronic products (such as watches and clocks), toys, garments and textiles, plastic products, and a range of other goods. The toy industry in the PRD has a world production share in excess of 60 per cent. Watches produced in Shenzhen alone in 2003 accounted for more than 40 per cent of the global market. Much of this output stems from investment by foreign entities and is geared to the export market. The PRD economic zone accounts for approximately one-third of China's trade value.

Nearly 5 per cent of the world's goods were produced in the Greater PRD in 2001, with a total export value of US$289 billion. Over 50 000 Hong Kong companies have plants there, according to a 2002 survey.

The export-led economy and Shenzhen Port development
When China started its open-door policy, Shenzhen was selected as the first of the special economic zones (SEZs) in China in 1979 due to its proximity to Hong Kong. The location was chosen to attract industrial investments from Hong Kong, which is nearby and has a similar culture. The concept proved a great success, propelling the further opening up of China and continuous economic reform. Shenzhen eventually became one of the largest cities in the PRD region, with 8.27 million people (see Appendix Figure 7A.4 and Appendix Table 7A.5). Shenzhen has also become one of the economic powerhouses of China, as well as the largest manufacturing base in the world.

Shenzhen was a fishing village before 1979, with 30 000 people. It has started a large number of infrastructure construction projects during the past 27 years. Between 1979 and 2006, Shenzhen used 705 billion RMB of its fixed assets investment with an average annual growth rate of 36.4 per cent. The investments were mainly spent on transportation infrastructure construction, including railway, airport, expressway, seaports and subway. Shenzhen has already developed a transportation system to connect inland China, Hong Kong and overseas. The construction of Shenzhen Airport started in May 1989 and it opened in September 1991. In 2004, Shenzhen Airport already ranked as the second largest in air cargo handled and fourth largest in passengers transported in China. Shenzhen Port, opened in 1994, also ranked as fourth-largest container port in the world from 2004. Such infrastructure development provides a great environment for FDI. It also greatly enhances Shenzhen's attractiveness as a gateway to the South China manufacturing centre.

During past decades, Shenzhen has achieved not only great urban expansion, but also economic development and the creation of global economic linkages. Between 1978 and 2001, the annual growth rate of GDP, industrial output value and foreign trade averaged 29.5 per cent, 45.4 per cent and 39.1 per cent, respectively.

The total number of multinational manufactures increased dramatically from 163 in 1984 to 2172 in 1990, and reached its peak – 6390 in 1994 – before slightly dropping to 4784 in 2000. The forces of foreign capital that have determined Shenzhen's urban outcomes and their impacts are enormous. In the last several years, foreign investment enterprises, for example, have employed over one-third of Shenzhen's labour force, contributed to three-quarters of its industrial output value and about 60 per cent of its exports and imports. It is multinational and foreign investors that drive Shenzhen's urban expansion and form its export-oriented economy.

Therefore Shenzhen was not only regarded as Hong Kong's factory, but a huge amount of containerized cargo had to be carried by trucks/barges to Hong Kong Port first, and then transported to overseas markets. This added greatly to trade costs in terms of transport and time. The rapid economic development of Shenzhen and the PRD economic zone have created a surge in container traffic.

Because of such urgent demand, Shenzhen ports were planned and constructed by the Shenzhen government from 1994. It is about 20 sea miles from Hong Kong to the south and 60 sea miles from Guangzhou to the north. Shenzhen ports consist of facilities in the following areas: Yantian, Shekou, Chiwan, Mawan, Dongjiaotou, Fuyong, Xiadong, Shayuchong and Neihe, where Yantian, Shekou and Chiwan are the major port terminals.

Yantian Port is the most important and biggest container port terminal in Shenzhen. The first phase of the project of Yantian port was finished and

Table 7.5   Container throughput of Shenzhen Port

Year	YICT		Shenzhen Port		Shenzhen's ranking in China	Shenzhen's ranking in the world
	(TEU)	Growth rate (%)	(TEU)	Growth rate (%)		
1994	13 000	0	179 000	0	8	
1995	106 000	715	284 000	59	7	
1996	353 509	233	589 000	107	4	
1997	638 000	80	1 148 000	95	2	35
1998	1 038 000	63	1 952 000	70	2	17
1999	1 600 000	54	2 978 000	53	2	11
2000	2 147 000	34	3 993 000	34	2	11
2001	2 700 000	26	5 076 000	27	2	8
2002	4 182 000	55	7 614 000	50	2	6
2003	5 258 000	26	10 652 000	40	2	4
2004	6 260 000	19	13 655 000	28	2	4
2005	7 660 000	22	16 197 000	19	2	4
2006	8 865 000	16	18 468 900	14	2	4

Note: YICT is Yantian International Container Terminals.

opened for operation in 1994. In the same year, Yantian Port handled 13 000 TEU container cargoes. Over ten years later, in 2006, it achieved 8.86 million TEU. Yantian Port serves close to 40 of the world's top shipping companies. Manufactured goods are shipped worldwide, reaching customers in Europe, America and Australia. With other ports in Shenzhen, Shenzhen Port group also ranked the fourth-largest container port in the world (see Table 7.5).

During the past two decades, Shenzhen has invested a total of more than 20 billion RMB on the port berth constructions and facility upgrading in order to meet the increasing demand caused by fast-growing international trade. Even so, Shenzhen ports are still becoming congested in terms of freight ton and container TEU (see Figures 7.20 and 7.21).

Shenzhen Port not only provides service to Shenzhen City; it is also a gateway to the South China manufacturing centre. Pingyan railway provides a dedicated rail link to Yantian Port. It offers an international logistics service from factory to port, connecting both the Beijing–Kowloon railway and the Beijing–Guangzhou railway. With this rail link, Yantian Port can extend its port services to inland catchments areas of China, which include Hunan, Sichuan, Yuannan and Guizhou (see Appendix Figure 7A.5).

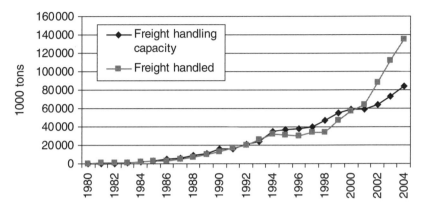

*Figure 7.20   Freight handling capacity and throughput of Shenzhen Port,
1980–2004*

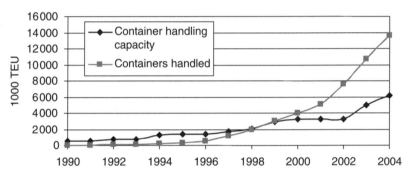

*Figure 7.21   Container handling capacity and throughput of Shenzhen
Port, 1990–2004*

In this way, it has also greatly reduced transport costs for international cargoes between the above provinces and overseas. Beforehand, these provinces' container cargoes mostly had to be carried to Shanghai Port and transported overseas. This would take a long time and high cost over land. Furthermore, due to serious congestion in Shanghai Port, these container cargoes still had to wait several days to load on to the container ship. Such a situation also impedes FDI to inland China. Table 7.6 gives examples to show that using Shenzhen Port can significantly save on transport costs for Yunnan, Guizhou and other southwestern provinces.

Shenzhen Port contributes to the export-led economic growth of South China by providing 'world-class' container terminal services to the shipping industry and export/import community. The modern port has

Table 7.6   Distance and transport fee for 10-ton container cargo by land transport

	Shenzhen		Shanghai	
	Distance (km)	Fee (RMB)	Distance (km)	Fee (RMB)
Kunming	1706	3410	3207	8800
Guiyang	1359	3498	3102	8000

Source: Data collected from Shenzhen Huandao Logistics Company and Shanghai Jingsu Logistics Development Co. Ltd.

enhanced Shenzhen's attractiveness as a gateway to the South China manufacturing centre.

Another important factor is that, unlike other ports whose investments were mainly from the Chinese central government, Shenzhen port investment was mainly from the Shenzhen local government and private sector, especially FDI from Hong Kong. FDI contributed greatly to Shenzhen port construction, amounting to 4.2 billion RMB FDI of the total 4.7 billion RMB investment in 2003. Shenzhen developed a successful approach to use FDI on infrastructure construction and support its export-led economy.

Shenzhen Port plays a very important role in the economic development of southern China. It is China's second-busiest container port after Shanghai, and the world's fourth largest, handling 18.5 million TEU in 2006, up 14 per cent on 2005. Shenzhen Port has three deep seaports at Yantian, Shekou and Chiwan. Container handling costs at Yantian and Shekou are about 30 per cent and 40 per cent cheaper than at Hong Kong Port, and have significantly reduced the trade cost between Shenzhen and overseas.

Furthermore, after the expressway and railway construction, Shenzhen Port connected the inland of China, especially southern China. Such infrastructure improvement made it possible for southern provinces to use Shenzhen Port to export to overseas more cheaply than using Shanghai Port. Meanwhile, FDI can go to the inland southern provinces due to the relatively convenient transportation and cheaper trade cost. Rising trade is increasing container cargo shipments from the southern provinces to Shenzhen Port. This makes it imperative for Shenzhen Port to improve its capacity and efficiency. Shenzhen City is constructing a new deep sea-route which will make Shenzhen Port open to traffic in all weather conditions for the fourth generation of container ships.

5. CONCLUDING REMARKS

In 1978, China opened the door to the outside world, and invigorated the national economy through reform. In order to attract foreign investment, the Chinese government invested a huge amount of money in infrastructure development. Most of these investments were allocated to coastal areas. Furthermore, the fastest-growing economy and international trade boom of the past three decades in China placed heavy demand on the infrastructure, especially transportation infrastructure. Transportation infrastructure construction achieved unprecedented development during the last few decades.

The export-led economy greatly triggered infrastructure development in China. With labour costs and land costs becoming more and more expensive in the coastal area, foreign investors began to look for new factory locations in inland China. Therefore the transportation condition of the inland provinces and their connections to coastal ports become very important factors for their location decisions. For this reason, the Chinese government has gradually shifted its infrastructure investment priority from the coastal area to the inland area in order to provide a better investment infrastructure environment.

In this process, China, with limited financial resources, gave high priority to infrastructure construction in the coastal area in order to attract FDI and to support export-led economic development. This created high demand and provided financial support for such development. Infrastructure construction and trade development both positively affect each other, although the poor condition and limited capacity of China's infrastructure are still serious problems.

Furthermore, in the case of Shenzhen port development, a new approach was used: not only government investment but also FDI, which addressed the shortage of financial resources, while the technology transfer brought by FDI also improved the infrastructure management level and efficient usage. For the Port of Shanghai, it showed that trade growth drove the needs of infrastructure development, which enhanced port competitiveness.

In order to promote exports and attract FDI, inland provinces have to offset the disadvantages of being far from seaports. Apart from the location disadvantage, inland provinces have their own comparative advantages, such as agricultural products, raw minerals and water resources. The inland provinces can benefit from international trade opportunities. However, the supplying enterprises in the inland provinces have to lower costs in order to get a competitive edge. The major components of their product costs are those associated with trade logistics, transportation and inventory. Besides the disadvantage arising from such direct transportation costs, there is also a substantial time delay for the delivery of goods from the inland provinces to the coastal ports, which leads to increased inventory costs for firms. This relatively longer delivery time is attributed to the lower quality of the transport infrastructure and lower efficiency in the logistics services and management in China, in particular in inland provinces.

Railway transportation is crucial for inland provinces, which are far from coastal seaports for international exports. Moreover, most inland provinces produce and export mineral ores and chemicals, which can be transported in bulk relatively cheaply by rail over long distances. Also containerized rail wagons for the high-value manufactured goods, such as electronics, will reduce delivery costs for manufactured products and hence enhance export competitiveness. However, the existing railway network does not adequately cover wider areas within the inland regions. In addition, the orientation of the rail connectivity seems to be eastwards, that is, towards the coast. There is a very limited rail connection to link the whole western region with other parts of China. Highways are relatively (to railway) flexible in terms of scheduling, and very important for the transfer of consumer goods from warehouse to distribution outlets in different cities. Shipping is the most economical mode of transportation for transporting goods over long distances. For most inland regions, multi-modal transportation[29] normally results in delays during transit, mainly due to the lack of a seamless logistics management system in China.

The cross-border infrastructure is also important, such as highways and railways. In addition, the development of transportation logistics linkages at the borders as well as the effectiveness and reliability of the trade facilitation and administrative procedures at the customs are crucial, which includes rationalization of the customs transit system aiming at the reduction of customs inspection and the simplification of the declarations and documentation process.

To summarize, infrastructure's role in facilitating trade and lowering trade costs has been significant for China in the last two decades. Seaport development is vital for the trade of the nation, while infrastructure such as roads, railways and waterways connecting the inland provinces of China and coastal ports or ports at the border are particularly important. The priority of infrastructure development depends on the location of production and exporting clusters.

NOTES

1.   Logistics infrastructure includes railways, highways, seaports, airports, inland waterways and warehouses.

2. Logistics services include trucking, air freight, rail transportation services, freight forwarding and other third-party logistics services, shipping, warehousing and distribution.
3. According to the World Bank (2007, p. 8) projection, GDP growth of China will be 11.3 per cent in 2007 and 10.8 per cent in 2008.
4. For comparison, in 1995 landlocked countries on average had an import share in GDP of 11 per cent, compared with 28 per cent for coastal economies (Limao and Venables, 2001, p. 451). The same figure for China in 1995 was 18.1 per cent, which is higher than for landlocked economies but lower than average for coastal economies. The figure for China reached 18.8 per cent in 2000 and 29.5 per cent in 2005. However, there are big differences among different provinces of the country. The ratios are higher in coastal regions than in hinterland regions.
    We calculated the ratios of exports to GDP for 31 provinces of China, which decline from the coastal east to the central and west of China. The ratios for Guangdong (87.2%), Shanghai (81.9%), Tianjin (60.7%), Jiangsu (55.0%), Zhejiang (46.8%) and Fujian (43.5%) are much higher than for other provinces. These coastal regions have become intensively involved in trade. The ratio for Xinjiang (15.9%) was much higher compared with other regions located in the west of China, such as Guizhou (3.6%). The reason is that cross-border trade has increased in Xinjiang in recent years. Yunnan and Guangxi, which also share borders with Viet Nam, Lao PDR and Myanmar, saw higher ratios compared with other inland provinces (see Appendix Table 7A.2 for details).
    Geographical location is the dominant factor in the extent to which regions are involved in trade. Coastal regions have a locational advantage, with good ports, proximity to waterways, and higher road, rail and airway intensity, while the inland regions, far from seaports and with poor rail and road infrastructure, incur very high transportation costs in moving goods to the ports. The correlation test on the relationship between transport infrastructure density and ratios of exports to GDP for 31 provinces in 2005 shows significant positive correlation. The correlation coefficients for expressway density (0.741) and road density (0.731) are higher than for inland waterway density (0.637) and railway density (0.480).
5. Take Shanxi Province, for example: due to the shortage of railway capacity, a huge amount of coal has to be transported by trucks to the highly industrialized eastern part of the country and the port of Qinhuangdao for export. Heavy trucks have also damaged the roads and caused congestion.
6. Source: based on data from Ju Tian Zheng Quan Institute (2003).
7. Trade costs can be divided into five parts in terms of cargo movement: (a) door to exporting port (seaport, airport and border port) of origin; (b) at port of origin; (c) from port of origin to port of destination; (d) at port of destination; (e) from port of destination to door.
8. Freight and insurance are shown as a value in this data set; freight cannot be separated from insurance. The rates of shipping insurance are mostly determined by the distance between port of origin and port of destination. Other factors can affect the rates of insurance, such as route and competition, but they are relatively stable over time.
9. Focusing on trade costs incurred from inland area to seaports.
10. Focusing on infrastructure development and trade costs incurred at the Port of Shanghai and Port of Shenzhen.
11. US Imports of Merchandise database, which disaggregates imports at the 10-digit level. HS refers to Harmonized System. Thank to David Hummels for providing the data.
12. The compositional change from high weight–value goods to low weight–value goods will be analysed in the following section.
13. The next part of this section will show the dramatic decrease in trade costs for goods transported by air.
14. UNCTAD (2006), p. 72.
15. Based on US Imports of Merchandise database disaggregated at HS 10-digit level, the numbers of products imported from China were 6274 items in 1991, increasing to 26 976 items in 2004.

16. China's actual import tariff (unweighted average) decreased from 44.1 in 1991 to 35.2 in 1995, and 12.3 in 2002 (Rodrik, 2006, p. 4).
17. In terms of weight, the shares of cargo by ocean and by air were relatively constant in this period; only around 1 per cent of cargo transported by air in terms of weight.
18. Ministry of Communications, PRC (2007).
19. Includes 1108 berths with capacity over 10 000 tons.
20. According to the new expansion plan for Yangtze River Delta, seven more cities will join the Yangtze River Delta. They are: Wenzhou, Yancheng, Lianyungang, Wuhu, Maanshan, Hefei and Tongling. However, we just look at the YRD composed of 16 cities.
21. http://www.tdctrade.com.
22. The blueprint projects five years ago stated that Shanghai ports would handle a cargo throughput of about 200 million tons in 2005 and 280 million tons in 2010. Information from http://tpwebapp.tdctrade.com.
23. Concerning the competitiveness of the Port of Shanghai relative to the Port of Shenzhen in South China, there is very little competition between the two ports. The main reason is that they have different cargo sources. The cargo sources of the Port of Shenzhen are mostly from Guangdong and provinces located in Southwest China. In view of location, there should be intensive competitiveness between the Port of Shenzhen and the Port of Hong Kong.
24. For comparison, the cost for a 40-foot container transported from Chengdu to Shanghai is US$1200, from Shanghai to Long Beach US$2000, from Shanghai to the Philippines US$600. Information from Global Institute of Logistics, http://www.globeinsti.org.
25. The Yangtze River, stretching 6300 km through seven provinces and two cities, including Shanghai and Chongqing, is the main artery connecting the eastern, central and western regions, carrying 50% of China's inland cargo in tonnage terms and nearly 80% in terms of ton-mileage. The government sees the development of the transport infrastructure along the Yangtze River as part of the 'Great Development Plan for the West' launched in 2000 to develop 12 western provinces and cities, such as Chongqing, Yunnan, Sichuan, Tibet and Shaanxi. Therefore the shipping on the Yangtze River has been called the 'Golden Waterway'.
26. Take land utilization as an indicator of port efficiency, which shows that China has very low efficiency in land utilization. The figures for 2006 are: China 18 000 average TEU per acre/pa; Europe 6000 average TEU per acre/pa; USA 4500 average TEU per acre/pa. Information from Global Institute of Logistics, http://www.globeinsti.org.
27. Aguilar (2006).
28. Source: Wikipedia.
29. Goods are transported over land by railways or highways to the seaports before being loaded on to the ships.

REFERENCES

Aguilar, Wilmer E. (2006), 'China port and logistics challenges', presentation on 19 September, Shanghai.
Anderson, James E. and Eric van Wincoop (2004), 'Trade costs', *Journal of Economic Literature*, **42**(September), 691–751.
Brooks, Douglas H. and David Hummels (2007), 'Infrastructure's role in Asia's trade and trade costs', Finalization Conference on Infrastructure's Role in Reducing Trade Costs, ADBI, Tokyo, Japan, 25–26 June.
Carruthers, Robin (2003), 'Trade and logistics: evolution of a product line', http://www.worldbank.org.

Comtois, Claude (2006), 'Gateway development and port rivalry in the Yangzi River Delta', presentation at University of British Columbia, Canada, http://www.iar.ubc.ca.

De, Prabir (2007), 'Impact of trade costs in trade: empirical evidence from Asian countries', ARTNET Working Papers No. 26, UNESCAP, Bangkok.

Global Institute of Logistics (2006).

Hummels, David and Alexandre Skiba (2004), 'Shipping the good apples out? An empirical confirmation of the Alchian–Allen conjecture', *Journal of Political Economy*, **112**(6), 1384–402.

Hummels, David (2001), 'Time as a trade barrier', unpublished paper, Purdue University, USA.

Hummels, David (1999a), 'Have international transportation costs declined?', unpublished paper, University of Chicago, July, available at: https://gtap.agecon.purdue.edu/resources/download/1238.pdf.

Hummels, David (1999b), 'Toward a geography of trade costs', GTAP Working Paper 1162, Center for Global Trade Analysis, Department of Agricultural Economics, Purdue University, USA.

Ieda, Hitoshi and Liqiang Ma (2005), 'Issues of China transportation under the fast developing economy', *Journal of Civil Engineering*, *JSCE*, **90**(8), 35–6.

International Trade Institute of Singapore (2006), 'World Bank-funded project in China – trade and logistics development in 8 inland lagging provinces', available at http://www-wds.worldbank.org/external/default/WDSContentServer/WDSP/IB/2004/06/10/000112742_20040610113317/Rendered/PDF/278400v140China0lagging0prov.pdf.

Ju Tian Zheng Quan Institute (2003), 'Report on China's Transport Industry', available at http://www.jtfund.com/fund/append/11808jtys.doc.

Limao, Nuno and Anthony J. Venables (2001), 'Infrastructure, geographical disadvantage, transport costs, and trade', *The World Bank Economic Review*, **15**, 451–79.

Ministry of Communications of People's Republic of China (2007), 'Report on Development of China's Highways and Waterways in 2006', available at http://www.moc.gov.cn/zhuzhan/tongjixinxi/fenxigongbao/tongjigongbao/200710/t20071017_436569.html (Chinese version only).

Rodrik, Dani (2006), 'What's so special about China's exports?', NBER Working Paper No. 11947, National Bureau of Economic Research, Cambridge, MA.

Survey data from Shenzhen Huandao Logistics Company and Shanghai Jingsu Logistics Development Co., Ltd, available at http://www.sz-hbhy.com/tielu.htm (Chinese version only).

United Nations Conference on Trade and Development (UNCTAD) (2006), *Review of Maritime Transport 2006*, New York and Geneva: United Nations Conference on Trade and Development.

World Bank (2003), 'Trade and logistics in East Asia: a development agenda (vol. 6 of 6): China: trade and logistics development in 8 inland provinces', Report No. 27840, East Asia Region Transport Sector (EASTR) Working Paper, No. 3, World Bank, Washington.

World Bank (2007), 'China quarterly update – September 2007', World Bank Office, Beijing.

APPENDIX   MAPS AND STATISTICAL INFORMATION

Figure 7A.1   Map of China

Table 7A.1   Major economic indicators of China, 2006

Major economic indicators	Value	Growth (%)
Area (km², million)	9.6	
Population (million)	1 314.50	
GDP (RMB billion)	20 940.70	10.7[a]
Urban per capita disposable income (RMB)	11 759	10.4[a]
Rural per capita disposable income (RMB)	3 587	7.4[a]
Fixed assets investment[b] (RMB billion)	9 347.20	24.5
Added value of industrial output[c] (RMB billion)	7 975.20	16.6[a]
Consumer goods retail sales (RMB billion)	7 641.00	13.7
Consumer price index		1.5
Urban unemployment rate (%)		4.1
Exports (US$ billion)	969.1	27.2
by foreign-invested enterprises (US$ billion)	563.8	26.9
Imports (US$ billion)	791.6	20.0
by foreign-invested enterprises (US$ billion)	472.6	22.0
Trade surplus (US$ billion)	+177.5	
FDI		
number of new projects	41 473	−5.8
utilized amount (US$ billion)	63.0	4.5
Foreign currency reserves (US$ billion)	1 066.3	30.2

Notes:
[a] Real growth.
[b] Urban investments in fixed assets.
[c] All state-owned and other types of enterprises with annual sales over RMB 5 million.

Sources: The National Bureau of Statistics, Ministry of Commerce, and General Administration of Customs.

Table 7A.2   Import and export value of commodities by places of destination or origin in China by region

Region	2000			2005			2000–2005
	Trade value (US$ billion)	Share in total (%)	Ratio of exports to GDP (%)	Trade value	Share in total (%)	Ratio of exports to GDP	Annual growth of trade (%)
National total	**474.3**	**100.00**	**20.79**	**1421.91**	**100.00**	**34.09**	**24.60**
Guangdong	175.49	37.00	78.75	439.18	30.90	87.23	20.10
Shanghai	54.7	11.50	46.12	181.5	12.80	81.18	27.10
Tianjin	17.16	3.60	43.56	54.63	3.80	60.66	26.10
Jiangsu	49.19	10.40	24.85	238.48	16.80	55.03	37.10
Zhejiang	31.52	6.60	26.66	123.81	8.70	46.82	31.50
Fujian	22.96	4.80	27.26	56.8	4.00	43.45	19.90
Beijing	24.24	5.10	39.97	53.49	3.80	36.72	17.10
Liaoning	20.07	4.20	19.25	47.04	3.30	23.97	18.60
Shandong	28.25	6.00	15.05	89.12	6.30	20.40	25.80
Xinjiang	2.59	0.50	7.31	8.3	0.60	15.85	26.30
Hainan	1.09	0.20	12.82	2.12	0.10	9.36	14.10
Ningxia	0.53	0.10	10.20	1.18	0.10	9.29	17.30
Heilongjiang	3.99	0.80	3.69	10.47	0.70	9.02	21.30
Hebei	5.49	1.20	6.04	19.33	1.40	8.86	28.60
Anhui	3.69	0.80	5.92	9.26	0.70	7.91	20.20
Shanxi	2.79	0.60	6.23	9.09	0.60	6.92	26.60
Shaanxi	2.39	0.50	6.53	6.15	0.40	6.86	20.80
Chongqing	1.85	0.40	5.19	4.23	0.30	6.72	18.00
Yunnan	1.88	0.40	4.98	5	0.40	6.23	21.50
Guangxi	2.28	0.50	6.01	5.76	0.40	5.78	20.30
Jilin	2.99	0.60	5.71	7.36	0.50	5.58	19.80
Hubei	3.89	0.80	3.75	9.99	0.70	5.56	20.80
Tibet	0.15	0.00	7.99	0.13	0.00	5.39	−2.40
Sichuan	2.78	0.60	2.88	7.67	0.50	5.22	22.50
Jiangxi	2.05	0.40	4.95	4.96	0.30	4.93	19.30
Qinghai	0.23	0.00	3.52	0.49	0.00	4.87	16.70
Hunan	2.99	0.60	3.71	6.96	0.50	4.71	18.40
Gansu	0.69	0.10	3.49	2.99	0.20	4.62	34.00
Henan	3.12	0.70	2.41	9.07	0.60	3.94	23.70
Inner Mongolia	2.39	0.50	5.73	5.3	0.40	3.73	17.30
Guizhou	0.86	0.20	3.50	2.04	0.10	3.56	18.90

Source: Calculated based on data from *China Statistical Year Book*, 2006, Table 18-12.

Table 7A.3   Per capita GDP by region

Region	GDP per capita (US$)				Annual growth (%)
	1990	1995	2000	2005	1990–2005
National Total	**343.70**	**604.24**	**949.22**	**1713.93**	**11.3**
Shanghai	1235.57	2268.35	4173.15	6283.68	11.5
Beijing	1019.82	1566.88	2713.08	5547.57	12.0
Tianjin	757.02	1234.34	2173.49	4368.20	12.4
Zhejiang	443.64	966.83	1626.04	3381.84	14.5
Jiangsu	439.66	874.03	1422.13	2998.16	13.7
Guangdong	530.40	1017.24	1556.46	2982.90	12.2
Shandong	379.45	689.50	1154.21	2453.21	13.3
Liaoning	564.06	823.85	1356.06	2317.35	9.9
Fujian	368.58	812.72	1401.36	2276.21	12.9
Inner Mongolia	309.00	435.76	709.32	1993.60	13.2
Hebei	306.28	532.15	925.66	1804.51	12.6
Heilongjiang	423.98	654.41	1034.26	1762.03	10.0
Jilin	365.03	528.56	827.09	1629.45	10.5
Xinjiang	376.11	577.06	902.35	1600.16	10.1
Shanxi	319.45	427.37	620.53	1525.32	11.0
Hubei	325.31	498.38	868.28	1395.44	10.2
Henan	228.09	396.72	657.61	1385.06	12.8
Chongqing			622.95	1340.63	
Hainan	332.20	625.67	832.77	1327.07	9.7
Hunan	269.28	415.52	681.17	1272.75	10.9
Ningxia	291.23	398.52	584.53	1249.92	10.2
Qinghai	325.72	410.73	614.49	1226.24	9.2
Shaanxi	259.45	340.44	549.50	1208.42	10.8
Jiangxi	237.08	369.18	585.98	1152.39	11.1
Tibet	266.77	286.43	550.71	1112.59	10.0
Sichuan	237.08	368.94	577.89	1106.00	10.8
Guangxi	222.86	395.64	521.72	1072.79	11.0
Anhui	247.11	401.99	587.92	1059.00	10.2
Yunnan	255.90	364.51	560.13	956.46	9.2
Gansu	229.76	273.98	463.62	912.75	9.6
Guizhou	169.34	221.89	321.56	616.72	9.0

Note: In 1997, Chongqing was removed from Sichuan Province and promoted to the status of provincial-level municipality, like Beijing, Tianjin and Shanghai.

Source: China Economic Information Network: http://www.cei.gov.cn/.

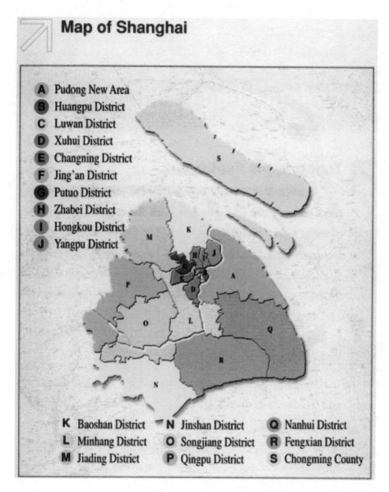

Notes:
* **Area (2004)**   6341 km²   0.06% of PRC total territory
* **Population (2005)**   17.78 million   1.39% of PRC total
* **GDP (2005)**   US$111.75 billion   4.63% of PRC total
* **GDP per capita (2005)** US$6283.68   367% of PRC average
* **Trade (2005)**   US$181.50 billion   12.8% of PRC total

Source: Shanghai Statistics (by the end of 2005). http://www.stats-sh.gov.cn/english/shgl/zrdl/zrdl.htm.

Figure 7A.2   Major economic indicators of Shanghai

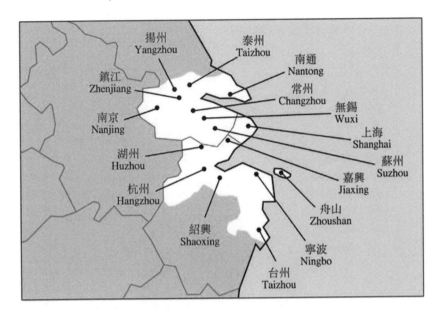

Notes:
* **Area**   109 961 km²   1% of PRC total land area
* **Population**   82.7 million (2005)   6.3% of PRC total
* **GDP**   US$414.5 billion (2005)   19% of PRC total
* **GDP per capita**   US$5015   US$1714 for PRC as a whole
* **Retail sales**   US$131.1 billion   16% of PRC total
* **Industrial output** US$333.7 billion   25.4% of PRC total
* **Exports**   US$276 billion   36% of PRC total
* **Imports**   US$227 billion   32% of PRC total
* **Actually used FDI** US$26.3 billion   43% of PRC total

Source: China Economic Information Network: http://www.cei.gov.cn/.

Figure 7A.3   The Yangtze River Delta

Table 7A.4 Major economic indicators of the Yangtze River Delta, 2005

Cities	Land area (km²)	Population (mn)	GDP (US$ bn)	GDP growth (%)	Per capita GDP (US$)ᵃ	Industrial outputᵇ (US$ bn)	Retail sales (US$ bn)	Exports (US$ bn)	Actual FDI (US$ bn)
YRD Total	**109 961**	**82.7**	**414.5**	**13.4**	**5 015ᵃ**	**781.4**	**131.1**	**276.0**	**26.30**
Shanghai	6 341	13.6	111.7	11.1	8 236	206.0	36.3	90.7	6.80
Nanjing	6 582	6.0	29.4	15.1	4 990	49.6	12.3	14.2	1.40
Suzhou	8 488	6.1	49.1	15.3	8 148	120.9	11.0	72.8	5.10
Wuxi	4 788	4.5	34.2	15.1	7 606	69.8	10.1	15.5	2.00
Changzhou	4 375	3.5	15.9	15.2	4 541	30.6	5.4	6.1	0.70
Yangzhou	6 634	4.6	11.3	15.0	2 471	17.7	3.7	1.9	0.50
Zhenjiang	3 847	2.7	10.6	15.0	3 978	16.2	2.9	2.0	0.60
Nantong	8 001	7.7	18.0	15.1	2 326	26.2	6.5	5.8	1.50
Taizhou	5 797	5.0	10.0	15.0	1 997	14.8	2.9	1.3	0.50
Hangzhou	16 596	6.6	35.9	13.0	5 474	66.4	11.9	19.8	1.70
Ningbo	9 365	5.6	29.9	12.5	5 389	59.7	9.3	22.2	2.30
Jiaxing	3 915	3.3	14.2	13.1	4 235	26.6	4.6	7.0	1.20
Huzhou	5 817	2.6	7.9	14.1	3 055	13.1	2.9	2.0	0.70
Shaoxing	8 256	4.4	17.7	13.3	4 062	39.2	4.7	8.1	0.90
Zhoushan	1 440	1.0	3.4	15.0	3 531	3.5	1.2	1.0	0.03
Taizhou	9 411	5.6	15.3	13.4	2 738	21.2	5.4	5.2	0.30

Notes:
ᵃ GDP per capita of the YRD is calculated based on the GDP and population figures.
ᵇ Industrial output of industrial enterprises with an annual sales income of over RMB 5 million.

Sources: *Statistical Yearbooks* of Shanghai, Jiangsu and Zhejiang, 2006, http://www.tdctrade.com.

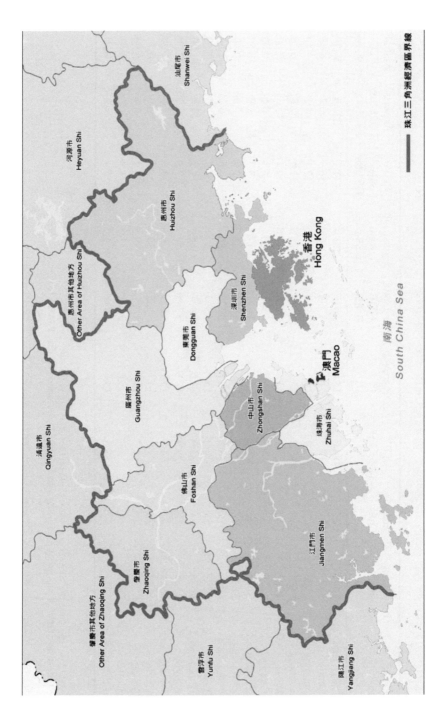

汕尾市
Shanwei Shi

河源市
Heyuan Shi

惠州市
Huizhou Shi

惠州市其他地方
Other Area of Huizhou Shi

东莞市
Dongguan Shi

深圳市
Shenzhen Shi

香港
Hong Kong

广州市
Guangzhou Shi

清远市
Qingyuan Shi

佛山市
Foshan Shi

中山市
Zhongshan Shi

澳門
Macao

珠海市
Zhuhai Shi

肇庆市
Zhaoqing Shi

肇庆市其他地方
Other Area of Zhaoqing Shi

江門市
Jiangmen Shi

云浮市
Yunfu Shi

阳江市
Yangjiang Shi

南海
South China Sea

珠江三角洲經濟區界線

226

Notes:

- **Area**   41 698 km²   0.4% of China's total land area
- **Population**   27.1 million   2.1% of China's total
- **GDP**   US$164.0 billion   8.5% of China's total
- **GDP per capita**   US$6043   US$1714 for China
- **Retail sales**   US$51.5 billion   8.3% of China's total
- **Industrial output**   US$282.8 billion   12.4% of China's total
- **Exports**   US$182.4 billion   30.7% of China's total
- **Imports**   US$227 billion   32% of China's total
- **Actually used FDI**   US$26.3 billion   43% of China's total

Source: http://www.hydrocarbons-technology.com/projects/guangdong/guangdong5.html.

Figure 7A.4   The Pearl River Delta

Table 7A.5   *Major economic indicators of the Pearl River Delta, 2004*

Cities	Land area (km²)	Population (mn)	GDP (US$ bn)	GDP growth (%)	Per capita GDP (US$)	Gross industrial output (US$ bn)	Retail sales (US$ bn)	Exports (US$ bn)	Actual FDI (US$ bn)
Total PRD[a]	**54 653.60**	**27.14**	**164.02**	**n.a.**	**6043**	**282.81**	**51.51**	**182.44**	**9.00**
Guangzhou	7 434.40	7.38	49.73	15.00	6 799	60.94	20.24	21.47	2.40
Shenzhen	1 952.80	1.65	41.36	17.30	7 161	78.65	11.06	77.84	2.35
Zhuhai	1 687.80	0.86	6.60	13.80	5 056	15.26	2.17	9.04	0.47
Foshan	3 848.50	3.51	20.01	16.30	5 758	40.25	6.55	13.83	0.69
Jiangmen	9 451.00	3.86	10.08	12.20	3 720	15.98	4.70	5.08	0.51
Dongguan	2 465.00	1.62	13.96	19.60	8 699	31.21	2.16	35.19	0.97
Zhongshan	1 800.10	1.39	7.37	18.70	5 317	20.48	2.57	10.01	0.51
Huizhou	11 158.00	2.93	8.28	15.10	2 857	13.53	1.36	8.74	0.63
Zhaoqing	14 856.00	3.94	6.63	13.20	3 198	6.51	0.70	1.24	0.48

Notes: At current price and statistical coverage includes all state-owned and non-state-owned enterprises with an annual sales revenue over 5 million yuan.
[a] The sum of the nine cities.

Sources: *Statistical Yearbooks* of Shanghai, Jiangsu and Zhejiang, 2006, http://www.tdctrade.com.

228

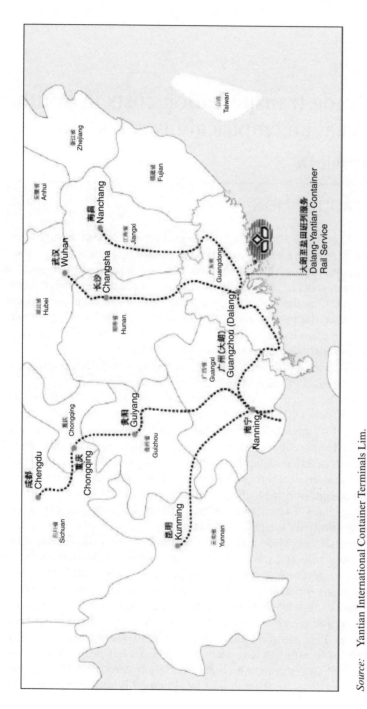

Source: Yantian International Container Terminals Lim.

Figure 7A.5   Railway connection to Yantian Port

8.   Trade transportation costs in South Asia: an empirical investigation*

Prabir De

1.   INTRODUCTION

As South Asia began to approach its second era of regional cooperation, the region witnessed a considerable rise in economic growth and regional trade.[1] Accompanying this growth has been an increase in demand for infrastructure services, for production, consumption and international trade purposes. In the coming years, South Asian merchandise exports, recorded under the provisions of the South Asia Free Trade Agreement (SAFTA), are expected to reach US$14 billion by the end of this decade, from the present volume of US$8 billion.[2] A failure to respond to this demand will cause bottlenecks and act as a check on South Asian trade from growing to its full potential – regionally and otherwise.

Realizing the urgent need for improved trade and transport facilitation for enhancing South Asian trade, the Heads of the South Asian Association for Regional Cooperation (SAARC) countries have been emphasizing the potential of an integrated transport system for the region.[3] They have stressed that higher intraregional trade will not be achieved until and unless the physical infrastructure and appropriate customs clearance and other facilitation measures, including multimodal transport operations, are in place. They also point out that in this effort, uninterrupted overland connectivity is equally important.

A substantial theoretical and empirical literature exists on the impact of poor infrastructure and trade facilitation measures on external trade and on income in developing countries. In general, trade liberalization and trade facilitation for external trade induce a substitution effect in consumption and production by changing the relative prices by way of a reduction in trade cost, and thereby better reallocate resources towards economically efficient uses. This literature has formed the basis for much of the policy advice offered to South Asian countries. Its focus has been on trade and transport facilitation steps, which are urgently needed in order to reduce transportation costs in general, and to eliminate border delays, enhance trade efficiency, effect technological upgradation at borders and train human resources for dealing with external trade in particular.

In a highly competitive world economy, transportation cost is a significant determinant of competitiveness, just as an integrated and efficient transport network plays a pivotal role in integrating a region.[4] An uninterrupted connectivity, therefore, will not only better integrate South Asia physically but will also reduce intraregional trade transportation costs. To date, South Asia as a region pays a huge amount for international transportation costs.[5] A number of studies also indicate that the benefits of trade liberalization have so far remained limited, since the region by and large has failed to reduce the trade transportation costs, both inland and international. The fact is that competitive advantage in both international and regional trade is increasingly being defined by logistics as other factors lose importance.

This chapter aims to estimate the trade transportation costs in South Asia. Transportation costs vary widely across both goods and countries. To a very large extent, the variability of transportation costs in South Asia depend on the performance of India's inland and international transportation infrastructure services, since intra-South Asia trade is largely driven by India alone.[6] The trade transportation efficiency of South Asia depends very significantly on how India's international border in the region is performing. At the same time, understanding the transportation costs is of particular interest because it enables a better evaluation of the required transport services of the region.

The rest of the chapter is organized as follows. Section 2 presents stylized facts on South Asian trade flows and trade transportation costs. Section 3 provides estimates of trade transportation costs for each of the South Asian countries, including data and methodology. Finally, conclusions are drawn in Section 4.

2.   INTRA-SOUTH ASIA TRADE FLOWS AND TRANSPORTATION COSTS: SOME STYLIZED FACTS

The growing importance of intraregional trade has always been an important policy agenda of SAARC. By concluding a free trade agreement (FTA) on 1 July 2006, South Asia has received growing attention as a region that is fast integrating with the global economy. However, the performance of South Asian countries in terms of intraregional trade is not encouraging. SAARC countries do not have significant trading activity with one another in spite of their geographical proximity.[7] The amount of intraregional trade

Table 8.1   Intra-South Asian trade in 2006

(a) Exports (US$ million)

	Bangladesh	India	Nepal	Pakistan	Sri Lanka	Total	Share (%)
Bangladesh		139.48	4.08	61.01	10.33	214.90	2.69
India	1892.55		974.19	752.82	2190.64	5810.20	72.70
Nepal	3.12	396.16		3.80	0.12	403.20	5.05
Pakistan	250.24	395.84	4.23		180.37	830.68	10.39
Sri Lanka	17.15	664.54	0.47	51.10		733.26	9.17
Total						7992.24	100.00

(b) Imports (US$ million)

	Bangladesh	India	Nepal	Pakistan	Sri Lanka	Total	Share (%)
Bangladesh		2144.63	3.43	163.22	11.59	2322.87	29.44
India	121.91		435.77	184.02	614.04	1355.74	17.18
Nepal	4.49	1071.61		4.65	0.52	1081.27	13.71
Pakistan	79.92	677.44	4.18		69.39	830.93	10.53
Sri Lanka	10.41	2153.42	0.13	135.67		2299.63	29.14
Total						7890.44	100.00

Source: Direction of Trade Statistics Yearbook 2006, IMF.

in South Asia is quite small relative to extraregional trade. However, India continues to have a dominant share in the region's exports and the distribution of merchandise trade in South Asia remains largely uneven.

Table 8.1 gives a sense of the trade flows in South Asia. Official intraregional exports in South Asia are about US$7.99 billion;[8] India alone contributes about 72.79 per cent of total intraregional exports. The remaining South Asian countries, namely, Bangladesh, Nepal, Pakistan and Sri Lanka, contribute less than 30 per cent. However, the scenario changes completely when we consider intra-South Asian imports. Bangladesh and Sri Lanka each share 29 per cent of these imports, whereas India contributes about 17 per cent. Pakistan is the only country having around a 10 per cent share in both intra-South Asian exports and imports. A large portion of India's merchandise trade with South Asian countries is carried overland. For example, about 63.10 per cent of India's US$5.81 billion exports to South Asia in 2006 were carried by road, 18.90 per cent by sea, 13.30 per cent by rail, 3.20 per cent by air, and 1.50 per cent by inland water transport (Table 8.2). Obviously, the overall transportation efficiency of the

Table 8.2   Modal composition of India's merchandise: trade with South Asian countries in 2005

Transport mode	Share (%)
Road	63.10
Sea	18.90
Rail	13.30
Air	3.20
Inland water transport	1.50
Total	100.00

Note: Average over India's trading partners in South Asia, namely, Bangladesh, Bhutan, Maldives, Nepal, Pakistan and Sri Lanka.

Source: De (2007).

South Asian countries depends on how India's international land border in South Asia is performing.

Since a large portion of intra-South Asian trade is centred on India, it is important to understand India's trade flows within the region. Table 8.3 (a, b) shows India's commodity-wise aggregate exports to and imports from selected South Asian countries for the financial year 2005–06.

Tables 8.3(a) and (b) deliver some important messages. First, India trades with South Asian countries in a large number of items. Fuels, mining and forest products, textiles and clothing, and food products are India's top three export commodities to South Asian countries. Their exports alone contribute about one-quarter of India's total exports to South Asia (Table 8.3(a)), whereas the shares of leather and leather products, and transport equipment in India's total exports to South Asia, are comparatively very low. India's two-way trade in South Asia in electrical and electronics is small (US$157.65 million). In automobile and components, it is comparatively high (US$431 million). India is a net importer of metal and metal products (US$104.64 million), and leather and leather products (US$6.89 million), and a net exporter in the other commodities.

Second, in the case of India's imports from South Asia, metal and metal products, textiles and clothing, and chemicals are the top three import commodities. Import of food products comes next. India's imports are relatively concentrated on these four commodities, which together account for about 55 per cent of India's total imports from South Asia.

Third, if we look at the country-wise breakdown of India's trade in South Asia, we get a mixed picture. Table 8.4 shows India's commodity-wise trade with its South Asian partners, for both imports and exports. While India's top

Table 8.3   India's merchandise trade with South Asian countries in 2005–06*

(a) Exports**

Commodity group#	Value	Share
	(US$ million)	(%)
Fuels, mining and forest products	1301.09	24.84
Textiles and clothing	702.53	13.41
Food products	496.99	9.49
Chemicals and chemical products	460.00	8.78
Automobiles and components	428.75	8.19
Iron and steel	352.93	6.74
Rubber and plastics	226.65	4.33
Machinery and mechanical appliances	171.56	3.28
Pharmaceuticals	138.05	2.64
Metal and metal products	137.86	2.63
Electrical and electronics	120.35	2.30
Paper and pulp	77.22	1.47
Transport equipment	27.42	0.52
Leather and leather products	2.97	0.06
Miscellaneous	593.86	11.32
Total	5238.23	100.00

(b) Imports**

Commodity group	Value	Share
	(US$ million)	(%)
Metal and metal products	242.50	19.18
Textiles and clothing	168.36	13.32
Chemicals and chemical products	148.87	11.78
Food products	140.42	11.11
Iron and steel	65.14	5.15
Rubber and plastics	61.53	4.87
Electrical and electronics	37.30	2.95
Fuels, mining and forest products	24.10	1.91
Paper and pulp	17.56	1.39
Machinery and mechanical appliances	11.69	0.92
Leather and leather products	9.86	0.78
Pharmaceuticals	5.35	0.42
Automobiles and components	2.11	0.17
Transport equipment	0.69	0.05
Miscellaneous	328.66	26.00
Total	1264.14	100.00

Table 8.3   (continued)

Notes:
* Excluding India's trade with Afghanistan, Bhutan and Maldives.
** Does not consider trade in agriculture.
\# Commodity groups were calculated based on Appendix Table 8A.1.

Source: Calculated based on Export–Import Databank, Ministry of Commerce and Industry, Government of India.

three export commodities to Bangladesh are textiles and clothing, food products, and fuels, mining and forest products, for Nepal they are fuels, mining and forest products, automobiles and components, and pharmaceuticals. In the case of Pakistan, India's exports are primarily driven by chemicals, rubber and plastics, and food products, whereas fuels, mining and forest products, automobiles and components, and textiles and clothing drive India's exports to Sri Lanka. What emerges is that India's exports to South Asian countries are largely driven by three commodity groups, namely, textiles and clothing, food products, fuels, mining and minerals. In the case of India's imports from South Asian countries, textiles and clothing, chemicals and products, food products, iron and steel, and metal and products are the major commodities. Most obviously the competitiveness of each of these commodity groups is very sensitive to trade costs and the reliability of logistics.

Therefore we find that (i) India's exports to South Asia are more diversified, compared to India's imports from the region, (ii) India's two-way trade in South Asia in fuels, mining and forest products, textiles and clothing, food products, and chemicals is relatively higher than that of other commodities, and (iii) India's exports of fuels, mining and forest products are crucial for the growth of South Asia in general and Nepal and Sri Lanka in particular.

From the pattern of intra-South Asia merchandise trade flows, some sort of trade interdependence on a limited variety of goods can be inferred. This may increase if regional trade is allowed to grow by removing barriers to trade.[9] Since South Asian countries suffer from supply-side bottlenecks, high transportation costs act as a serious constraint to enhancing the merchandise trade flow in South Asia. We now look at some stylized facts on the incidence of transportation costs in South Asia.

The World Bank, in its *Doing Business Database*,[10] found that the cost of trade in South Asia is comparatively very high. In terms of time, the region's performance is just above that of Sub-Saharan Africa (Table 8.5(a)), in both exports and imports, whereas in terms of costs, the region's performance is better than that of Central Asia but worse than that of Latin America. As noted in Table 8.5(b), South Asia still takes about 34.40

Table 8.4 India's trade with selected South Asian countries in 2005–06

Commodity group	Bangladesh				Nepal			
	Export		Import		Export		Import	
	Value (US$)	Share (%)	Value (US$)	Share (%)	Value (US$)	Share (%)	Value (US$)	Share (%)
Food products	324.55	19.50	15.97	12.57	26.45	3.08	52.92	13.93
Fuels, mining and forest products	185.28	11.13	1.59	1.25	414.65	48.22	7.38	1.94
Chemicals and products	107.78	6.48	40.72	32.06	40.40	4.70	47.79	12.58
Electrical and electronics	50.91	3.06	2.74	2.16	19.59	2.28	4.39	1.16
Iron and steel	129.77	7.80	0.89	0.70	37.82	4.40	49.39	13.00
Metal and products	37.94	2.28	4.21	3.31	7.41	0.86	21.14	5.57
Machinery and mechanical appliances	60.16	3.61	1.17	0.92	30.91	3.59	2.55	0.67
Leather and products	0.54	0.03	2.42	1.91	0.38	0.04	3.18	0.84
Paper and pulp	16.11	0.97	0.07	0.06	13.06	1.52	1.89	0.50
Pharmaceuticals	23.54	1.41	0.00	0.00	45.64	5.31	5.17	1.36
Rubber and plastics	49.74	2.99	1.90	1.50	22.66	2.63	41.45	10.91
Textiles and clothing	381.85	22.94	51.65	40.66	26.40	3.07	71.72	18.88
Automobiles and components	79.86	4.80	0.02	0.02	55.36	6.44	0.78	0.21
Transport equipment	0.22	0.01	0.00	0.00	1.15	0.13	0.00	0.00
Miscellaneous	216.11	12.98	3.68	2.90	118.09	13.73	70.10	18.45
Total	1664.36	100.00	127.03	100.00	859.97	100.00	379.85	100.00

Commodity group	Pakistan				Sri Lanka			
	Export		Import		Export		Import	
	Value (US$)	Share (%)	Value (US$)	Share (%)	Value (US$)	Share (%)	Value (US$)	Share (%)
Food products	87.47	12.69	34.54	19.24	58.52	2.89	36.99	6.40
Fuels, mining and forest products	45.51	6.60	0.73	0.41	655.65	32.38	14.40	2.49
Chemicals and products	235.08	34.11	24.31	13.54	76.74	3.79	36.05	6.24
Electrical and electronics	3.19	0.46	1.53	0.85	46.66	2.30	28.64	4.96
Iron and steel	37.71	5.47	0.54	0.30	147.63	7.29	14.32	2.48
Machinery and mechanical appliances	7.28	1.06	0.06	0.03	73.21	3.62	7.91	1.37
Metal and products	7.59	1.10	6.57	3.66	84.92	4.19	210.58	36.45
Leather and products	0.21	0.03	1.71	0.95	1.84	0.09	2.55	0.44
Paper and pulp	0.10	0.01	0.05	0.03	47.95	2.37	15.55	2.69
Pharmaceuticals	5.97	0.87	0.03	0.02	62.90	3.11	0.15	0.03
Rubber and plastics	87.50	12.70	1.91	1.06	66.75	3.30	16.27	2.82
Textiles and clothing	77.68	11.27	35.72	19.89	216.60	10.70	9.27	1.60
Automobiles and components	0.39	0.06	0.06	0.03	293.14	14.48	1.25	0.22
Transport equipment	0.00	0.00	0.00	0.00	26.05	1.29	0.69	0.12
Miscellaneous	93.55	13.57	71.80	39.99	166.11	8.20	183.08	31.69
Total	689.23	100.00	179.56	100.00	2024.67	100.00	577.70	100.00

Source: As for Table 8.3.

237

Table 8.5   Trading across borders: cost and time in 2006

(a) Region

Region or economy	Cost to export (US$ per container)	Rank	Cost to import (US$ per container)	Rank
OECD	811.00	1	882.60	1
East Asia & Pacific	884.80	2	1037.10	2
Middle East & North Africa	923.90	3	1182.80	3
Latin America & Caribbean	1067.50	4	1225.50	4
South Asia	1236.00	5	1494.90	5
Europe & Central Asia	1450.20	6	1589.30	6
Sub-Saharan Africa	1561.10	7	1946.90	7

Region or economy	Time for export (days)	Rank	Time for import (days)	Rank
OECD	10.50	1	12.20	1
Latin America & Caribbean	22.20	2	27.90	3
East Asia & Pacific	23.90	3	25.90	2
Middle East & North Africa	27.10	4	35.40	4
Europe & Central Asia	29.20	5	37.10	5
South Asia	34.40	6	41.50	6
Sub-Saharan Africa	40.00	7	51.50	7

(b) South Asia

Economy	Cost to export (US$ per container)	Rank*	Cost to import (US$ per container)	Rank*
Sri Lanka	797	1	789	1
India	864	2	1 244	3
Bangladesh	902	3	1 287	4
Pakistan	996	4	1 005	2
Maldives	1 000	5	1 784	5
Bhutan	1 230	6	1 950	7
Nepal	1 599	7	1 800	6
Max	4300 (Tajikistan)		4565 (Zimbabwe)	
Min	265 (Tonga)		333 (Singapore)	

Economy	Time for export (days)	Rank*	Time for import (days)	Rank*
Maldives	15	1	21	2
Pakistan	24	2	19	1
Sri Lanka	25	3	27	3

Table 8.5   (continued)

(b) South Asia

Economy	Time for export (days)	Rank*	Time for import (days)	Rank*
India	27	4	41	5
Bangladesh	35	5	57	7
Bhutan	39	6	42	6
Nepal	44	7	37	4
Max	105		139	
Min	3		3	

Notes:
* Rank in South Asia.
** For definitions, refer to *Doing Business Database 2007*, available at www.doingbusiness.org.

Source: Doing Business Database 2007, World Bank.

days for exports and 41.50 days for imports, whereas Sub-Saharan Africa takes about 40 days for exports and 51.50 days for imports. In terms of costs, an export consignment takes US$1236 per container in South Asia, whereas US$1494 is the cost of importing one loaded container. In general, South Asia performs fairly poorly, compared to the OECD benchmark, in both time and cost.

Within South Asia, there is also high variation in cost and time of trading across borders. Nepal is the most expensive country in terms of export and import of containerized cargo, whereas Sri Lanka is the least expensive, even lower than the OECD average. In terms of time, the performance of South Asian countries is not impressive. At the two extremes are Nepal and Bangladesh, which take 44 days to export and 57 days to import, respectively. India appears in the middle, in terms of time for both exports and imports. Sri Lanka's performance in costs of exports and imports is impressive but certainly not in terms of time. Time delay in shipment for both exports and imports appears to wipe out the benefits of cost advantages in Sri Lanka.

The aforesaid aggregate estimates of transportation costs and time do not reveal much about the magnitude of transaction costs and time at the border. These become especially important as a large portion of South Asia's trade is passed through a land border. This is particularly true of the trade between India and Bangladesh.

The situation in respect of South Asian countries is highly volatile and continuous to be unsatisfactory. For example, India's overland trade with

Table 8.6　Transaction time and cost for India's overland exports to Bangladesh

Particulars	Subramanian and Arnold (2001) Survey year: 1998	Das and Pohit (2006) Survey year: 2002	De and Ghosh (2006) Survey year: 2005
Transaction costs (% of shipment value)*	–	10.38	16.80
Border crossing delays (days)**	2.5	3.63	3.92
Types of documents required at border (no.)	29	–	17
Copies of documents required at border (no.)	118	–	67

Notes:
* Consider costs taken at Petrapole (Indian border point) to cross the border, unloading at Benapole (Bangladesh border point) and crossing the border after unloading at Benapole.
** Considers only time taken at Petrapole to clear goods, unloading at Benapole, and crossing the border after unloading at Benapole.
*** Data for 1998 and 2002 are collected from Subramanian and Arnold (2001), and Das and Pohit (2006), respectively; data for 2005 are taken from De and Ghosh (2006).

Source:　De and Ghosh (2008).

Bangladesh involves high trade transaction costs. Border delay in terms of time for India's exports to Bangladesh at the border (here, Petrapole in India; Benapole in Bangladesh) has not shown any change during the period 1998 to 2005 (Table 8.6). On the one hand, delays in terms of time at the border increased from 2.5 days in 1998 to 3.92 days in 2005, and on the other, the costs of transaction increased from 10.38 per cent in 2002 to 16.80 per cent in 2005. One of the major reasons for high transaction time (and also costs) of India's exports to Bangladesh is cumbersome and complex cross-border trading procedures and the rent-seeking economy that impede trade at the border (Das and Pohit, 2006; De and Ghosh, 2008; De and Bhattacharya, 2007a, 2007b).[11] At the same time, complex requirements in cross-border trade increase the possibility of corruption. All this leads to high transaction costs at the border. As a result, informal trade in South Asia has grown sharply, and has in many cases exceeded the formal trade volume.[12] The loss to industry and consumers in general on account of trade transaction costs is considerable.

To sum up, the 'border effects' impose significantly higher transportation costs for exporters in South Asia. Therefore the region is likely to gain by expanding intraregional trade through complementary investments in infrastructure, continued policy reforms, and other policy initiatives that facilitate trade at the border. What is more, eliminating border obstacles would contribute to trade integration in South Asia.

3. TRADE TRANSPORTATION COSTS: REGIONAL PROFILE

3.1 Data and Methodology

The cost of transportation of merchandise from one country to another in South Asia is a combination of two major components: inland and international transportation costs. Understanding the unit freight rate in these two legs will help us to discover the variation in cost of transportation across commodities in South Asia.

An important aspect of trade costs is the difficulties in obtaining accurate measures of transportation costs. Due to paucity of trade cost data, the problem is exacerbated when one attempts to measure the transportation costs in the context of South Asia. Unlike the USA, which gathers Census and Transportation data, South Asian countries do not compile international trade data by transport modes and countries. Many measures have been used to deal with transportation cost. The most straightforward is the difference between the c.i.f. (cost, insurance and freight) and f.o.b. (free on board) quotations. Their difference is a measure of the cost of getting an item from an exporting country to an importing country. However, the c.i.f./f.o.b. factor is calculated for those countries that report the total value of imports at c.i.f. and f.o.b. values, both of which involve serious measurement error.[13] The measure aggregates overall commodities imported, so it is biased if high transport cost countries systematically import lower transport cost goods. This would be particularly important if we were using exports, which tend to be concentrated in a few specific goods. It is less so for imports, which are generally more diversified and vary less in composition across countries. To avoid measurement errors in the c.i.f./f.o.b. ratio, we estimate transportation costs by using the open-source freight database of Maersk Sealand, which contains information on bilateral freight rates, both inland and international, by both commodities and countries.[14] The usual caveat is that the freight rates considered in this chapter are the gross rates and not the negotiated rates that the shipping line entered into. The negotiated rates happened to be lower than the gross rates. These gross rates are collected for shipment of a 20-ft container (TEU) between the major container ports of origin and the destination countries from the historical freight rate database of Maersk Sealand (2007). The rates are quarterly averaged for the years 2000 and 2005, and include container handling charges, documentation fees, government taxes and levies, etc. of both the trading partners.

In this chapter we follow the methodology adopted by Hummels (1999) and rely on the Maersk Sealand (2007) database. The Hummels methodology is useful to estimate the magnitude of transportation costs. There will obviously be problems of concordance, if not checked at the start of the trade compilation. We tackle this particular problem in two ways. First, we classify the commodity groups at the 4-digit HS level and create a set of 18 commodities for which freight rates at the country level in bilateral pairs are available from Maersk Sealand (2007). Second, we draw the freight rates for each commodity group, both the international and inland legs of the journey, from Maersk Sealand.

To give a better shape to the freight rates, we made three assumptions. First, since a large part of India's trade with Pakistan is passed through a third country, we took the freight rate between India and Pakistan via Dubai.[15] Second, Nepal, being a landlocked country, conducts its trade with Pakistan and Sri Lanka through the port of Kolkata. So we have always added an additional freight mark-up for export and import of Nepal's cargo passed through Kolkata Port except for the country's trade with India and Bangladesh, which is carried overland. Third, we consider that the trade between India, Bangladesh and Nepal is carried overland and draw the overland freight rate from the CONCOR.[16]

In order to evaluate the incidence of transportation costs, our analysis follows the following three steps: (i) aggregation of the freight rates, (ii) estimation of the *ad valorem* transportation costs, and (iii) the weight-value ratio of trade and transportation costs.

Aggregation of freight rates
We first estimate the country-wise freight rate, which is a weighted average of all commodity groups across all trading partners for both international and inland shipments of a container from one country to another. We use equations (8.1) and (8.2) to estimate the country-wise freight rate (weighted average) per container for both inland and international shipment.

$$F_{ij} = \frac{\sum_k Q_{ij}^k f_{ij}^k}{\sum_k Q_{ij}^k} \tag{8.1}$$

$$F_i = \frac{1}{n}(F_{ij}) \tag{8.2}$$

where F_i represents the weighted average freight rate per container of country i, which is averaged over all commodity groups across all trading partners of country i, F_{ij} denotes the weighted average freight rate per container for country i for import of commodity k from country j, Q_{ij}^k stands for import of commodity k in TEU by country i from country j, f_{ij}^k represents the freight rate per TEU of import of commodity k by country i from country j, k is the commodity traded (at the 4-digit HS level) between partners i and j, and n is number of bilateral trading partners of i. We collect f_{ij}^k for inland and international transportation separately. F_i is estimated from the 4-digit HS level for imports of country i from its partner for the year 2005.[17]

Estimation of *ad valorem* transportation costs

We estimate the *ad valorem* transportation costs (both international and inland) for shipment of a container from one country to all its trading partners. The *ad valorem* (trade-weighted) inland and international transportation costs provide us with US$ transport cost per US$ of import and its commodity distribution across countries. We use equation (8.3) to estimate commodity distribution of *ad valorem* inland transportation cost (*AdvInlTC*) for import of country i from country j, whereas equation (8.4) is used to estimate the commodity distribution of *ad valorem* international transportation costs (*AdvIntTC*).

$$AdvInlTC_i^k = \frac{\sum_k Q_{ij}^k f_{ij}^{inland}}{\sum_k M_{ij}^k}*100 \qquad (8.3)$$

$$AdvIntTC_i^k = \frac{\sum_k Q_{ij}^k f_{ij}^{international}}{\sum_k M_{ij}^k}*100 \qquad (8.4)$$

where $AdvInlTC_i^k$ and $AdvIntTC_i^k$ represent inland and international *ad valorem* transportation costs respectively for country i for commodity k, Q_{ij}^k stands for import of commodity group k in weight (here, in TEU) by country i from country j, f_{ij}^{inland} represents inland freight rate per TEU for import of commodity k by country i from country j, $f_{ij}^{international}$ represents international freight rate per TEU for import of commodity k by country i from country j, M_{ij}^k stands for import of commodity group k in value (here, in US$) by country i from country j, k is the commodity traded at the 4-digit HS level. The transportation costs are estimated for k commodity groups for imports of country i from its partner for the year 2005. Commodity composition of inland and international transportation costs are estimated as a percentage of total import.

The weight–value ratio of trade

In order to evaluate transportation needs, one has to describe regional trade in terms of weight. We calculate the weight–value ratio for South Asian countries for their regional trade with the help of equation (8.5).[18]

$$w_{it} = \sum_k S_{ikt} w_k \tag{8.5}$$

where w_k is the median weight–value ratio for each HS 4-digit commodity k in imports (exports) for the year 2005, S_{ikt} is the share of product k in the trade bundle of country i at time t, and w_{it} is the aggregate weight–value ratio for country i's imports for the year t.

Data

The data are reported in HS classification code at the 4-digit level, or 3029 goods, and include shipment values and quantities for five South Asian countries, namely, Bangladesh, India, Nepal, Pakistan and Sri Lanka. Commodity-wise freight rates for inland and international shipment were collected from Maersk Sealand (2007), whereas countries' imports at the 4-digit HS level were collected from COMTRADE (UN, 2007).[19] Quantity data are missing for approximately 12 per cent of total South Asian regional trade flows for the year 2005. The usual caveat applies. We estimate the transportation costs only for regional trade flows. However, the estimated rates may substantially vary if the countries' trade with the rest of the world (other than South Asia) is considered in this chapter. The aggregation of transportation costs is inevitable due to the coarseness of observations of complex underlying phenomena.

3.2 Regional Trade Transportation Costs

Aggregated freight rates

The country-wise freight rates (weighted average) per container for both inland and international shipment were derived using equations (8.1) and (8.2). Figure 8.1 provides the aggregated freight rates, and the same at commodity levels is captured in Table 8.7. The following observations are worth noting.

First, we find that the aggregated freight rates vary across South Asian countries for their regional trade. Since a larger portion of South Asian trade is carried overland, the incidence of inland freight is much higher than the international (ocean) freight. It ranges from US$1676 per TEU in Nepal to US$110 per TEU in Sri Lanka, with Pakistan occupying the middle ground.

Second, the international freight rates of Nepal, India and Bangladesh are lower than the South Asian average of US$193 per TEU. Pakistan has the highest international freight rate, at US$718 per TEU.

Third, the inland freight rates in India, Nepal and Bangladesh are much higher than the South Asian average of US$1328 per container. Nepal came out as the country with the highest freight rate and seems to be paying

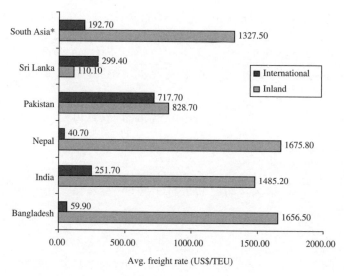

Note: * South Asia average for imports.

Figure 8.1 Aggregated average freight rates in 2005 (weighted average)

a higher price for being landlocked. For the other countries, ranking changes significantly, but Sri Lanka remains among the countries with the lowest inland freight rates.

Fourth, the commodity-wise weighted average of freight rates in Table 8.7 and the same in both legs of the journey, as recorded in Appendix Table 8A.2, show that the dispersion in freight rates across countries is not wide, except for Sri Lanka. We also note that barring Sri Lanka, the variation in freight rates (weighted average) across goods is also not large in South Asia.

Fifth, the inland transportation cost is the major component of overall transportation costs in South Asia; about 88 per cent of total trade transportation costs are incurred by the inland leg of the journey.

Sixth, there is high variation in the composition of freight rates. The composition of inland and international freight rates is quite similar in Bangladesh and Nepal. Everywhere the inland leg of the journey is the key element. It is however totally different in Sri Lanka, where the international leg of the journey constitutes the entire transportation.

Finally, there is not much variation across commodities when we consider the share of inland freight rate in total freight rate, while the international freight rate varies across commodities. However, in no case does the share of international freight rate exceed that of the inland freight rate. Therefore, what emerges is that the inland leg of the journey is much more

Table 8.7   Aggregated freight rate (weighted average), US$ per TEU*

Commodity group	Bangladesh	India	Nepal	Pakistan	Sri Lanka	Total
Agriculture and food products	1696.10	1856.10	1672.20	1303.50	427.00	1496.70
Chemicals	1683.10	1556.40	1681.30	1230.10	403.70	1588.80
Electrical and electronics	1692.30	1491.70	1670.00	1677.10	391.60	1331.70
Fuels, mining, and forest products	1699.20	1725.70	1670.00	1669.70	390.50	1504.50
Iron and steel	1671.10	1658.30	1670.00	1734.00	420.00	1468.90
Leather and products	2024.40	1776.30	1670.00	3324.10	1026.90	1902.70
Machinery and mechanical appliances	1720.70	1673.50	1670.50	1663.50	394.20	1363.30
Metal and products	1791.80	1584.80	1671.50	1673.20	395.70	1379.10
Paper and pulp	1676.30	1516.70	1672.60	1709.80	390.10	1282.70
Pharmaceuticals	1750.40	1738.60	1690.50	1206.80	409.60	1266.60
Rubber and plastic	1728.90	1705.70	1670.00	1640.20	454.40	1443.10
Textiles and clothing	2065.50	1654.90	1749.40	1674.10	554.10	1688.20
Transport equipment	1710.90	1795.50	1679.70	1505.30	395.40	1081.00
Miscellaneous	1925.00	1534.00	1670.00	1425.10	397.70	1552.80
Total	1716.40	1736.90	1676.60	1546.50	409.50	1510.20

Note: * Both inland and international freight rate.

important than the international leg in South Asian regional trade transportation.

Estimated *ad valorem* transportation costs
We turn now to estimate the *ad valorem* equivalent rate of transportation costs with the help of equations (8.3) and (8.4). We measure the *ad valorem* transportation costs (both international and inland) for imports by combining both inland and international transportation costs. The *ad valorem* (trade-weighted) transportation costs provide us with a US$ transport cost per US$ of import and its commodity distribution across countries.

Table 8.8 (a)–(c) provides evidence on the level and distribution of trade transportation costs for each importer by commodity across seven Asian

Table 8.8   *Estimated* ad valorem *transportation costs, 2005 (% of import value)**

(a) Total transportation costs (inland + international)

Commodity group	Bangladesh	India	Nepal	Pakistan	Sri Lanka	Total
Agriculture and food products	57.70	29.90	188.60	29.10	11.80	63.42
Chemicals and products	19.20	17.80	84.60	9.40	4.80	27.16
Electrical and electronics	2.20	4.90	0.00	1.40	0.50	1.80
Iron and steel	29.00	22.60	60.50	16.80	4.90	26.76
Leather and products	3.20	2.80	4.80	10.60	0.90	4.46
Machinery and mechanical appliances	1.90	1.10	8.40	1.50	0.60	2.70
Metal and products	11.50	4.80	29.20	12.50	2.10	12.02
Paper and pulp	23.10	80.50	67.80	9.80	5.50	37.34
Pharmaceuticals	0.80	3.30	5.20	0.50	0.40	2.04
Rubber and plastic	10.20	8.50	4.20	10.10	2.70	7.14
Textiles and clothing	6.90	13.00	45.10	8.80	1.30	15.02
Transport equipment	3.90	0.30	0.00	49.00	0.50	10.74
Total	14.13	15.79	41.53	13.29	3.00	17.55

(b) Inland transportation costs

Commodity group	Bangladesh	India	Nepal	Pakistan	Sri Lanka	Total
Agriculture and food products	56.60	21.80	188.30	15.80	3.00	39.50
Chemicals and products	18.90	15.50	84.60	5.00	1.30	52.00
Electrical and electronics	2.20	4.30	0.00	0.80	0.10	1.70
Iron and steel	29.00	21.50	60.50	8.60	1.30	28.00
Leather and products	2.50	2.50	4.80	6.60	0.60	2.60
Machinery and mechanical appliances	1.80	1.00	8.40	0.80	0.20	2.30
Metal and products	10.50	4.00	29.20	6.70	0.60	5.80
Paper and pulp	23.00	69.20	67.70	5.10	1.60	27.10
Pharmaceuticals	0.70	3.30	5.20	0.30	0.10	1.80
Rubber and plastic	9.70	8.20	4.20	5.50	0.60	5.90
Textiles and clothing	5.20	11.40	45.00	4.70	0.30	9.90
Transport equipment	3.80	0.30	0.00	29.00	0.10	1.30
Total	28.10	25.00	42.90	24.20	1.40	33.70

(c) International transportation costs

Commodity group	Bangladesh	India	Nepal	Pakistan	Sri Lanka	Total
Agriculture and food products	1.20	8.20	0.30	13.30	8.70	7.00
Chemicals and products	0.20	2.30	0.00	4.40	3.50	2.50

Table 8.8   (continued)

(c) International transportation costs

Commodity group	Bangladesh	India	Nepal	Pakistan	Sri Lanka	Total
Electrical and electronics	0.00	0.60	0.00	0.70	0.30	0.20
Iron and steel	0.00	1.10	0.00	8.10	3.60	1.60
Leather and products	0.70	0.30	0.00	4.00	0.30	0.60
Machinery and mechanical appliances	0.10	0.00	0.00	0.70	0.40	0.20
Metal and products	1.00	0.80	0.00	5.80	1.50	1.00
Paper and pulp	0.10	11.30	0.10	4.70	4.00	3.70
Pharmaceuticals	0.00	0.00	0.00	0.20	0.30	0.20
Rubber and plastic	0.50	0.30	0.00	4.60	2.00	2.00
Textiles and clothing	1.70	1.60	0.10	4.10	1.10	1.40
Transport equipment	0.10	0.00	0.00	20.00	0.30	0.60
Total	1.00	4.20	0.10	21.00	3.70	4.60

Note: * Trade weighted over all South Asian partners.

countries for the year 2005, and Figure 8.2 shows the aggregate *ad valorem* rate for South Asia. The following broad features are worth noting.

1. The trade-weighted *ad valorem* transportation cost for all goods is lowest in the case of Sri Lanka (3 per cent in 2005) and highest in the case of Nepal (41.53 per cent in 2005). Nepal is landlocked, and thus pays a high price for transportation.
2. Transportation costs are lower for manufactured goods than for traditional commodities. In general, South Asian countries, except Sri Lanka, stand out as having exceptionally high freight rates in traditional commodities such as agriculture and food products, and paper and pulp. Agriculture and food products incur the highest transportation costs (63.42 per cent) in South Asia, while electrical and electronics have the lowest transportation costs (1.80 per cent).
3. The *ad valorem* transportation cost varies across commodities and countries. For example, transportation costs for imports of chemicals, agriculture and food products, iron and steel, and metal are comparatively very expensive in Nepal and Bangladesh. Similarly, India experiences relatively higher transportation costs for imports of paper and pulp (80 per cent) from South Asia. Transportation costs for imports of high-end manufacturers such as electrical and electronics appear to be low. Perhaps the low level of intra-South Asian trade in these two categories could explain the low transportation costs.

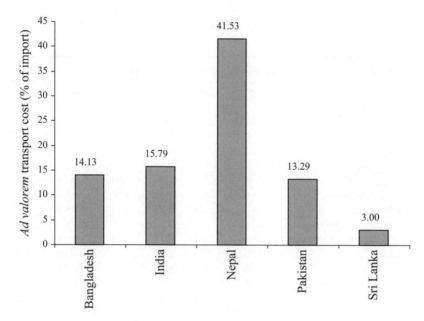

Note: Trade weighted over all South Asian partners.

Figure 8.2   Estimated ad valorem *transportation costs by country in 2005 as a percentage of imports*

4. The variation in *ad valorem* transportation costs across countries and commodities is influenced by inland infrastructure facilities since the inland leg of the journey is the crucial determinant of total transportation costs in South Asia.
5. The South Asian countries have a comparatively high incidence of inland transportation costs *vis-à-vis* international transportation costs (the exception being Sri Lanka) where the variation across countries and commodities is influenced by differences in inland freight rates, and by a country's domestic transport services responsible for the movement of goods. The costs will be higher if we consider the regulatory constraints that are often a significant impediment to trade (Arnold, 2007). To sum up, the variations in inland transportation costs therefore have a significant influence on regional trade transportation costs in South Asia.

The weight–value ratio of trade

The weight–value ratio of a product is a major determinant of the transportation expenses a country faces (Hummels and Skiba, 2004).[20] The

Table 8.9   Estimated net (import–export) weight–value ratio (kg/US$) in 2005

Commodity group	Bangladesh	India	Nepal	Pakistan	Sri Lanka	Total
Agriculture and food products	3.22	−0.92	7.89	−1.55	0.65	9.29
Chemicals and products	1.43	−0.82	−4.83	−0.92	0.10	−5.04
Electrical and electronics	0.00	0.01	0.00	0.00	0.01	0.02
Fuels, mining, and forest products	−0.01	2.56	−3.49	−1.48	−0.72	−3.15
Iron and steel	0.39	0.14	−0.38	0.03	−0.44	−0.26
Leather and products	0.00	−0.01	0.00	−0.06	−0.64	−0.70
Machinery and mechanical appliances	−0.01	0.01	−0.07	0.01	−0.01	−0.08
Metal and products	−0.05	−0.13	0.04	−0.01	0.11	−0.04
Paper and pulp	−0.04	−0.13	−0.38	0.00	0.10	−0.44
Pharmaceuticals	0.05	0.01	−0.06	0.00	−0.01	−0.01
Rubber and plastic	−0.08	0.02	0.06	−0.24	0.26	0.02
Textiles and clothing	0.29	−0.34	−4.40	0.55	−0.46	−4.36
Transport equipment	−0.04	0.02	0.00	−0.31	−0.03	−0.36
Total	5.14	0.46	−5.70	−4.09	−0.81	−5.00

transportation of heavier goods will certainly cost more than that of lighter goods. If a country (or a region) is a net importer of weights, it will have a net deficit in transportation costs.[21] We calculate the weight–value ratio for South Asian countries for their regional trade by means of equation (8.5). We report the estimated net (import–export) weight–value ratio (measured in kg per US$) for each South Asian country in Table 8.9, while Appendix Table 8A.3 provides the estimated weight–value ratio for imports and exports separately.

Since most of the South Asian countries are geographically interlinked, and include a large country like India, it is helpful to understand the relationship between transport cost and weight–value ratio, which will help us to evaluate the transportation needs in South Asian countries more precisely. The following patterns are worth noting.

1. South Asian countries by and large are importers of weights (Table 8.9). Except Bangladesh, which is a net exporter of weights, and India, the other South Asian countries are net importers in their regional trade. In the case of commodity groups, except agriculture and food products, South Asia is mostly a net importer of weights. Bangladesh and Nepal are net exporters of agriculture and food products, and

Table 8.10   Estimated weight–value ratio (kg/US$) in 2005 by bilateral partners

Exporter	Importer					
	Bangladesh	India	Nepal	Pakistan	Sri Lanka	Total
Bangladesh		2.195	0.252	0.015	0.613	3.075
India	2.716		3.322	2.241	0.946	9.226
Nepal	7.351	8.127		0.863	0.584	16.924
Pakistan	2.613	3.850	0.517		1.351	8.330
Sri Lanka	0.884	1.550	0.654	0.828		3.917

India of fuels, minerals and forest products, presumably because of their lower imports in these commodity groups.

2. Nepal's imports are comparatively heavy, which leads to a negative weight–value ratio. In contrast, Bangladesh and India are importers of lesser weights from South Asia. Since India's imports are semi-finished raw materials and intermediate products, it shows a negative weight–value ratio in agriculture and food products, chemicals, leather, paper and pulp, metal and textiles and clothing.

3. Most of the trade between India, Bangladesh and Nepal is driven by heavier commodities (Table 8.10). At the bilateral level, Nepal, a small, landlocked economy, imports weights from Bangladesh and India and incurs considerably higher transportation expenses. This also indirectly indicates that land border dealing in overland trade between India, Nepal and Bangladesh is certainly overcrowded, and faces cross-border delays and higher transaction costs. Recall the findings of Table 8.6, where the field survey results indicated that the time delays at the India–Bangladesh border increased from 2.5 days in 1998 to 3.92 days in 2005, and the costs of transaction at the border also increased from 10.38 per cent in 2002 to 16.80 per cent in 2005.

4. The heavier the good, the larger the transportation cost in South Asia. Alternatively, South Asian countries import higher weights, thereby implying frequent transport congestion and higher trade transportation costs.

5. The estimated *ad valorem* transportation costs at bilateral levels outweigh the applied customs tariffs for most of the South Asian countries, except in three cases: (i) Bangladesh's imports from India, (ii) India's imports from Sri Lanka, and (iii) Sri Lanka's imports from India.

Table 8.11   *Estimated bilateral* ad valorem *total transportation costs in 2005*

Importer	Exporter	*Ad valorem* transport costs (%)*	Applied tariff (%)**
Bangladesh	India	30.50	39.54
	Nepal	6.20	4.46
	Pakistan	17.40	15.64
	Sri Lanka	20.70	18.56
India	Bangladesh	29.40	15.87
	Nepal	48.20	22.66
	Pakistan	45.00	24.35
	Sri Lanka	11.90	23.29
Nepal	Bangladesh	81.90	9.05
	India	63.10	14.70
	Pakistan	24.10	10.40
	Sri Lanka	18.80	15.43
Pakistan	Bangladesh	21.10	6.58
	India	53.60	7.91
	Nepal	16.60	6.83
	Sri Lanka	15.60	6.58
Sri Lanka	Bangladesh	13.20	6.81
	India	5.00	9.20
	Nepal	12.00	11.72
	Pakistan	5.90	3.76

Notes:
* Represented by total transportation costs as percentage of import value.
** Weighted-average tariff, drawn from World Bank WITS (2008).

From the foregoing discussion, we derive three important conclusions: (i) the heavier the good, the larger the transportation cost in South Asia. Alternatively, South Asian countries import higher weights, thereby implying frequent transport congestion and higher trade transportation costs; (ii) the incidence of transport costs in South Asia is higher than the tariff incidence. South Asian countries pay more towards trade transportation costs, compared to customs tariff; and (iii) the costs of trade transportation increase if the country is landlocked (e.g. Nepal).

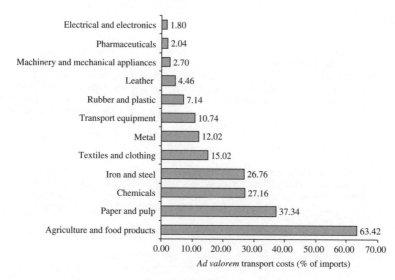

Figure 8.3 *Estimated* ad valorem *transportation costs by commodity in 2005, as a percentage of imports*

4. CONCLUDING REMARKS

The purpose of this chapter has been to estimate and explain the magnitude of transport costs for a set of South Asian countries. The estimation shows that trade transportation costs across South Asia are very expensive and vary across goods and countries. The cost of trade transportation increases if the country is landlocked (here, Nepal). Our empirical findings also tell us that the land border in South Asia is overcrowded and needs special attention in order to reduce time delays and transaction costs.

The findings of this chapter have strong policy implications for South Asian countries. They highlight a broad range of possible improvements in border crossing that can stimulate growth in trade. Countries in South Asia must give the utmost priority to reduction in inland transportation costs when formulating any trade-enhancing policy. In order to maximize the benefits in terms of faster trade growth, the costs of trading across the border must be reduced by removing infrastructure bottlenecks. Obviously, South Asia must give adequate attention to infrastructure development since better infrastructure brings down transportation costs and thus stimulates trade.

NOTES

* An earlier version of this chapter was presented at the Asian Development Bank Institute (ADBI) Conference on 'Trade Costs in Asia', held at Tokyo, 25–26 June 2007. The author acknowledges the comments and suggestions of David Hummels, Douglas Brooks, Susan Stone and Ajitava Raychaudhury. Bhisma Rout provided excellent research assistance. The author sincerely acknowledges the financial support provided by the ADBI for carrying out this study. The views expressed by the author are his personal views. The usual disclaimers apply.

1. The South Asian economy has been growing at an average rate of 6 per cent per annum and intra-South Asia export has been rising at an annual average rate of 7 per cent since 2001.

2. SAFTA has been in place since 1 July 2006 and will be fully operational by 2016. SAFTA includes about 5500 tariff lines, taking into account both agriculture and industrial products. According to the Government of India, SAFTA would lead to growth in intra-regional trade from US$6 billion in 2006 to US$14 billion in 2010 (Government of India, 2006).

3. See the Declaration of the 14th SAARC Summit, New Delhi, 3–4 April 2007.

4. See, e.g., Polak and Heertje (1993).

5. See, e.g., Wilson and Ostuki (2007) and De (2008), among others.

6. Except for Pakistan, India is the largest trading partner of the South Asian countries; India alone shares 73 per cent of South Asian exports (US$5.81 billion in 2006).

7. For example, intraregional trade in ASEAN at present is about 20 per cent per annum, from a mere 5 per cent in early 1990s, whereas in South Asia today it is only 5 per cent, and that too has been hovering in the same position for the last decade and a half. Therefore the economies in the region have not yet engaged in higher trading among themselves; 5 per cent of intraregional official trade in 2006 is none the less disappointing.

8. However, including Afghanistan, Bhutan and the Maldives, intra-South Asian trade increased to about US$8.20 billion in 2006. This does not include informal trade among the South Asian countries, which would bring the rate up to about 10 per cent (see, e.g., Taneja et al., 2005).

9. See, e.g., Panagariya (1999), Srinivasan (2002), World Bank (2004), RIS (2004), USAID (2005), Ahmed and Ghani (2007), to name a few.

10. The database corresponds to the year 2006. Although this database is related to shipment of a container of textiles and clothing, it also provides a general idea of transportation costs in South Asia.

11. These observations are also well captured in a large sample (220 firms across the country) by the Reserve Bank of India (RBI, 2006), according to which procedural delay in trade transaction is the major reason for rising time delays and costs for India's exports.

12. See, for example, Taneja et al. (2005).

13. This is popularly known as the 'matched partner' technique. In most cases it produces serious measurement errors. Hummels and Lugovskyy (2006) have shown that the technique is subject to enormous measurement error and produces time series variation that is orthogonal to actual variation in shipping costs.

14. Not all the freight rates were collected from Maersk Sealand. There are some modifications as well. In the case of trade between India, Bangladesh and Nepal, the freight rates for both the inland and the international leg of the journeys were collected from Container Corporation of India (CONCOR), New Delhi. All others used Maersk Sealand.

15. Due to lack of information, we have omitted the portion of the overland trade carried between India and Pakistan, which is a minor part of about US$1 billion official total trade between the two countries.

16. However, this is not to deny that a small portion of India–Bangladesh trade in goods to the extent of 10 per cent of total merchandise trade per annum is also carried by sea.

Due to lack of proper information on sea freight volume, we were compelled to consider that the entire trade between India and Bangladesh is carried overland.

17. See Appendix Table 8A.1, which provides the commodity classification adopted in this chapter. In general, COMTRADE does not provide trade weight at the 2-digit HS level. It comes from the 4-digit HS level only. So we have to classify the commodity groups at that level. This classification of commodity groups follows the WTO's classification, which is reported in its *Annual Report 2006*. We exclude trade in agriculture.

18. Here, the methodology follows Brooks and Hummels (2007).

19. Systematic data on South Asia's imports by origin and commodity are not available. The problem becomes more acute when one looks for trade in weight in TEUs. As a result, we had to rely on Maersk Sealand, which provides freight rates for commodities at the bilateral level. Since COMTRADE does not provide trade in TEU, we had to convert the weight in kg into weight in TEU. This was done based on the author's personal communication with Mr S Ghosh, formerly Sr Vice President, International Navigation Association (PIANC), Brussels, and presently Managing Director, Consulting Engineering Services Pvt Ltd (CES), New Delhi. The conversion rate we used here was 12 000 kg ≅ 1 TEU to get a loaded 20-foot container (popularly known as FCL), sourced from PIANC.

20. Hummels and Skiba (2004) commented that a 10 per cent increase in the product weight–value ratio leads to a 4 per cent increase in the *ad valorem* shipping cost.

21. This is ideally true if the trade is undertaken at the c.i.f. price.

REFERENCES

Ahmed, S. and E. Ghani (2007), 'South Asia's growth and regional integration: an overview', In S. Ahmed and E. Ghani (eds), *South Asia Growth and Regional Integration*, New Delhi: Macmillan, pp. 3–42.

Arnold, J. (2007), 'The role of trade facilitation in export growth', in S. Ahmed and E. Ghani (eds), *South Asia Growth and Regional Integration*, New Delhi: Macmillan, pp. 191–235.

Brooks, D. and D. Hummels (2007), 'Infrastructure's role in Asia's trade and trade costs', paper presented at the Finalization Conference on 'Infrastructure's Role in Reducing Trade Costs', organized by the Asian Development Bank Institute (ADBI), held in Tokyo, 25–26 June.

Das, S. and S. Pohit (2006), 'Quantifying transport, regulatory and other costs of Indian overland exports to Bangladesh', *World Economy*, **29**(9), 1227–42.

De, P. (2005), 'Cooperation in the regional transportation infrastructure sector in South Asia', *Contemporary South Asia*, **14**(3), 267–88.

De, P. (2007), 'Facilitating overland trade in South Asia', paper presented at the Regional Conference on 'Economic Cooperation in SAARC: SAFTA and Beyond', organized by RIS and SACEPS, New Delhi, 19 March.

De, P. (2008), 'Realising the gains from full regional connectivity in South Asia: the transport costs dimension', *Man and Development*, **30**(1), 27–44.

De, P. and B. Bhattacharya (2007a), *Prospects of India–Bangladesh Bilateral Economic Engagement: Implications for South Asian Regional Cooperation*, Discussion Paper no. 78, Asian Development Bank Institute (ADBI), Tokyo.

De, P. and B. Bhattacharya (2007b), *Deepening India–Bangladesh Economic Cooperation: Challenges and Opportunities*, Discussion Paper no. 130, Research and Information System for Developing Countries (RIS), New Delhi.

De, P. and B. Ghosh (2006), *On Assessing Transaction Costs of Trade at Border: An analysis on Indian exports to Bangladesh*, mimeo, Asian Institute of Transport Development, New Delhi.

De, P. and B. Ghosh (2008), 'On reassessing transaction costs of trade at border: an analysis of Indian exports to Bangladesh', *Economic and Political Weekly*, **43**(29), 19–25 July.

Government of India (2006), *India's Trade in SAFTA*, mimeo, Ministry of Commerce and Industry, New Delhi.

Hummels, D. (1999), Toward a geography of trade costs, Working Paper, University of Chicago.

Hummels, D. and V. Lugovskyy (2006), 'Are matched partner trade statistics a usable measure of transportation costs?', *Review of International Economics*, **14**(1), 69–86.

Hummels, D. and A. Skiba (2004), 'Shipping the good apples out? An empirical confirmation of the Alchian–Allen conjecture', *Journal of Political Economy*, **112**, 1384–402.

Maersk Sealand (2007), *Historical Shipping Rates Database*, available at http://www.maerskline.com.

Panagariya, A. (1999), 'Trade policy in South Asia: recent liberalization and future agenda', *World Economy*, **22**(3), 353–78.

Polak, J. and A. Heertje (1993), *European Transport Economics*, Oxford: Blackwell.

Research and Information System for Developing Countries (RIS) (2004), *South Asia Development and Cooperation Report 2004*, New Delhi: RIS.

Reserve Bank of India (RBI) (2006), *Report on the Survey on Impact on Trade Related Measures on Transaction Costs of Exports*, Balance of Payments Statistics Division, Department of Statistical Analysis and Computer Services, Mumbai.

Srinivasan, T.N. (2002), *Trade, Finance and Investment in South Asia*, New Delhi: Social Science Press.

Subramanian, U. and J. Arnold (2001), *Forging Subregional Links in Transportation and Logistics in South Asia*, Washington, DC: World Bank.

Taneja, N., M. Sarvananthan, B.K. Karmacharya and S. Pohit (2005), 'Informal trade in India, Nepal and Sri Lanka', in M. Khan (ed.), *Economic Development in South Asia*, New Delhi: Tata McGraw-Hill, pp. 54–114.

United Nations (UN) (2007), *COMTRADE Database*, UN Statistical Division, New York.

US Agency for International Development (USAID) (2005), *South Asian Free Trade Area: Opportunities and challenges*, Washington, DC.

Wilson, J.S. and T. Ostuki (2007), 'Cutting trade costs and improved business facilitation in South Asia', in S. Ahmed and E. Ghani (eds), *South Asia Growth and Regional Integration*, New Delhi: Macmillan, pp. 236–70.

World Bank (2004), *Trade Policies in South Asia: An overview*, Report 29949, vol. 2, Washington, DC.

World Bank (2008), *World Integrated Trade Solution (WITS) Database*, Washington, DC, available online at www.wits.org.

APPENDIX

Table 8A.1   Classification of commodity groups

Commodity group	Corresponding 2/4-digit HS (2002)	Remarks
Agriculture products	01–24, 50–53	Taken at 4-digit HS
Food	16–23	excluding HS 01 and HS 06
Fuels, mining and forest products	25–27, 44	Taken at 4-digit HS, excluding HS 45
Chemicals	28–36, 38	
Pharmaceuticals	30	Taken at 4-digit HS,
Rubber and plastics	39–40	excluding HS 37
Leather	41–43, 64	
Paper and pulp	47–48	
Textiles and clothing	54–63	Taken at 4-digit HS,
Iron and steel	72–73	excluding HS 64–67, 71
Metal	68–70, 74–81	
Machinery and mechanical appliances	82–84	Taken at 4-digit HS, excluding HS 8415, 8418, 8471, 8473
Electrical and Electronics	85, 90, 91, 92, 95	Taken at 4-digit HS, including HS 8415, 8418, 8471, 8473
Office and telecom equipment	8517–8548	
Electronic integrated circuits	8542	
Transport equipment	86–89	
Automobiles and components	87	

Table 8A.2 Aggregated freight rates: 2005

(a) Inland transportation

Commodity group	Bangladesh	India	Nepal	Pakistan	Sri Lanka
	(US$ / TEU)				
Agriculture and food products	1662	1350	1670	706	110
Chemicals	1662	1355	1681	656	110
Electrical and electronics	1663	1318	1670	899	110
Fuels, mining, and forest products	1662	1698	1670	890	110
Iron and steel	1670	1578	1670	894	110
Leather	1573	1564	1670	2072	691
Machinery and mechanical appliances	1656	1620	1669	890	110
Metal	1633	1334	1670	894	110
Paper and pulp	1668	1303	1669	890	110
Pharmaceuticals	1648	1736	1690	699	110
Rubber and plastic	1647	1642	1670	891	110
Textiles and clothing	1560	1449	1744	892	110
Transport equipment	1659	1664	1680	890	110

(b) International transportation

Commodity group	Bangladesh	India	Nepal	Pakistan	Sri Lanka
	(US$ / TEU)				
Agriculture and food products	34	506	2	598	317
Chemicals	21	202	0	574	294
Electrical and electronics	29	174	0	778	282
Fuels, mining, and forest products	37	27	0	780	281
Iron and steel	2	80	0	840	310
Leather	452	213	0	1253	336
Machinery and mechanical appliances	65	54	1	774	284
Metal	159	251	2	779	286
Paper and pulp	8	214	3	820	280
Pharmaceuticals	102	3	0	508	300
Rubber and plastic	82	64	0	749	344
Textiles and clothing	506	206	5	782	444
Transport equipment	52	132	0	615	285

Table 8A.3   Estimated weight–value ratio (kg/US$) in 2005

(a) Country aggregates by commodities (import)

Commodity group	Bangladesh	India	Nepal	Pakistan	Sri Lanka	Total
			(kg/US$)			
Agriculture and food products	1.17	3.88	2.38	3.64	1.06	12.13
Chemicals	0.36	1.25	5.12	1.01	0.09	7.83
Electrical and electronic	0.02	0.05	0.00	0.00	0.01	0.08
Fuels, mining, and forest products	0.88	2.63	3.49	2.66	0.77	10.43
Iron and steel	0.14	0.25	0.52	0.08	0.54	1.54
Leather	0.00	0.01	0.00	0.06	0.64	0.71
Machinery and mechanical appliances	0.02	0.00	0.07	0.00	0.01	0.11
Metal	0.09	0.19	0.10	0.02	0.05	0.45
Paper and pulp	0.04	0.20	0.42	0.00	0.06	0.71
Pharmaceuticals	0.00	0.00	0.06	0.01	0.01	0.08
Rubber and plastic	0.14	0.10	0.01	0.32	0.08	0.65
Textiles and clothing	0.15	0.61	4.64	0.06	0.55	6.00
Transport equipment	0.04	0.00	0.00	0.31	0.03	0.39
Total	3.08	9.23	16.92	8.33	3.92	41.47

(b) Country aggregates by commodities (export)

Commodity group	Bangladesh	India	Nepal	Pakistan	Sri Lanka	Total
			(kg/US$)			
Agriculture and food products	4.40	2.96	10.27	2.09	1.71	21.42
Chemicals	1.78	0.43	0.29	0.09	0.19	2.79
Electrical and electronics	0.01	0.07	0.00	0.00	0.01	0.10
Fuels, mining, and forest products	0.87	5.18	0.00	1.19	0.05	7.29
Iron and steel	0.53	0.39	0.14	0.11	0.10	1.28
Leather	0.00	0.00	0.00	0.00	0.00	0.01
Machinery and mechanical appliances	0.00	0.01	0.00	0.01	0.00	0.03
Metal	0.04	0.06	0.13	0.02	0.16	0.40
Paper and pulp	0.00	0.07	0.04	0.00	0.16	0.27
Pharmaceuticals	0.05	0.01	0.00	0.00	0.00	0.07
Rubber and plastic	0.06	0.12	0.06	0.09	0.34	0.67
Textiles and clothing	0.44	0.27	0.24	0.61	0.08	1.64
Transport equipment	0.00	0.02		0.01	0.00	0.03
Total	8.21	9.68	11.23	4.24	3.11	36.47

Index

IPC (Indonesia Port Company)
119–21, 141–2

Javorcik, B.S. 12

Krugman, P. 78

Levinson, M. 37
Limao, N. 14, 80

Malaysia 12, 148–74
  FDI 157–62
  infrastructure and trade costs
    167–73
  trade patterns 162–7
  transport infrastructure 149–57
Manchin, M. 1, 2, 79
manufacturing sector
  share of FDI, Malaysia 160–62
  trade patterns, Malaysia 162–7
margins of trade expansion 30
Mumbai, port costs 46–8

neoclassical trade theory 76–7
networks 10–11
new market testing, use of air
  transport 28
new trade flows 30–33
new trade theory 77
non-commercial ports, Indonesia 119
Nordås, H.K. 5, 79

Obstfeld, M. 78
ocean freight rates 8–9, 80–85, 102–3

Pearl River Delta 208–9
Penang, port costs 46
People's Republic of China, *see* China
Piermartini, R. 5, 79
port activity, Indonesian ports 135–6
port competitiveness 9–10, 113–44
  indicators 115–16
  Indonesia 131–44
port costs 41–4
  effect of infrastructure investments
    7–8, 44–5, 46, 49–58
port hinterlands 115
  Indonesia 135–6
port infrastructure
  Indonesia 136–7

investment 44–5, 46, 49–58,
  114–15
  effect on trade costs 40–58
  India 51–6
Port Klang 156
Port of Tanjung Pelepas (PTP) 155
port users, Indonesian ports 138–41
ports, Asia 39–41
  China 189
  congestion 13
  Indonesia 116–31
  Malaysia 154–7
privatization, Indonesian ports 122,
  142–3, 144
profitability, effect of trading distance
  79
Prusa, T. 33
public ports, Indonesia 119
public service obligation (PSO),
  Indonesia 143

rail transport
  China 185, 215
  Malaysia 152–3
Ray, D. 120
regional distribution of FDI, Malaysia
  161–2
regional infrastructure coordination
  14–15
regional trade transportation costs,
  South Asia 244–52
regulations, Indonesian ports 140–41
river transport, China 186, 189
road development
  China 186
  and E&E exports, Malaysia 171–2
  Malaysia 151–2
Rogoff, K. 78

SAARC (South Asian Association for
  Regional Cooperation) 230
Samuelson, P.A. 77, 78
Schaur, G. 29
seaports, *see* ports
Shanghai Port 202–8
  congestion problems 13
  port costs 46
Sharma, K. 159
Shenzhen Port 202, 208–13
shipping costs, *see* transport costs